THE DEVIL IN DC

THE
DEVIL
IN DC

WINNING BACK THE COUNTRY
FROM THE BEAST IN WASHINGTON

CHERYL K. CHUMLEY

 WND Books

THE DEVIL IN DC

Published by WND Books, Washington, DC. WND Books is a registered trademark of WorldNetDaily.com, Inc. ("WND").

Book designed by Mark Karis and Vi Yen Nguyen

Paperback ISBN: 978-1-944229-10-8
eBook ISBN: 978-1-944229-11-5

Library of Congress Cataloging-in-Publication Data

Names: Chumley, Cheryl K., 1968- author.
Title: The devil in DC : winning back the country from the beast in
Washington / Cheryl K. Chumley.
Description: Washington, D.C. : WND Books, [2016] | Includes bibliographical
references and index.
Identifiers: LCCN 2015033802| ISBN 9781942475149 (hardcover) | ISBN
9781942475156 (e-book)
Subjects: LCSH: Political culture--United States. | Christianity and
politics--United States. | Christianity and culture--United States.
Classification: LCC JK1726 .C48 2016 | DDC 320.520973--dc23
LC record available at http://lccn.loc.gov/2015033802

Printed in the United States of America
15 16 17 18 19 20 XXX 9 8 7 6 5 4 3 2 1

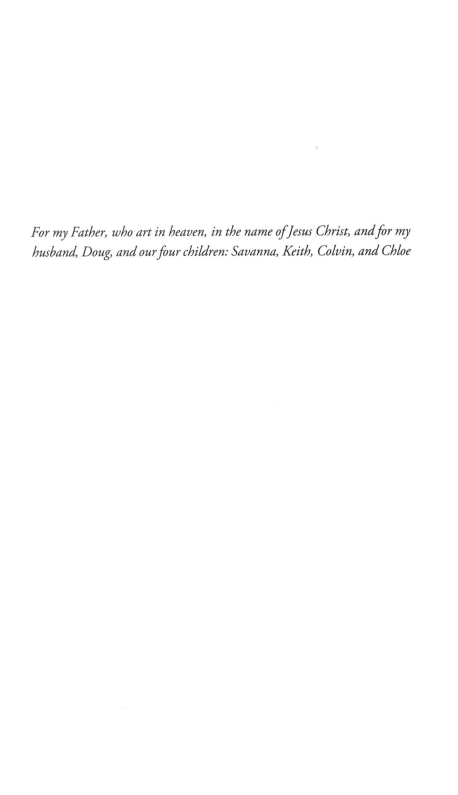

For my Father, who art in heaven, in the name of Jesus Christ, and for my husband, Doug, and our four children: Savanna, Keith, Colvin, and Chloe

CONTENTS

ACKNOWLEDGMENTS

GOV. MIKE HUCKABEE, thank you, thank you, and thank you again—not just for the foreword and career support, but for standing firm in the faith among a nation of mockers. Believe me, people notice that and draw strength.

PASTOR MICHAEL EDWARDS of Heritage Baptist Church in Woodbridge, Virginia, thank you for your prayers, guidance, and excellent preaching and teaching—for allowing God to work through you so obviously and thoroughly. If only the country and church had more like you. If only.

DR. CHUCK HARDING, missionary, evangelist, and the founder of Awake America, your voice and cause are truly inspiring. Hurry and get your book out there; the nation needs the wake-up call.

CARL GALLUPS, senior pastor of Hickory Hammond Baptist Church in Milton, Florida, top-selling author, conservative pundit, and nationally known defender of the Christian faith, it's such an honor to have your assistance in this endeavor. I can truly say I hope our paths cross again soon.

ROBERT SCOTT BELL, host of the Robert Scott Bell Show, a sensational radio broadcast devoted to advancing freedom and liberty in all walks of life, thank you for your insights, contributions to this book and the country, and the chance to converse on so many, many shows.

JONATHAN EMORD, an author and constitutional attorney with an amazing legal mind and an even more admirable character, you are one of the last great American patriots. I can't tell you how much I appreciate your years of encouragement, career support and, even more significantly, kindness and friendship.

JOHN TAYLOR, president of Virginia Institute for Public Policy and of Tertium Quids, I've said it before and now say it again: You're one of the fiercest fighters for freedom I know and it's an honor to count you and your wife, LYNN, among my rather small circle of friends.

PAMELA GELLER, brilliant columnist; outspoken pundit; founder editor, and publisher of AtlasShrugs.com; and president of the American Freedom Defense Initiative, you're an American of whom the Founding Fathers would be proud. Thank you, Pamela. You're uncompromising and principled and I love it.

SAM SORBO, who along with her husband, KEVIN, unknowingly provides many with great inspiration, in bold defense of the faith, I am very thankful for the endorsement.

MICHAEL SAVAGE, a very grateful and humble thank you. You've been on the forefront of this fight for decades, and I hope God blesses all your endeavors. We certainly need your voice; more importantly, your courage and love for country.

JENNIFER WISHON, White House correspondent for Christian Broadcast Network, you're a cut above the rest, a true gem, and I truly appreciate your professionalism and personality.

ALAN GOTTLIEB, Second Amendment Foundation founder, and JOHN WOOLLEY of the American Presidency Project, thank you both so much for the permissions and, in John's case, the fascinating chat. And appreciation to the Center for Responsive Politics for the same.

JOSEPH FARAH and ELIZABETH FARAH, the wind beneath WND, thank you for your faith. It's touching, encouraging, and humbling all rolled into one. And I look forward to a God-blessed, long-running professional partnership. You two are top-notch.

GEOFFREY STONE, RENEE CHAVEZ, MICHAEL THOMPSON, MARK KARIS and the rest of the editing, publishing, and marketing crew of WND, thank you for your long hours, incomparable skills, and dedication and commitment. To you, it's your job. To me, you're godsends, and I'd be hard-pressed to have any success as an author at all without your help.

DENNIS AND RUTH ZICKO, in Duxbury, Massachusetts, once more, thank you. You've done excellent work—don't you agree? Appreciate the years of love and laughter; looking forward to many more of the same.

And finally, to my reasons for living: SAVANNA, KEITH, COLVIN, CHLOE, and my husband, DOUG. You guys are the greatest family a person could have. And DOUG CHUMLEY, an especial heaping of love for you—the James 5:20 of modern-day America.

FOREWORD

In early 2015, I watched with growing alarm as gay rights activists around the nation—aided and abetted by a complicit, weak media—unleashed an attack of epic proportions against Indiana governor Mike Pence for signing into law the Religious Freedom Restoration Act, a measure that simply underscored the First Amendment rights of individuals and business owners.

Soon after, these same forces turned an attacking eye to my home state, Arkansas, over a similar bill that was winding through the legislature.

My views of the matter were widely reported. I told Megyn Kelly on a Fox News segment broadcast the first week of April that the furor ignited by the RFRA was simply "a manufactured crisis by the Left," and that "if they manufactured as many products as they do crises like this one, which is an utterly phony attempt to create some kind of division, 92 million Americans who are jobless would have jobs."[1]

I stand by that view, even in the face of *Obergefell v. Hodges*, the US Supreme Court ruling that swept gay marriage into all fifty states.

Indiana and Arkansas, the US Supreme Court, and the

whole gay rights movement are just small cogs in a larger wheel of America's troubles. The larger wheel is actually this: Our nation is crumbling because we're rapidly losing what used to be our greatest asset—the idea that our rights as individuals come from God, not government. And once we let government think it's the one in charge, not God, then we're headed for a free fall of constitutional demise, where individual rights play second fiddle to the power-hungry lusts of the political class. The solution?

I actually referenced this larger wheel, and its solution, during that same interview with Megyn Kelly, when I talked about my hope for Christians to step up, speak up, and help save this great republic of ours. I truly believe if Christians really wanted to, they could make a real change, a real difference, and they could help push back some of these leftist attacks on our most fundamental of liberties.

This is where *The Devil in DC: Winning Back the Country from the Beast in Washington* comes in—and this is why *The Devil in DC* is such an important book to read.

I first met author Cheryl Chumley on my program on Fox News in 2014, when she came on to discuss her first book, *Police State USA: How Orwell's Nightmare Is Becoming Our Reality*, and the many ways government had in fact become America's new god. Her follow-up, *The Devil in DC*, now takes the fight of patriotic Americans to an even higher level, appealing to Christians and those of faith to get in the ring, jump in the fight. And what I really like about this book is it then shows them just how to do it.

Chumley lays it out bluntly, cutting through the political chatter and partisan bickering to make clear this basic premise:

The fate of our nation is being decided by a battle of principalities, not a war of Republican versus Democrat. And without God in charge—without recognizing God as our leader—we're doomed. She then goes on to explain, chapter by chapter and point by point, just how a concerned patriot, Christian warrior, or faithful servant of God might fight the forces of progressivism and evils that are invading our nation, and reignite and reawaken the same spirit that drove the Founding Fathers to boldly dismiss their king and declare allegiance to their Creator, first and foremost.

We need more of that spirit in this country. We need more people of faith getting off the sidelines and demanding their government stay in check. Without that, we can only expect more Indianas—more Arkansases—more constitutional hits, dings, dents, and chips.

We need a government that's subservient to God, not a government that arrogantly rules on self-interest, and self-interest alone.

Read *The Devil in DC*. It'll teach you how to humble this overbearing government of ours and, at the same time, suggest specific ways to bring back God as our recognized leader.

—MIKE HUCKABEE, FORMER GOVERNOR OF ARKANSAS

INTRODUCTION

THE TIME TO FIGHT IS NOW

Dream with me.
Imagine an America . . .

where the fruits of one's labors are not stolen by an oppressive tax system and a greedy political force;

where the public school systems actually teach logical math, grammatical English, and truthful history, not new math, English as a Second Language, and propagandized history;

where politicians and elected leaders are constrained not only by an informed, emboldened populace but also by a personally ingrained set of morals and values that prick their consciences and prod their behaviors;

where television, movies, and the entertainment and media industries don't constantly bombard with sexually graphic messages that treat the likes of adultery, homosexuality, and promiscuity as normal and fun;

where those of Christian faith aren't treated as despicable bigots for insisting on the rights of religious freedom and for opposing activities like gay marriage, that run counter to biblical teachings;

where poverty isn't so much a political program but rather an opportunity for a church- or community-based solution, or even an individual solution;

where the Constitution still matters, justice is blind, and the rule of law is applied as equally to the president of the United States as to the salesperson in the store, the homemaker in the house, and the homeless on the street; and

where service to the nation is conducted in a manner that sets God's full glory on display, inadvertently or purposely, by men and women who abide by the most basic of biblical commands: do unto others as you would have them do unto you.

This is the America we should seek, for ourselves, for our children, for our children's children, and so on, for as long as God blesses our country to thrive and survive.

We've strayed quite a bit from this vision. And getting back will certainly not prove an overnight venture—or even a one-year achievement. It'll take a long, hard slog against some forces of wickedness that have been plotting and planning America's constitutional demise for decades, biding time until opportunity presented as seemed right—like the long-running degradations from the progressive movement, for example. But we can fight—and we can determine not to quit.

God set us on this hill. It seems only logical He'd like to keep us there.

Confess. Repent. Pray. Those are the first steps to bringing our country back under the auspices of God. And after?

Hopefully, some of the subsequent suggested actions outlined in this book will prove both inspiring and guiding.

Ecclesiastes teaches of "a time to love, and a time to hate; a time for war, and a time for peace" (Eccl. 3:8). Right now, with the turmoil swirling about America, this is a time to fight—a time for war. Will you do your part?

ONE

PARTISAN POLITICS WON'T WIN THE NATION

For the kingdom is the Lord's: and he is the governor among the nations. —PSALM 22:28 KJV

In June 2014, Rep. Eric Cantor's political star—the one that had shone for years on Capitol Hill, lighting the way for him to assume the role of second most powerful Republican in the House—fell from grace. In a shock election, he lost a Republican primary race to newcomer Dave Brat, a then economics professor at Randolph-Macon College in Ashland, Virginia, who possessed little in his background that would have warned of his ability to take down a sitting Majority leader.[1]

And yet, Brat did—by about 11 percent, no less. He went on to win the House seat against his Democratic challenger that November. Cantor, whose loss was partly attributed by many to his embrace of an immigration reform seen by his conservative base as a sellout to President Obama and Democrats, went on to a cushy, well-paid position with the investment firm Moelis and Company.[2]

But in the end, the voters spoke.

It's not the only time they did during that same time period.

In August 2014, Congress closed for a five-week recess and members headed home, carting an approval rating with American voters that stood at 6 percent.

Six percent.

That is, only 6 percent of likely US voters thought Congress was doing a good or excellent job, compared to 65 percent who regarded its performance as downright poor, Rasmussen Reports found. That poor showing wasn't just a blip. Congress came back to Capitol Hill that September dragging the same low rating on its back—and that's after dragging around single-digit approval numbers for years, as far back as April 2011.[3]

Why?

Part of the reason for the long-running subpar performance rating was due to voter backlash to Obamacare—first, from those who opposed the creation of the massive federal program, and then, from those who watched in despair the disastrous rollout and wished for a return to simpler medical provider times. In fact, Rasmussen reported that the negative marks given to Congress spiked to 75 percent in November 2013, at the height of the rollout disaster.[4] Part of the reason, too, was the sluggish economy that dogged President Obama's administration, as well as the frequently heated, oft-vicious rhetoric emanating from Capitol Hill on a score of issues, from Benghazi to the IRS to the emerging conflicts in Syria and Iraq.

But Rasmussen itself pointed to an even deeper schism.

"Just eight percent (8%) of voters think most members of Congress get reelected because they do a good job representing their constituents. Sixty-seven percent (67%) think it's because election rules are rigged to benefit incumbents," the polling outlet reported. "Sixty-three percent (63%) of voters also still think most members of Congress are willing to sell their vote for either cash or a campaign contribution, and 59% think it's likely their own representative already has."[5]

Only 13 percent of respondents to the survey believed the majority of members of Congress were truly beholden to their constituents, and that their lawmakers' votes, for example, weren't for sale.[6]

ONLY 13 PERCENT . . . BELIEVED THE MAJORITY OF MEMBERS

OF CONGRESS WERE TRULY BEHOLDEN TO THEIR CONSTITUENTS.

Pretty dim. Call it the Eric Cantor blues. But that's how voters have pretty much felt since 2012, Rasmussen reported.

How's that for an American consensus?

This is a significant finding—one that underscores a long-forgotten Founding Father intent for our nation: the creators of our Constitution never wanted a political party system.[7] They simply wanted voters to cast ballots for the president, the vice president, and so forth, with the candidate with the largest tally winning the respective political seat. Never mind Republican; forget about Democrat. The Founders thought political parties would just muddy the process, bring rancor and partisanship, and ultimately leave voters stranded and abandoned, disenfranchised from their own government.[8] Here's how John Adams put it: "Parties and Factions will not Suffer, or permit improvements to be made. As Soon as one Man hints at an improvement his Rival opposes it. No sooner has one Party discovered or invented an Amelioration of the condition of Man or the order of Society, than the opposite Party, belies it, misconstrues it, misrepresents it, ridicules it, insults it, and persecutes it."[9]

"PARTIES AND FACTIONS WILL NOT SUFFER, OR PERMIT IMPROVEMENTS TO BE MADE. . . . NO SOONER HAS ONE PARTY DISCOVERED OR INVENTED AN AMELIORATION OF THE CONDITION OF MAN OR THE ORDER OF SOCIETY, THAN THE OPPOSITE PARTY, BELIES IT, MISCONSTRUES IT, MISREPRESENTS IT, RIDICULES IT, INSULTS IT, AND PERSECUTES IT." –JOHN ADAMS

Wiser words couldn't be spoken today. Isn't that exactly the atmosphere that emanates from Capitol Hill? Rasmussen would say yes. So would Gallup, which found in its own poll in late 2013 that only 26 percent of Americans—a new low for this question—believed the two parties adequately represented the will of the voters.[10]

The real impact to the American public from all this political bickering is that issues of importance get pushed to the side. Oppose Obamacare? That makes you an enemy of the poor.

Oppose amnesty for illegal immigrants? That makes you an enemy of the downtrodden. Oppose progressive policies put forth by President Obama, like his massive food stamp entitlements or his free college visions? That makes you a racist. And with Hillary Clinton heating up the political scene once again, expect those who oppose her policies to be labeled sexist or antiwoman. See how it works? Political partisanship means battle—and political claws dig deep.

It's as George Washington said in his farewell address, harking back to the horrible political fights he had witnessed in Europe: "The alternate domination of one faction over another, sharpened by the spirit of revenge, natural to party dissension, which in different ages and countries has perpetrated the most horrid enormities, is itself a frightful despotism."[11]

The interesting aside is that as much as the Founders hated the idea of a two-party political system, it didn't take them long to create one—the Federalists versus the Democratic-Republicans, in 1796. The latter, headed by Thomas Jefferson, despised what he characterized as the Federalist elitism that came right off the lands of Europe, right from the hands of aristocrats, and he wanted nothing more than to lay the groundwork for this new nation to be composed of independent thinkers, unfettered by class considerations. Federalists, meanwhile, led by John Adams, thought of themselves as the party of good governance and order—and Democratic-Republicans as rabble-rousing rebels, dangerous to the blossoming nation. Interestingly, the views espoused by Jefferson resonated in the South; those of Adams, in the New England states. But ultimately, Adams won by a narrow margin, and—voilà!—the two-party political system took root in America.[12]

Since, this root has only grown into a two-party grab fest for money and power.

Check out the list of "Top Organization Contributors" compiled by Open Secrets to show the breakdown of donations by party from 2002 to 2014, and the level of partisanship each donor displays, as based on the accumulated percentages of gifts to one party over another.[13]

It's not that this list is shocking in terms of what firms and fields traditionally donate to Democrats, versus what firms and fields generally give to Republicans. What is a bit of a surprise, however, is how heavily tilted twenty-five of the total one hundred listed organizations are toward Democrats—the same party that has always pointed fingers at the Republicans as standing in the camp of lobbyists and wealthy business owners.[14]

While both Democrats and Republicans were recipients of some deep-pocketed groups in the years leading up to 2015, it was the Democrats—not the GOP—that received much larger donations from single organizations. In fact, of the top twenty-five donors on the list that was compiled to reflect Federal Election Commission data through March 2015, only a handful provided more money to Republicans than Democrats. Democrats, far and away, received the bulk of money from the heaviest hitting of donating groups.[15]

Information posted on *OpenSecrets* changes with election filings. But the big takeaway from watching, over the course of months, how the money from outside organizations really seems to pile in the Democrats' camps is this: Liberals may try to bill themselves as the party of the blue-collar and the bulwark to the little people. But when it comes to bringing in the bucks,

RANK	ORGANIZATION	TOTAL CONTRIBUTIONS	% TO LIBERALS	% TO CONSERVATIVES
1	SERVICE EMPLOYEES INTERNATIONAL UNION	$222,434,657	99%	1%
2	ACTBLUE	$160,637,963	100%	0%
3	AMERICAN FEDN of ST/CNTY/MUNIC EMPLOYEES	$93,830,657	99%	1%
4	NATIONAL EDUCATION ASSN	$92,972,656	97%	4%
5	FAHR LLC	$75,289,659	100%	0%
6	AMERICAN FEDERATION of TEACHERS	$69,757,113	100%	1%
7	LAS VEGAS SANDS	$69,440,942	0%	100%
8	NATIONAL ASSN of REALTORS	$68,683,359	49%	52%
9	CARPENTERS & JOINERS UNION	$67,778,534	94%	7%
10	INTL BROTHERHOOD of ELECTRICAL WORKERS	$63,572,836	99%	2%
11	UNITED FOOD & COMMERCIAL WORKERS UNION	$63,229,927	100%	1%
12	AT&T INC	$61,004,110	42%	58%
13	LABORERS UNION	$57,644,241	94%	6%
14	PERRY HOMES	$55,482,749	0%	100%
15	GOLDMAN SACHS	$52,230,718	54%	47%
16	AMERICAN ASSN FOR JUSTICE	$48,004,160	93%	7%
17	CONTRAN CORP	$45,763,122	1%	99%
18	AFL-CIO	$45,587,534	98%	3%
19	SOROS FUND MANAGEMENT	$44,442,608	98%	2%
20	UNITED AUTO WORKERS	$44,054,732	100%	1%
21	COMMUNICATIONS WORKERS of AMERICA	$43,240,737	100%	1%
22	TEAMSTERS UNION	$43,065,898	95%	5%
23	PLUMBERS/PIPEFITTERS UNION	$42,777,845	96%	4%
24	ADELSON DRUG CLINIC	$42,521,518	0%	100%
25	NEWSWEB CORP	$40,253,121	99%	1%

For a complete listing of the top 100 organizations go to https://www.opensecrets.org/orgs/list.php

Democrats do very well with outside sources, from unions to lawyers, and they really have a leg up on Republicans.

That's not to say Republicans, as a party, are the poor and downtrodden. GOPers get some pretty hefty donations of their own from the likes of the financial sectors, Koch Industries, and the gas and oil interests.[16]

But either way, the constituent's in the cold.

Special-interest groups, PACs, and private companies nowadays have a lot more sway in the political process than the single voter. That's a large part of why the political candidate who holds such promise on the campaign trail doesn't seem so appetizing after a few months on Capitol Hill—he or she often has donors to thank and debts to pay, in the form of political favors, political concessions, and the granting of political access.

The solution to all this special-interest trading is simple: voters should stop funding the main political parties.

THE SOLUTION TO ALL THIS SPECIAL-INTEREST TRADING IS SIMPLE: VOTERS SHOULD STOP FUNDING THE MAIN POLITICAL PARTIES.

The Republican Party doesn't care about your particular interest—except in cases where it happily coincides with the party's overarching interests.

Think about it. If a political candidate gets thousands of dollars from a company with a lobbyist presence on Capitol

Hill, thousands more from a PAC with similar influence in the halls of Congress, and a supporting political party guarantee to launch several get-out-the-vote drives in key spots around the country, how much does the thirty-five dollars from Joe Q, an electrician from flyover country, really matter? Or the twenty dollars from the elderly retiree in southern Florida?

It doesn't, of course.

One justification for the two-party political system is that one is supposed to serve as a watchdog over the other—and that they both perform checks and balances on each other and alert the public to whatever failings and problems crop up.

Another touted benefit of the two-party system is that it helps keep government organized, in the federal arena and at both state and local levels. It's supposed to bring cohesion by giving candidates from all walks of life a chance to rally around certain key party principles and present a united front to voters—who then aren't flummoxed at the ballot boxes with long lists of candidate names with fuzzy or unknown platforms. Voters can just vote the party ticket with confidence that most of their values are being represented by the listed candidates.

So goes the theory, anyway.

But if that were true, the Republican Party wouldn't have so many RINOs—Republicans In Name Only—and quasi-conservative candidates usurping the previously core conservative values in recent years, demanding concessions from voters and compromise with Democrats on immigration, gay marriage, the debt ceiling and budget, and even abortion. Remember Speaker John Boehner's concessions to President Obama on the budget and federal debt levels?[17] Or Sen. Marco Rubio's call for amnesty—without calling it amnesty?[18]

If that were true, too, the Republican Party wouldn't have so many Republicans turning on other Republicans—wouldn't have the likes of former White House adviser Karl Rove or Sen. John McCain publicly attacking the likes of former Alaska governor Sarah Palin or Sen. Ted Cruz, just because they happen to represent principles that stray from establishment GOP lines.

Remember former president George W. Bush's reach-out to one of the Republican Party's supposed staunchest political enemies, the left-of-left senator Ted Kennedy, for help in forming a federal education plan?[19] This same Republican president also gave America a massive entitlement expansion in the form of a federal prescription drug plan; a Democratic dream-come-true with the American Dream Downpayment Act for federally subsidized housing;[20] and a nomination to the US Supreme Court—Harriet Miers—who shocked conservatives with a legal background that included staunch support for affirmative action.[21] All this while Republicans under the Bush presidency held the Senate for four and a half years and the House for six. Some of that liberal agenda, including the Miers nomination, was actually brought forth when the Republicans held a triple sweep of White House, House, and Senate.[22]

With all that in mind, answer this: What are voters really getting in return for funding the Republican Party versus the Democratic Party: A government that works for them? A political system that sticks with the rules of the Constitution?

The correct answer is C, nothing but betrayal.

Stop funding the parties.

A smarter political investment is to give to the nonpartisan, nonprofit groups that do the real fighting for the average

American—that really do care about Joe Q. and Jane Q. and that have the guts to take their concerns to the belly of the political beast and fight.

STOP FUNDING THE PARTIES. INSTEAD GIVE TO THE NONPARTISAN, NONPROFIT GROUPS THAT DO THE REAL FIGHTING FOR THE AVERAGE AMERICAN—AND THAT HAVE THE GUTS TO TAKE THEIR CONCERNS TO THE BELLY OF THE POLITICAL BEAST AND FIGHT.

Here's an example of how a private organization can pick up the fight where the political party–tied powers-who-be fail—on the matter of asset forfeitures, where government entities can take private properties without having to go through the normal court process.

The Institute for Justice, a nonprofit civil rights organization with a libertarian bent, joined forces with the law firm Kairys, Rudovsky, Messing & Feinberg and filed a class-action lawsuit in August 2014 against the city of Philadelphia, the Philadelphia Police Department, and the Philadelphia district attorney's office alleging abuse of asset forfeiture laws.[23] Thousands of city residents have seen their properties and homes confiscated—in some cases, without even any criminal charges filed—because of federal forfeiture laws that allow law enforcement agents to seize items they deem as being used in the commission of a crime. The laws were originally intended to give the Department of

Justice and US Marshals Service easier methods to dissuade and prosecute drug-related crimes. But the kicker is participating law enforcement agencies get to keep portions of the seized properties, and the laws have quickly morphed into cash-cow opportunities for governments.

In Philadelphia, city coffers were being boosted by $6 million each year from forfeitures. Between 2002 and 2012, the Philadelphia district attorney's office seized more than three thousand vehicles, almost twelve hundred homes and other real estate properties, and $44 million in cash.[24]

So where's the government on this issue?

Sen. Rand Paul in mid-2014 introduced a bill to scale back civil asset forfeitures, the Fifth Amendment Integrity Restoration Act, FAIR. In it, he called for changes in federal law so that government would have to provide convincing evidence of a crime before seizing and keeping property.[25] The bill also "would remove the profit incentive for forfeiture by redirecting forfeiture assets from the Attorney General's Asset Forfeiture Fund to the Treasury's General Fund," and thereby cut out the equitable sharing of seized properties that occurs among federal, state, and local law enforcement entities.[26]

The bill was introduced on July 23, read twice, and sent to the Judiciary Committee—with no cosponsors.[27]

In other words, its chances for passage are slim to none. Shortly after introducing the bill, Paul got busy with the business of running for president, leaving few voices on Capitol Hill to take up the anti–asset forfeiture chant.

Don't expect state or local governments to step in and help ease civil forfeiture laws in Philadelphia, or around the nation, either. These public officials actually have a vested interest in keeping the status quo and seem only too willing to ignore the ramifications for the citizens who actually pay their salaries. As Justice Don Willett wrote in a dissenting opinion in a civil forfeiture case in Texas, "When agency budgets grow dependent on asset forfeiture . . . constitutional liberties are unavoidably imperiled."[28]

Now enter the Institute of Justice, with a big wake-up call of a lawsuit to shake these oppressive government practices. Good.

A lawsuit might prove just the tool to bring about quicker reforms in asset forfeiture laws. At the very least, Philadelphia residents will feel that someone is actually in the trenches and fighting for them—something they likely haven't felt for years from the people they elect and pay to represent their constitutional rights.

So imagine this scenario in your backyard and consider: Which would help your cause more—giving money to the Republican or Democratic Party, or to the Institute for Justice?

Exactly. It's a no-brainer, right?

It's also a surefire way to humble those in the political world. Take away their money, and they lose their carte blanche, devil-may-care, independent attitudes. Suddenly, politicians will need voters once again.

Biblically speaking, Matthew 6:24 addresses this point: "No one can serve two masters, for either he will be devoted to the one and despise the other, or he will be devoted to the one and despise the other. You cannot serve God and money."

If our government is supposed to be an "of, by and for the people" system, where those elected are beholden to the interests of the people—as put forth by the laws of the Constitution—then wouldn't a godly form of American government be one where the governing class upholds those principles? Too often, our political leaders go for the money over the principle—the cash-waving lobbyist, donor, and special interest over the individual, the rule of law, and the limits of the Constitution. A good dose of humble pie, administered by way of smart political donations, could do wonders for our out-of-control government.

The Institute for Justice's suit against asset forfeiture is just one example of a nonprofit or private group fighting the good fight for the average American.

How about Judicial Watch and its repeated Freedom of Information Act requests to get to the root of Benghazi, and the White House's response to the September 11, 2012, terrorist attack that left four Americans—including Ambassador J. Christopher Stevens—dead?[29] Or the American Center for Law and Justice, with its fight to defend the concept of God-given rights and religious liberties, both domestically and abroad—a cause that saw ACLJ members in August 2014 band together and demand US government action against the slaughter of Christians by Islamic State terrorists?[30]

If the White House had its druthers, it would have continued to turn a blind eye to the Christian persecution. In fact, ACLJ's call for action came right around the time President Obama, back from his golfing vacation on Martha's Vineyard, admitted during a nationally televised press conference that his White House had yet to form a strategy about ISIS.[31] And that press conference came on the heels of another Obama statement made a few months earlier, when he referred to ISIS with scorn—a "JV team," in fact.[32]

It's amazing the power the private sector has to shine light on what government wants to hide or dismiss.

IT'S AMAZING THE POWER THE PRIVATE SECTOR HAS TO SHINE

LIGHT ON WHAT GOVERNMENT WANTS TO HIDE OR DISMISS.

Even some left-leaning groups do some good work when it comes to curbing federal powers and pushing back against unconstitutional actions. The American Civil Liberties Union, for example, has hit hard on the issue of emerging technology and the dangers of a surveillance state, as well as on police militarization tactics that have left innocent Americans injured and dead.[33]

Here are some more possibilities, to get the ball rolling:

- CHURCH. Give to your local place of worship, first and foremost. Politics, government, and the state of the Constitution don't matter so much to the poor, the hungry, and the homeless. And no matter how much the Democratic and Republican parties promise to help these suffering segments of American society, the church is better positioned to deliver speedy, targeted aid. Besides, giving to church carries a blessing. Consider this, from God's explanation of what constituted fasts that were pleasing to Him:

> "Is not this the fast that I choose: to loose the bonds of wickedness, to undo the straps of the yoke, to let the oppressed go free, and to break every yoke? Is it not to share your bread with the hungry, and bring the homeless poor into your house, when you see the naked, to

cover him, and not to hide yourself from your own flesh? Then shall your light break forth like the dawn, and your healing shall spring up speedily, your righteousness shall go before you, the glory of the Lord shall be your rear guard. Then you shall call, and the Lord will answer, you shall cry, and he will say, 'Here I am.'" (Isa. 58:6–9)

In that vein, it would seem not just godly, but practical as a nation, to give money to the church and stay in God's good graces, in the expectant light of receiving His blessings.

- THE NATIONAL RIFLE ASSOCIATION, and similar gun rights groups. After years of Second Amendment attacks from President Obama and his administration, does any doubt remain about the crucial need for concerted lobbyist effort to protect one of America's most basic of constitutional rights?

- THE SOUTHEASTERN LEGAL FOUNDATION, THE AMERICAN LAND RIGHTS ASSOCIATION, AND THE PROPERTY AND ENVIRONMENT RESEARCH CENTER. The first two get right in the legal mix and help landowners defend their properties from overreaching government entities; the third offers creative, free-market solutions to the whole private-property-versus-environmental-protection debate.

- FREEDOM WATCH, a political advocacy group with a pretty hard-core conservative edge, unafraid to take on the big players in Washington, DC, and elsewhere.

- THE RUTHERFORD INSTITUTE, an organization that bills itself as "dedicated to the defense of civil liberties and human rights," run by one of America's most respected, knowledgeable, and tireless attorneys, John Whitehead.

- HILLSDALE COLLEGE, a Michigan-based facility for higher learning that offers free online courses on the Constitution to anyone who requests. What could be a better tool in the fight for America's soul than a nation of patriotic believers who know the law of the land, and how to properly apply it?

- AMERICAN RED CROSS. Or the Salvation Army. Donate to their disaster relief programs—make the bureaucratic, ineffective Federal Emergency Management Agency moot.

- THE HERITAGE FOUNDATION, CATO INSTITUTE, CAPITAL RESEARCH CENTER, MANHATTAN INSTITUTE FOR POLICY RESEARCH, CLAREMONT INSTITUTE, and the host of other think tank organizations that provide in-depth studies, white papers, talking points, and research documents on most of the pressing political and cultural issues of the day.

- THE ELECTRONIC FRONTIER FOUNDATION, a nonprofit dedicated to fighting for freedom of speech and for civil liberties, particularly in the digital arena.

- THE PACIFIC LEGAL FOUNDATION, a decades-old public interest, nonprofit legal outfit dedicated to fighting for just the same principles the Founders wanted, and that former president Ronald Reagan embraced.

- CONCERNED WOMEN FOR AMERICA, a conservative group that promotes biblical values and traditional views.

These are but a few. Hundreds, if not thousands, more possible donor sources exist in the private and nonprofit sectors—sources that would make far better use of your hard-earned money than the big political parties. The added benefit of donating to such groups is that the amount is limitless, and often, private. As the Center for Responsive Politics reported: "Spending by organizations that do not disclose their donors has increased from less than $5.2 million in 2006 to well over $300 million in the 2012 presidential cycle and more than $174 million in the 2014 midterms."[34]

But really, the bigger point is this: funding the two main political parties is a loser of a move. Those who care about the fate of the Constitution and the state of this nation ought to instead put their money into causes that truly fight for its principles—that fight for the little guy the document's supposed to protect—and not into the bottomless pit of Capitol Hill bureaucracy and growing cesspool of state legislatures.

Jesus told His followers, "Render to Caesar the things that are Caesar's and to God the things that are God's" (Luke 20:25). Well, here's a thought: The positions politicians hold and the money they use to conduct their oft-unconstitutional business come from the people. *We are politicians' "Caesar."*

But they're not treating us that way, are they?

So how about going right into the belly of the beast and running for political office ourselves? Think of the impact: more Christians with biblical compasses exerting direct influence at all levels of government. That's a pretty powerful scenario.

But barring that, grabbing back the power of the purse from those who seek to use and abuse it for wrongful purposes is still a dramatic and bold move that will not only secure the attention of the leading political class, but also zonk them with a wake-up that says, we want a more godly government.

TWO

CHARITY KEEPS US FREE

Give a man a fish and you feed him for a day; teach a man to fish and you feed him for a lifetime. —UNKNOWN ORIGIN

Davy Crockett, an American frontiersman of mythological proportions who went on to serve three terms in the US Congress between 1827 and 1835, was faced with a legislative request to appropriate a sum of money to the widow of an honored naval officer. His congressional colleagues, by and large, were in favor of the bill and as such, delivered several impassioned speeches aimed at showcasing the touted compassionate roots of their legislative cause.

Then, it was Crockett's turn to speak—and his reported words silenced the room:

Mr. Speaker, I have as much respect for the memory of the deceased and as much sympathy for the sufferings of the living, if suffering there be, as any man in this House, but we must not permit our respect for the dead or our sympathy for a part of the living to lead us into an act of injustice to the balance of the living. I will not go into an argument to prove that Congress has no power to appropriate this money as an act of charity. Every member upon this floor knows it. We have the right, as individuals, to give away as much of our own money as we please in charity, but as members of Congress we have no right so to appropriate a dollar of the public money.[1]

Crockett then went on to make the case that the government did not owe a debt to the deceased officer—that his pay had never been in arrears. He further raised some very valid questions: If we pay this widow, what about all the other widows? Do we pay them similarly? Aren't they equally deserving?

"I do not wish to be rude," he concluded, "but I must be plain. Every man in this House knows it is not a debt. We cannot, without the grossest corruption, appropriate this money as the payment of a debt. We have not the semblance of [constitutional] authority to appropriate it as a charity."[2]

Following, the bill failed and the widow didn't get paid by taxpayers. But the story's not ended.

Edward Sylvester Ellis, whose book tells this story, reported that later, a man stormed into Crockett's office to demand—as he put it—"what devil had possessed him to make that speech" and bring about the defeat of the bill.[3]

In response, Crockett recounted how a farmer in his legislative district, named Horatio Bunce, had once chastised him for a vote he had made to appropriate twenty thousand dollars for Georgetown fire victims. Bunce demanded that he point to the place in the Constitution that gave "any authority to give away the public money in charity."[4] Crockett couldn't, and he stumbled to provide an adequate reply.

But Bunce wasn't having any of Crockett's politicking.

"If you have the right to give to one, you have the right to give to all; and, as the Constitution neither defines charity nor stipulates the amount, you are at liberty to give to any and everything which you may believe, or profess to believe, is a charity, and to any amount you may think proper. You will very easily perceive what a wide door this would open for fraud and corruption and favoritism, on the one hand, and for robbing the people on the other," Bunce lectured. "No, Colonel, Congress has no right to give charity. . . . The people have delegated to Congress, by the Constitution, the power to do certain things. To do these, it is authorized to collect and pay moneys, and for nothing else. Everything beyond this is usurpation, and a violation of the Constitution."[5]

It was that dressing-down that Crockett had in mind when he spoke so vehemently against awarding a taxpayer gift to the naval officer's widow. Bunce's constitutional arguments were so sound that the lesson shocked Crockett's core and stuck.

That's a somewhat long story to make only this brief, blunt point: the proper role of America's government is to uphold law, not serve as a charity.

The proper moral role of America's people, on the other hand, is to serve others as they would want to be served themselves—to help those of lesser fortune, ability, and circumstance.

Proverbs 31:8–9 tells us: "Open your mouth for the mute, for the rights of all who are destitute. Open your mouth, judge righteously, defend the rights of the poor and needy." If we are indeed a nation founded on Judeo-Christian ideals, that's a simple command right from God. If we're a nation that's trying to return God to the place of leadership in this country, we ought to do this—and this, from Matthew 5:42: "Give to the one who begs from you, and do not refuse the one who would borrow from you."

Following these principles not only keeps America right with God, but also goes far toward reining in Big Government. If we supply the needs of the needy, they won't have to turn to government and demand so many taxpayer services.

In other words, let's not allow government to be the source where people with problems automatically turn, if those same problems might be addressed through the private sector or by charity. And "charity" can mean either the 501c(3) organizations or the more biblically defined acts of kindness that God expects from all of us.

Our government has no right to take from one to give to another for causes of compassion, or to push through some ideal of equality where none truthfully exists.

GOVERNMENT HAS NO RIGHT TO TAKE FROM ONE TO GIVE TO ANOTHER FOR CAUSES OF COMPASSION, OR TO PUSH THROUGH SOME IDEAL OF EQUALITY WHERE NONE TRUTHFULLY EXISTS.

Our government has no right to kick off endeavors aimed more at righting some perceived wrong that doesn't affect any but the select few.

Our government is not supposed to bestow, but rather protect.
Yet, look at how our government's grown over the years.
The website USA.gov provides an A-to-Z listing of hundreds of
our nation's federal departments and agencies, and while some
are worthwhile and constitutional—like the Air Force and the
Army—others are just head-scratchers.

Among the ones that would spin Davy Crockett in his
grave: the Administration on Aging, which bills itself on its
website as an advocacy organization "for older persons and their
concerns."[6] The African Development Foundation "provides
grants to community groups and small enterprises" for underserved communities in Africa.[7] The Office of Fair Housing and
Equal Opportunity makes policies "to ensure that all Americans
have equal access to the housing of their choice."[8] The James
Madison Memorial Fellowship Foundation provides fellowships
to train those pursuing master's degrees in how to teach the US
Constitution to students.[9]

But why do taxpayer dollars have to be used to further the
interests of the elderly among the political classes? The Meals on
Wheels America nonprofit provides both companionship and
food deliveries to needy senior-aged adults.[10] The Independent
Transportation Network nonprofit gives rides to those age sixty
or higher, as well as to the blind, seven days a week and twenty-
four hours a day, using funds from dues, contributions, and
other private sources.[11] The Pets for the Elderly Foundation helps
match shelter pets with lonely elderly individuals and pay the
adoption fees to give the animals welcoming homes.[12] The AARP
Foundation provides a multitude of services to those aged fifty or
higher, ranging from financial counseling to legal representation
in cases of age discrimination and abuse.[13] That's but a few.

Why does the force of federal government need to be tapped to regulate the laws guiding fair housing, when there's a little thing called the Tenth Amendment—"The powers not delegated to the United States by the Constitution, nor prohibited by it to the States, are reserved to the States respectively, or to the people"—which would seem to render moot the feds' authority to regulate housing at all and instead put it in the hands of the states?

But that aside, plenty of charities, nonprofits, and private groups can step in and meet the housing needs of most Americans. Habitat for Humanity is a terrific organization that builds homes for those in dire need—but selectively. The nonprofit vets candidates to determine which are most committed toward long-term financial stability, and even requires those selected for the program to pitch in, pick up a hammer, and help with the physical construction of their own homes.[14]

Mercy Housing assists families, seniors, veterans, and those with disabilities and illnesses—including people with HIV and AIDS—find affordable rental properties in choice spots around the nation.[15] The National Housing Law Project is a national legal advocacy center to represent low-income and minority tenants fight housing-related injustices, as well as help them expand their access to affordable housing.[16] The Leadership Conference on Civil and Human Rights is a nonprofit that fights for social justice on a variety of matters, including housing.[17] That's only a drop in the bucket of what's out there, and plenty more exist at the state and regional levels.

The Housing Association of Nonprofit Developers, for instance, is a multistate nonprofit dedicated to building more affordable housing in the high-priced Washington, DC, region.[18] Shelter Partnership, Inc. is a nonprofit that seeks to end homelessness in Los Angeles County, California.[19]

The list can certainly go on, but the main point is this: where government is, private charities and nonprofits could easily go—and in many instances, have already gone.

Just look at the government-run African Development Foundation. Why do US tax dollars have to be siphoned for overseas ventures aimed, no doubt, at fulfilling some social justice experiment? Certainly, those living in Africa could use some assistance. But as Davy Crockett learned by listening to the constitutional lesson from one of his constituents, the question is whether or not the rightful purpose of American tax dollars is to be given to those in need, simply because they need. Once again, the private or charity sectors could easily serve in this capacity. Save the Children is a nonprofit with a mission to feed starving children around the world and in Africa.[20] Charity International is a Christian-based organization that helps fight hunger, poverty, and homelessness around the world, with a special emphasis on African famine relief.[21] Africare is a nonprofit with a simple mission: "to improve the quality of life for the people of Africa."[22]

It's not only clear government has overreached into areas better left to the private sector, but it's also evident that if more gave to charities, by way of time or money, we could make much of government irrelevant.

The James Madison Memorial Fellowship program offers a good example of what happens when government steps into a role where it doesn't really belong.

Congress established the James Madison Memorial Fellowship Foundation in 1986 as an independent agency of the executive branch. Funding for the program, which provides up to twenty-four thousand dollars per fellow to pursue their master's degrees, and requires, in return, a teaching commitment, comes from contributions from individuals, businesses, and foundations—as well as from congressional appropriations.[23] In 2014 alone, fifty-one were selected for the fellowship program; the complete list of those chosen since 1986 hits in the hundreds.[24]

But the idea of siphoning federal taxpayer dollars to the executive branch for the purpose of awarding money to master's degree minds so they can teach the Constitution raises some interesting red flags; first and foremost, wouldn't the Founders themselves see such an expenditure as antithetical to their views of proper government? No doubt.

Yet there's another problem to consider. What if taxpayer dollars are being used to teach the Constitution in a manner that's inconsistent with these same taxpayers' own interpretations of the document? A taxpayer with an originalist viewpoint, in line with that of Supreme Court justice Antonin Scalia—who has vehemently stated on several occasions "the Constitution is not a living organism," most recently in March 2015—would hardly appreciate money being awarded to someone with a liberal or progressive mind-set. Yet this is exactly what's occurred.

Not only does the Foundation's website emphasize America's democracy over its republic—red flags to ideological fans of Scalia[25]—but it also showcases this very notion of America as a democracy in at least one female fellow's lessons plan, used during her 2003 program of study. It was entitled "The Progressive Movement (1890–1919) and WWI (1914–1920)," and in it, she wrote of the "strength of a democracy [being] dependent upon public deliberation and having a voice in government" and of the need for "laws in a democracy . . . to establish order, provide security and manage conflict."[26]

But remember: our Founding Fathers didn't want a democracy. They saw a democracy as a rule by the simple majority, susceptible to change with the winds, and a republic as a government run by law, where rights come from God and therefore exist in perpetuity. Fisher Ames called democracy "a volcano which conceals the fiery materials of its own destruction."[27] Noah Webster advised that "our citizens should early understand that the genuine source of correct republican principles is the Bible, particularly the New Testament, or the Christian religion."[28]

"OUR CITIZENS SHOULD EARLY UNDERSTAND THAT THE GENUINE SOURCE OF CORRECT REPUBLICAN PRINCIPLES IS THE BIBLE, PARTICULARLY THE NEW TESTAMENT, OR THE CHRISTIAN RELIGION." —NOAH WEBSTER

But thanks to the James Madison Memorial Fellowship Foundation, taxpayers in at least one instance were paying for a participant to learn and teach the concept of America's government as the very thing the Founders warned against, a democracy. And once again, the basic mission of the James Madison fellowship—to teach the Constitution—could easily be fulfilled outside of government. Hillsdale College provides free online tutorials on the topic.[29] The Heritage Foundation offers a detailed online constitutional tutorial.[30] The Cato Institute provides a free, twelve-course audio home study course on all things liberty, including one specific to the US Constitution.[31] All provide copies of the Declaration of Independence and Constitution in pocket-size versions at low cost. A taxpayer-funded government program is hardly needed in this regard.

Another reason to balk at the idea of government serving in private-sector roles is the potential for waste. It's easy to throw tax dollars at a problem; reaching into one's own pocket, however, seems to bring out the budget-conscious in most of us.

> ANOTHER REASON TO BALK AT THE IDEA OF GOVERNMENT SERVING IN PRIVATE-SECTOR ROLES IS THE POTENTIAL FOR WASTE. IT'S EASY TO THROW TAX DOLLARS AT A PROBLEM; REACHING INTO ONE'S OWN POCKET, HOWEVER, SEEMS TO BRING OUT THE BUDGET-CONSCIOUS IN MOST OF US.

In 2011 the Government Accountability Office published a 345-page report on government waste at the federal level, particularly in the area of overlapping service.[32] The document explained the existence of eighty different agencies to help disadvantaged people obtain transportation; another eighty aimed at helping people with their entrepreneurial endeavors; twenty more dedicated to aiding the homeless; forty-seven more for job training; and seventeen different Federal Emergency

Management Agency grant programs.[33]

Just slashing at some of the duplicity would go far toward reining in government and saving taxpayer dollars. But a good portion of these programs could be made obsolete at the federal level by an increased private sector and charitable organization involvement, especially when these entities join forces with the more local levels of government.

The American Red Cross is certainly less bureaucratic than FEMA; likewise, chambers of commerce and regional unemployment offices are much more responsive to those seeking business and job-related assistance than the US Economic Development Administration. And where would a homeless man have better luck getting a bowl of soup—from the offices of the US Interagency Council on Homelessness, or from a church or nonprofit shelter down the road?

Let's reel in the federal government. One act of charity at a time. As Deuteronomy puts it:

> If there is among you a poor man, one of your brethren, in any of your towns within your land which the Lord your God gives you, you shall not harden your heart or shut your hand against your poor brother, but you shall open your hand to him, and lend him sufficient for his need, whatever it may be. . . . For the poor will never cease out of the land; therefore I command you. You shall open wide your hand to your brother, to the needy and to the poor, in the land. (15:7–8, 11 RSV)

A nation that abided by that biblical command wouldn't have to worry about an ever-swelling government-run social welfare system.

In 2009, when President Obama entered office, about 32 million Americans took part in the federal government's Supplemental Nutrition Assistance Program—or, food stamps. In January 2012, the number of food stamp recipients surpassed 46 million.[34] By March 2014, that number hadn't changed much, and the Department of Agriculture reported 46.1 million program participants.[35] Just look at these numbers; they're horrific for a nation that's supposed to be the light of the world,

SUPPLEMENTAL NUTRITION ASSISTANCE PROGRAM PARTICIPATION AND COSTS
(DATA AS OF AUGUST 7, 2015)

FISCAL YEAR	AVERAGE PARTICIPATION	AVERAGE BENEFIT PER PERSON	TOTAL COSTS
	1,000s	$1,000s	Millions of $
1969	2,878	6.63	250.50
1970	4,340	10.55	576.90
1975	17,064	21.40	4,618.70
1980	21,082	34.47	9,206.50
1985	19,899	44.99	11,703.20
1990	20,049	58.78	15,447.26
1995	26,619	71.27	24,620.37
2000	17,194	72.62	17,054.02
2005	25,628	92.89	31,072.11
2010	40,302	133.79	68,283.47
2011	44,709	133.85	75,686.53
2012	46,609	133.41	78,410.61
2013	47,636	133.07	79,933.40
2014	46,537	125.35	74,157.71

For a complete chart go to http://www.fns.usda.gov/sites/default/files/pd/SNAPsummary.pdf

the bastion of free-market capitalism and wealth opportunities.

With the surge under Obama, it's no wonder he earned the moniker "food stamp president." After six years of his administration, food stamp enrollment rose by some 17 million over the White House days of George W. Bush. As a matter of fact, taxpayers spent $74 billion on SNAP in fiscal 2014 alone—and that's actually down from 2013, when we all paid about $80 billion. By comparison, taxpayers in 1969 only spent $250 million that year on SNAP.

What's going on in this great country of ours?

Since President Lyndon Johnson's 1964 declaration of war on poverty, the United States taxpayer has shelled out trillions of dollars for all kinds of entitlement programs. The House Budget Committee detailed some of the shocking numbers for fiscal year 2012 and found the total cost for ninety-two different antipoverty programs hit right at $799 billion.[36]

WAR ON POVERTY BY THE NUMBERS

PROGRAM AREA	# OF FEDERAL PROGRAMS	COST IN FY2012
CASH AID	5	$220 BILLION
EDUCATION & JOB TRAINING	28	$94.4 BILLION
ENERGY	2	$3.9 BILLION
FOOD AID	17	$105 BILLION
HEALTH CARE	8	$291.3 BILLION
HOUSING	22	$49.6 BILLION
SOCIAL SERVICES	8	$13 BILLION
VETERANS	2	$21.8 BILLION
TOTALS	92	$799 BILLION

Source: http://budget.house.gov/waronpoverty/

The US Senate Committee on the Budget, meanwhile, reported in December 2012 the total welfare spending for those in poverty figured out to about $168 per day per household.[37]

A lot of this higher poverty spending occurred under the most progressive-minded president we've had since Jimmy Carter—President Obama. The Cato Institute reported in April 2012 that welfare spending under Obama increased by 41 percent, to more than $193 billion each year.[38] And for what?

As Cato put it: "Despite this government largess, more than 46 million Americans continue to live in poverty. Despite nearly $15 trillion in total welfare spending since . . . 1964, the poverty rate is perilously close to where we began."[39]

In other words, throwing taxpayer money at the poverty problem just isn't working. It is just a way for politicians to buy votes and launch feel-good campaigns, all the while avoiding the difficult economic decisions that should be part and parcel of good and moral governance. Even President Bill Clinton, as liberal as he was, recognized the need to rein in government entitlement spending and in 1996 signed into law a welfare reform that saw expenditures in this area drop from 3.4 percent of GDP in 1990–1991, to 2.4 percent of GDP in 2000.[40]

It's not enough. Our nation is groaning under the weight of entitlement spending, yet we keep spending. And we keep spending because politicians don't have the boldness of leadership necessary to right the US rudder in this regard.

Benjamin Franklin hit the nail on the head when he wrote:

> I am for doing good to the poor, but I differ in opinion of the means. I think the best way of doing good to the poor, is not making them easy in poverty, but leading or driving them out of it.

In my youth I travelled much, and I observed in different countries, that the more public provisions were made for the poor, the less they provided for themselves, and of course became poorer. And, on the contrary, the less was done for them, the more they did for themselves, and became richer.[41]

Wise words. Now compare them with Obama's during his January 2015 State of the Union speech, when he said, "I want to spread [the] idea all across America . . . that two years of college becomes as free and universal in America as high school is today."[42]

The federal government is not our nanny or our parent. It's not our caretaker or a cradle-to-grave provider. We need to turn back time to a point where can-do attitudes ruled, pull-yourself-up-by-the-bootstrap actions reigned, and government was kept in its place—if only as a means of keeping individual freedoms intact.

With so many accustomed to government handouts, and so many now reliant on subsidized living, the idea of overnight abolishment of federal agencies and departments that provide entitlements may be a bit optimistic. But those concerned with the state of government spending—and with the federal power grab into unconstitutional arenas—can lead by example, and take action now, one step at a time.

In short, charity can help keep America free.

Don't like tax dollars being used for food stamps? Help feed the hungry. Donate money or time to the local shelter.

Don't want the federal government spending money to promote some social justice ideal of fair housing? Pick up a hammer and help out Habitat for Humanity.

Think FEMA's a bureaucratic nightmare that only wastes tax dollars? Volunteer to host a family displaced by flood or fire. Or send in some money to a private or nonprofit disaster relief fund.

The need's everywhere. As Jesus said, "You always have the poor with you" (Matt. 26:11).

One key to a free America, and to a country that's righteous in God's eyes, is to keep government from being the main provider.

THREE

PUTTING THE BIBLE BACK IN SCHOOLS

Now, the education of our children is of national concern, and if they are not educated properly, it is a national calamity. —DWIGHT D. EISENHOWER, THE PRESIDENT'S NEWS CONFERENCE, JULY 31, 1957

On April 9, 1965, and as part of his "War on Poverty," President Lyndon B. Johnson signed into law the Elementary and Secondary Education Act, one of the most far-reaching federal education initiatives to ever pass Capitol Hill muster. Notably, the bill took only a few months to move from introduction to passage.[1] ESEA, or Public Law 89-10, basically gave the thumbs-up to federal spending for public schools to bolster K–12 initiatives. Since its passage, it's been reauthorized several times.

Then came President George W. Bush's No Child Left Behind Act, the 2001 White House–pressed education reform that was aimed at implementing more expansive test-driven accountability standards for states to implement in schools nationwide. NCLB was simply the latest iteration of ESEA.

It mandated that schools that received certain federal dollars for low-income students had to show adequate yearly progress (AYP) in student performance, tracked via testing, or else face consequences ranging from warnings to state takeovers.[2]

Many saw NCLB as an unprecedented federal step into state and local domains. Bush didn't disagree that the initiative was ambitious, declaring soon after NCLB became law that a "new era" of public education had just been ushered into America. His comrade in education reform arms, the very liberal Democratic senator Edward Kennedy and bill sponsor, spoke similarly of the legislative endeavor, saying during floor discussion of NCLB that it represented the "defining issue about the future of our nation."[3]

Not all were so enamored. Critics called it a bold federal encroachment with impossibly high standards and state mandates. Some teachers and students, meanwhile, detested the test-after-test-after-test demands that seemed to crush classroom creativity and squash independent thinking, and that required educators to prove their worth through the achievement of certain credentials and classroom scores.[4] The next test always loomed; the next government assessment always beckoned. In short, NCLB really yanked education out of the hands of locals and put it in the control of bureaucrats.[5]

Next up: Common Core—or, the Common Core State Standards Initiative of 2009, a joint project of the National Governors' Association Center for Best Practices and the Council of Chief State School Officers.[6] Those two groups, using recommendations from other organizations that had determined America's students were at risk of falling behind global rankings in math and English—and also using $35 million provided by the Bill and Melinda Gates Foundation—released in the 2009–10 time frame their final reports that would become known as Common Core.[7] The initiative was quickly adopted by almost all fifty states.

ONCE COMMON CORE WAS ADOPTED, IT DIDN'T TAKE LONG FOR THE FEDERAL HEAVY-HANDEDNESS TO BEGIN, AND THE LUSTER OVER THE PROGRAM TO DIM. TEXAS, WHICH NEVER DID SIGN ON TO IT, TOOK THE LEAD IN SOUNDING THE ALARMS ON COMMON CORE TO THE REST OF THE STATES.

But it didn't take long for the federal heavy-handedness to begin, and the luster over the program to dim. Texas, which never did sign on to it, took the lead in sounding the alarms on Common Core to the rest of the states. Texas governor Rick Perry called it "an effort to undermine states' authority to determine how their students are educated."[8]

Mass dissension from the states really arose when President Barack Obama tied the adoption and achievement of Common Core standards to schools' receipt of Race to the Top grant dollars.[9]

The carrot-and-stick approach was perceived by states—especially those led by Republican governors—as a way for Obama to simply ram through his own vision of education reform from the bureaucratic comfort of his White House seat. By the end of 2014, several states had moved to repeal Common Core.[10]

Louisiana governor Bobby Jindal, meanwhile, filed a federal lawsuit, alleging that the Department of Education had basically blackmailed states by demanding they adopt Common Core or lose out on school grant dollars. He said, to a national newspaper, "Common Core is the latest effort by big government disciples to strip away state rights and put Washington, D.C. in control of everything. What started out as an innovative idea to create a set of baseline standards that could be 'voluntarily' used by the states has turned into a scheme by the federal government to nationalize curriculum."[11]

The issue grew even hotter in the months that followed. In February 2015, at the Conservative Political Action Conference, or CPAC, attendees and participants struck the heavy-handed tone that the standards needed to get the boot.[12]

Okay—so what's the point of running down all this history?

Simply to drive home this basic idea: America needs to wake up to all the federally imposed education of our youth that's going on.

For decades now this country has seen the control of children's education taken—sometimes slowly, sometimes with jarring efficiency—out of the hands of parents and local schools, and put with much ceremony and fanfare into the hands of Big Government. That's the same as banking our nation's future on the federal government.

"WHOEVER HAS THE YOUTH HAS THE FUTURE." —ADOLF HITLER

Remember: it was Adolf Hitler who wrote in *Mein Kampf* that "whoever has the youth has the future."[13] And it was Hitler who forced teachers to swear an oath of allegiance to him and to instruct students in ways that would secure the future of his Third Reich for generations to come—beginning with the importance of obedience to authority, and the Nazi Party oversight of all school curriculum and textbooks.[14]

The importance of the education of our youth cannot be overstated.

Compare Hitler's vision to what Benjamin Franklin saw as an ideal school for the newly formed nation, when he wrote in October 1749 his "Proposals Relating to the Education of Youth in Pennsylvania" of the importance of instruction in a range of topics—from penmanship, letter writing, and drawing, to geography and several histories—so that "[we] might supply the succeeding Age with Men qualified to serve the Publick with Honour to themselves and to their Country."[15] But also among his proposals? That morality be part of formal instruction.

Franklin wrote that morality should be taught "by descanting and making continual Observations on the Causes of the Rise or Fall of any Man's Character, Fortune, Power . . . the Advantages of Temperance, Order, Frugality, Industry, Perseverance . . . Indeed the general natural Tendency of Reading good history, must be, to fix in the Minds of Youth deep Impressions of the Beauty and Usefulness of Virtue of all Kinds, Publick Spirit, Fortitude."[16]

His reason was pretty basic. "The good Education of

Youth has been esteemed by wise Men in all Ages, as the surest Foundations of the Happiness both of private Families and of Common-wealths," he wrote.[17]

MODERN-DAY SCHOOLS DISPARAGE THE IDEA OF TEACHING ANYTHING

TO DO WITH MORALITY OR VIRTUE—OR, GOD FORBID, GOD.

Yet modern-day schools disparage the idea of teaching anything to do with morality or virtue—or, God forbid, God. Instead, this is what we get:

Parents in Chicago in November 2014 were horrified to learn that a proposed sexual education curriculum that educators were considering for fifth graders included instructions on how to use female condoms for anal sex—and that was just a drop in the bucket of some of the shocking suggested courses of study.[18]

A few months later, in February 2015, Pennsylvania parents were equally outraged to learn their Monessen Middle School children were handed word-search puzzles based on the sexually graphic book and film *Fifty Shades of Grey*, which included disturbing scenes of bondage and sadomasochism. Some of their search words? Bondage. Handcuffs. Leather cuffs. Spanking. Those were the tamer ones. Others were much more explicit, so explicit, in fact, that when reporting on this story the *New York Daily News* blurred out several of the more graphic items.[19]

Meanwhile, a father in Fort Lauderdale, Florida, in May 2014 was dismayed to discover his twelve-year-old son's teacher had chastised him for bringing a Bible to school to read in his free time, ordering him to the front of the class and demanding he use the telephone on her desk to call home. The Park Lakes Elementary School teacher then left a terse voice mail for the boy's parents about his "religious book," and made clear that "he's not permitted to read those books in my classroom," Fox News reported. The Liberty Institute stepped in to represent the boy and his family and fight for his religious rights.[20]

SO, GRAPHIC AND EXPLICIT SEXUAL TEACHINGS ARE A-OK. BUT THE BIBLE'S NOT. THIS IS WHAT OUR NEXT GENERATION IS LEARNING IN GOVERNMENT-SPONSORED SCHOOLS.

So, graphic and explicit sexual teachings are A-OK. But the Bible's not. This is what our next generation is learning in government-sponsored schools.

Childhood education rightly—constitutionally and morally—belongs under the purview of the parents. It does not belong under the control of the White House and Congress, or even with the federal Department of Education, a bureaucratic nightmare formed in 1979 under President Jimmy Carter that, according to the Tenth Amendment, does not even have the constitutional right to exist.[21] Where does the Constitution give the federal government the right to collect taxes for schools and oversee their operations? As the Tenth Amendment states, "The powers not delegated to the United States by the Constitution, nor prohibited by it to the States, are reserved to the States respectively, or to the people." Clearly, the Founding Fathers never intended for federal hands to guide and control the formal teachings of our nation's youngest and most vulnerable.

Neither does the role of education belong in the hands of the myriad of unions that now serve as enablers for the worst in teaching by clamping the ability of locals to make crucial contract decisions.

Who can forget the vicious attacks waged by the teachers' unions against Wisconsin governor Scott Walker in 2011 when he dared scale back collective bargaining rights for educators?[22] Activists and union supporters took off work—many even flocking from other states—and took over the Capitol, basically setting up camp, refusing to leave, acting more like Occupy Wall Street thugs than respectable members of educated society.

As conservative radio talker Rush Limbaugh described in a February 2011 broadcast, "Folks, I don't think the people in Wisconsin, the unions, the teachers and some of the protesters— I don't think they got the memo on civility. Have you seen what's going on? I mean this is Greece! It's Greece."[23] Limbaugh went on to describe some of the protesters' signs: One read, "Hosni + Hitler = Dictator Scott Walker." And another: "Down with dictators, one to go," with a picture of Hosni Mubarak, the former embattled president of Egypt, who resigned in February 2011 amid allegations of corruption and abuse of power, alongside a picture of Walker.

Truly, we must get the federal government, and its teachers' union sidekicks, out of our nation's schools.

But that's a well-worn argument, isn't it? And really, where has it brought us? If anything, the federal hand in schools has only grown heavier; the revolving door of union funding to politicians is spinning just as madly as ever.

It's time for a new tack.

"WITHOUT GOD, THERE COULD BE NO AMERICAN FORM OF GOVERNMENT,

NOR AN AMERICAN WAY OF LIFE." –DWIGHT EISENHOWER

Instead of focusing on what to take out of our schools, maybe we should shift tracks and look at something better to put in. As President Dwight Eisenhower said, "Without God, there could be no American form of government, nor an American way of life."[24]

So let's take that mantra and make it part of our schools' DNA. We need to bring Bible classes back to the public school system.

The US Supreme Court ruled in its 1963 *School District of Abington Township v. Schempp* that the Bible could "certainly [be] . . . worthy of study for its literary and historic qualities," even when "presented effectively as part of a secular program of education" in public school.[25] The same court affirmed in 1980 in *Stone v. Graham* that "the Bible may constitutionally be used in an appropriate study of history, civilization, ethics, comparative religion, or the like."[26]

Meanwhile, the American public is supportive of the idea.

Fully 81 percent of Americans participating in a 2014 survey by the Barna Group said morality is on the decline in the nation. The study, titled *The State of the Bible 2014*, further reported that 26 percent of those participants blamed this sorry condition on citizens' failure to read the Bible.[27] Another 50 percent thought the Bible had "too little influence" on US life—more than three times the ratio of those who thought it had "too much influence," about 16 percent.[28]

Perhaps most significantly, in 2013, this same survey found 66 percent of adults in the United States favored the Bible being taught in schools.[29]

Sixty-six percent.

So what's the holdup?

Fearful politicians, for one. Any mention of God in schools, of God in government, and most of today's political class heads for the exit doors. They're afraid of being sued.

In 2014, New Jersey senior Samantha Jones fought back an atheist attempt to remove the phrase "under God" from recitation of the Pledge of Allegiance in her Highland Regional High School.

The complaint was first made in February 2014 by a Monmouth County family who partnered with the American Humanist Association to sue the Matawan-Aberdeen Regional School District, claiming "under God" was discriminatory and violated the state's constitution. Jones stepped up to the plate and said that's not true—and then waged a court battle to keep the Pledge intact, with the assistance of the Becket Fund for Religious Liberty and other groups.[30]

In February 2015, she won her case, and told Fox News shortly after the ruling went public, "Ever since I was little, I've recited the Pledge of Allegiance because it sums up the values that make our country great. The phrase 'under God' protects all Americans—including atheists—because it reminds the government that it can't take away basic human rights because it didn't create them."[31]

The fact that she had to fight that battle at all, however, only showcases the cowardice of our politicians and government servants: one atheist cry, one threat of suit, and they crumble. Remember Michael Newdow, the atheist who took his objections to the phrase "under God" to court, alleging his daughter—who didn't even live with him, but rather with her mother, at a different residence—was being indoctrinated by the school during daily recitation of the Pledge? He took his objections to several courts, losing at the district level, winning on appeal, and finally landing on the desks of the US Supreme Court justices in 2004.[32] His 2004 *Elk Grove Unified School District v. Newdow* case sparked a national furor, and though he ultimately lost his fight to remove the phrase from use in public schools, it was only due to the Supreme Court's 5-3 determination that he lacked "prudential standing" to bring the case—and not due to any judicial finding that his argument was unsound.[33]

That's alarming. It shows just how influential a single committed atheist can be in knocking out any mention of God from the public arena.

Don't expect the battle to bring Bible courses into public schools to be any easier.

Naysayers will argue that bringing the Bible into classroom discussions violates the "separation of church and state standard"—even though the nation's highest court has already ruled the material is acceptable for certain uses in schools. They'll also throw arguments into the equation that demand equal access for other religious-based books, like the Qur'an.

Well, let them. We're not talking about Bible-thumping here. And we're not talking about mandated classes, but rather optional offerings.

The National Council on Bible Curriculum in Public Schools, an organization with a mission to bring elective Bible courses to public school systems around the nation—as comparative reading for literature and history—touts success with more than 2,500 high schools in thirty-nine states. The group said on its website that its "curriculum has been voted into 1,025 school districts . . . [and] over 625,000 students have already taken this course."[34]

This is the way to go, the direction we need to pursue.

As Noah Webster said, "The moral principles and precepts contained in the Scriptures ought to form the basis of all our civil constitutions and laws. All the miseries and evils which men suffer from vice, crime, ambition, injustice, oppression, slavery and war, proceed from their despising or neglecting the precepts contained in the Bible."[35]

Surely it's as important for our nation's children, who will grow into our nation's leaders and lawmakers, to receive publicly funded instruction in this regard as it is for them to word search on "bondage" and "spanking" and learn the proper techniques for female condoms.

"Train up a child in the way he should go: and when he is old, he will not depart from it." (Prov. 22:6 KJV)

Proverbs 22:6 is both a comfort and a warning. Those who teach their children of right and wrong, of godly principles versus satanic influences, of God and His Word, can take comfort that the rebellion years are simply a stage—their children will return in time to the correct path of their lives. That's the blessing.

But the warning, though unspoken, is this: those who teach their children an ungodly view of life, one where neither absolutes nor heavenly judge exist—and where teaching little kids about bondage and S&M makes perfect sense—can only expect these youth to carry those teachings into adulthood.

Train a child to believe God doesn't belong in the classroom, and he will grow to persecute those who bring their Bibles to school, or those who take an oath of government office that's "under God."

Train a child to see sex as just a fun pastime—just another word search subject, like names of baseball greats or American presidents—and she will grow to regard biblical ideas of marriage, morality, and sin as out-of-date, unnecessary, and foolish.

It's not hard to see the roots here. It's also not hard to see the finish line.

THE CHILDREN WE BREED WILL BE THE CHILDREN WHO SOON LEAD.

If our nation's laws are basically examples of our nation's collective morality—whether good or bad—then those laws ought to come from the hearts and minds of politicians and people who are properly trained and educated. We get the government we deserve; we get the government that reflects ourselves.

If we drive out God from our nation's schools, and elevate government to His position—and extinguish all flames of morality, virtue, and principle from the classrooms—it shouldn't be a surprise when the next generation of leaders is secular and selfish, beholden to their own interests. Neither should it surprise us when the upcoming political class pushes for cradle-to-grave entitlements, higher taxes and income distribution, and the radicalized separation of church and state.

So let's let Him back.

A little biblically based teaching in the schools could do wonders in training the next generation in the way it should go.

FOUR

THE BORDER BATTLE CANNOT BE CEDED

Those who forsake the law praise the wicked, but those who keep the law strive against them. Even men do not understand justice, but those who seek the Lord understand it completely. —PROVERBS 28:4–5

What does it mean to be a good Christian, a moral American citizen and a defender of godly principles on the issue of immigration?

That's definitely one of the most pressing issues of our time with a decision that looms large to the fate of our republic, our system of laws, and our ability to keep our government right with God. Luckily, the Bible offers guidance.

> When a stranger sojourns with you in your land, you shall not do him wrong. You shall treat the stranger who sojourns with you as the native among you, and you shall love him as yourself, for you were strangers in the land of Egypt; I am the Lord your God. (Lev. 19:33–34)

You shall not wrong a sojourner or oppress him, for you were sojourners in the land of Egypt. (Ex. 22:21)

Do not neglect to show hospitality to strangers, for thereby some have entertained angels unawares. (Heb. 13:2)

Many Christians have taken these passages, and others, to mean the United States has an obligation to provide for the illegal immigrants who cross our borders, some seeking new lives, new opportunities, and new family roots. The US Conference of Catholic Bishops even wrote a letter to Department of Homeland Security secretary Jeh Johnson in March 2014, pressing for new immigration reform that included amnesty and that phased out enforcement of existing deportation laws used by select communities around the nation. It read, in part:

We believe that legislation which provides a path to citizenship for as many as possible of the deserving members of the current undocumented population living in the United States would protect the integrity of immigrant families and communities and serve the security, social and economic interests of the United States. . . . The use of the Secure Communities program mandated for every jurisdiction and the 287(g) program has contributed to the increase in deportations and, in our view, undermined basic civil rights. We strongly believe these programs should be phased out, as they create fear and distrust in immigrant communities.[1]

Members and leaders of the Mormon, Protestant, and Jewish faiths have also pushed for amnesty-like provisions from the Obama administration based on moral principles and biblical citations.[2]

But it's hard to believe in a morality that teaches that breaking the law is okay.

> IT'S HARD TO BELIEVE IN A MORALITY THAT TEACHES THAT
>
> BREAKING THE LAW IS OKAY.

Our nation is the light on the hill—the bastion of freedom in a world of oppression and dictatorships. It's the land of the free, set aside at the earliest of stages for the "Glory of God," as the Pilgrims penned on November 11, 1620, in the Mayflower Compact:

> Having undertaken for the Glory of God and advancement of the Christian Faith and Honour of our King and Country, a Voyage to plant the First Colony in the Northern Parts of Virginia, do by these presents solemnly and mutually in the presence of God and one of another, Covenant and Combine ourselves together in a Civil Body Politic, for our better ordering and preservation and furtherance of the ends aforesaid.[3]

So if the first formal bit of governance on what was to become American soil was based on glorifying God and establishing a covenant with Him for the New World, how can it possibly be godly to give a free pass of amnesty to those who break the law to be here?

We reap what we sow. Allowing illegals free entry mocks those who took the difficult steps to become citizens, burdens the taxpayers for services that shouldn't even be rendered, and completely uproots the notions of law and order that are supposed to be guiding our government.

WE REAP WHAT WE SOW. ALLOWING ILLEGALS FREE ENTRY MOCKS THOSE WHO TOOK THE DIFFICULT STEPS TO BECOME CITIZENS, BURDENS THE TAXPAYERS FOR SERVICES THAT SHOULDN'T EVEN BE RENDERED, AND COMPLETELY UPROOTS THE NOTIONS OF LAW AND ORDER THAT ARE SUPPOSED TO BE GUIDING OUR GOVERNMENT.

Aside from that, sojourners, by definition, are temporary visitors. The biblical passages cited for regarding illegals as sojourners—and therefore morally worthy of US citizenship—aren't even valid arguments.

But the longer-term problem with turning our nation's immigration law on its head—and justifying that behavior as Christian or based on some spiritual and religious moral code—is that it dismisses the gift God has given us. America is exceptional; opening the doors for anybody and everybody to enter denies and degrades that gift of American exceptionalism.

Again, we reap what we sow.

Conservative columnist and author Ann Coulter wrote

in a piece on WND.com in late February 2015 that illegal immigrants were murdering more Americans than Islamic State terrorists ever would.[4] A couple of months later, in April, government watchdog Judicial Watch reported that according to anonymous sources, members of ISIS were operating a terror training camp in Mexico, just a few miles from El Paso. That report wasn't independently confirmed by members of the law enforcement community.[5] Regardless, the danger is there.

In 2010 the Department of Homeland Security sent out an alert to Texas law enforcement officials to keep an eye out for a suspected member of Al Shabaab, a terror group based in Somalia, who was believed to be plotting an illegal entrance into the United States through a vulnerable Mexico border spot. That warning came on the heels of another report just weeks earlier. The unsealing of court documents revealed a Somalian man was facing charges by federal authorities for running a smuggling operation to bring hundreds of Somalis from Brazil into the United States. Al Shabaab, which has a stated goal of imposing sharia law in Somalia, was designated a terrorist organization by the United States in 2008.[6]

Such examples only further Coulter's point—that illegal immigration is a far more critical issue to get ahold of than ISIS in keeping America safe and in constitutional check.

In the short term, open borders mean a welcome mat to criminals and, yes, terrorists. But it's the long term that's even more problematic. How long can our Constitution stand up to a constituency that doesn't understand the limited-governance standard the Founding Fathers set in place?

The more who come from countries that don't have a form of government based on the rule of law and the principle of limited governance, and who then win amnesty so they don't have to go the legal route of becoming citizens and learn the historical story of American exceptionalism, the less chance our republic has of standing. The time will come when the scales of balance will be tipped in this nation and those of an entitlement mind-set—those who hail from poverty-stricken and corrupt governments where the ingrained attitudes are all about hand-outs and income redistribution, not individual achievement and independence—will make up the majority.

That will then become the mind-set of the majority who vote in elections.

By logical extension, the winners of the elections will then be those who vow to represent that entitlement-minded majority and who advocate for such things as higher taxes and more social welfare spending. Our nation will crumble from within. Gone will be free-market capitalism; in its place will stand more government control.

Then what will we do? How will we turn back the country to its constitutional, limited government roots then?

Thomas Jefferson wrote brilliantly on this issue, pointing out the pitfalls of mass immigration, in his *Notes on the State of Virginia:*

> Every species of government has its specific principles. Ours perhaps are more peculiar than those of any other in the universe. It is a composition of the freest principles of the English constitution, with others derived from natural right and natural reason. To these nothing can be more opposed than the maxims of absolute monarchies. Yet, from such, we are to expect the greatest number of emigrants. They will bring with them the principles of the

governments they leave, imbibed in their early youth; or, if able to throw them off, it will be in exchange for an unbounded licentiousness, passing, as is usual, from one extreme to another. It would be a miracle were they to stop precisely at the point of temperate liberty. These principles, with their language, they will transmit to their children. In proportion to their numbers, they will share with us the legislation. . . . Suppose 20 millions of republican Americans thrown all of a sudden into France, what would be the condition of that kingdom? If it would be more turbulent, less happy, less strong, we may believe that the addition of half a million of foreigners to our present numbers would produce a similar effect here.[7]

Those words may have hailed from centuries ago, but they're just as true and applicable today.

Meanwhile, in the immediate, crime is a huge concern.

The soft-and-feely line of thought on immigration is that illegals pour into our nation because they're only trying to provide for their families—they're only trying to obtain jobs, homes, and economic stability, and to become fine, upstanding, and fully assimilated members of US society. That's no doubt true for some. But hardly all.

The Center for Immigration Studies (CIS) produced a report in 2009 based in part on Department of Homeland Security statistics that tracked the intersection of crime and illegal alien status, and found that 221,000 jail inmates around the nation were of noncitizen status—about 11 to 15 percent of those facilities' population. By contrast, only 8.6 percent of the nation's total adult population during that time frame were considered noncitizens. Those are just the state numbers. The Federal Bureau of Prisons reported that 26.4 percent of inmates in the federal penitentiary system were deemed noncitizens of the United States in that same year.[8]

"Between 1991 and 2007, enforcement of federal immigration laws became a growing priority in response to undocumented immigration," wrote the authors of the 2009 Pew Hispanic Center report "A Rising Share: Hispanics and Federal Crime." They went on, "By 2007, immigration offenses represented nearly one-quarter (24 percent) of all federal convictions, up from just 7 percent in 1991."[9]

A GOOD PORTION OF THE NATION'S JAIL AND PRISON CELLS ARE BEING FILLED BY THOSE WHO SHOULDN'T BE IN THE COUNTRY IN THE FIRST PLACE. —PEW HISPANIC CENTER

Further, the report showed that a good portion of the nation's jail and prison cells were being filled by those who shouldn't be in the country in the first place. Their crimes? "Among Hispanic offenders sentenced in federal courts" in 2007, "48% were sentenced for an immigration offense and 37% for a drug offense."[10]

By 2012, a separate and updated Pew Research Center report found that the number of illegal immigrants sentenced in federal courts for unlawful entry into the United States stood at 68 percent. Another 19 percent of illegals were sentenced to federal prisons for drug offenses in that same year.[11]

One conclusion to draw from all these numbers?

That the nation's prison population holds a heck of a lot of illegals, especially when the numbers are considered as a percentage of the known illegal immigration population residing in the country, outside of prison and jail walls.

The CIS warns that many of the data used to analyze the links between illegal immigration and crime rates are susceptible to error.[12] That makes sense given the various reporting and compiling methods used by all the different agencies, special interest groups, nonprofits, educational facilities, and others. But even low-balling the number of illegals imprisoned in state and federal facilities is alarming in this respect: it flies in the face of amnesty activists' contentions that people are only sneaking into America to secure employment, to help their families, and to live peacefully with their fellow citizens.

Even Mitt Romney, no bastion of strict constructionist interpretation of constitutional principles, remarked to a Manchester, New Hampshire, crowd in June 2007, "I very firmly believe that we have to make sure that we enforce our borders, that we have an employment verification system, and that those people who have come here illegally do not get an advantage to become permanent residents, they do not get a special pathway."[13]

Good idea.

Upsetting the laws of our nation shouldn't win the lawbreaker special access, and truthfully, those who cross the border into America by underhanded means are already lawbreakers, even if they don't commit any other crimes during their stays. And going after the employers who enable these illegals to not only come but stay in this country seems a good starting point to control our borders.

Each day an illegal border crosser stays on US soil is another day of criminal behavior. We should not allow politicians and special-rights groups to skew and convolute the fact that a law is a law, and a broken law, a broken law, by calling for compassion and slinging accusations of coldheartedness.

As John Adams said, during a statement for the defense at the Boston Massacre trial, "Facts are stubborn things; and whatever may be our wishes, our inclinations, or the dictates of our passions, they cannot alter the state of facts and evidence."[14]

Politicians on Capitol Hill have the luxury, not to mention the impudence, to slam Americans who oppose illegal immigrants and amnesty policies as heartless and uncaring for one main reason: they're largely sheltered from the ramifications of their legislative actions.

POLITICIANS ON CAPITOL HILL HAVE THE LUXURY, NOT TO MENTION THE IMPUDENCE, TO SLAM AMERICANS WHO OPPOSE ILLEGAL IMMIGRANTS AND AMNESTY POLICIES AS HEARTLESS AND UNCARING FOR ONE MAIN REASON: THEY'RE LARGELY SHELTERED FROM THE RAMIFICATIONS OF THEIR LEGISLATIVE ACTIONS.

Can you imagine the crackdown at the border if Malia Obama, the president's daughter, were ever injured by a drunken driver who was in the nation illegally? Just saying.

In August 2013, Cochise County sheriff's deputies found sixty-one-year-old National Park worker Karen Weston Gonzales bloody and unconscious on the bathroom floor near a picnic area inside Chiricahua National Monument in Arizona.[15] Her attacker, Gil Gaxiola, thirty-three, an illegal immigrant with a felony conviction, who had previously been deported, took off in her truck, leaving the rock he'd used to batter her at the scene.[16] Months later, he was arrested and charged with attempted first-degree murder, attempted second-degree murder, armed robbery, and multiple counts of aggravated assault, kidnapping, and theft. In February 2015, he was deemed incompetent to stand trial and ordered to attend a competency restoration program in hopes of getting him to a level of mental capacity where he can actually face his charges in a court of law.[17]

As for Gonzales?

She walks with a cane and was forced, due to the physical stresses brought on by her attacker, to quit her job at the park. And on the state of the border with Mexico, she had this to say in an NBC report: "It's not that safe. The closer you get to the border, the more unsafe it is."[18]

Her story isn't one that's likely to be shared by Sen. Harry Reid, who famously declared after emerging from a weekly lunch with fellow Democrats in July 2014, "The border is secure. [Sen.] Martin Heinrich talked to the caucus today. He's a border state senator. He said he can say without any equivocation the border is secure."[19] To put this in context, a month earlier, Reid and his wife, Landra, had just sold their Searchlight, Nevada, home for the cool price of $1.7 million, cheering how the buyer, Nevada Milling and Mining, would now be able to expand on the property and create sixty new jobs.[20]

Does this sound like the type of guy who worries about illegals breaking into his home at night, stealing his food, attacking his family, making off with his truck? Hardly.

But on immigration, politicians constantly talk out of both sides of their mouths, trying to guilt Americans into believing an open border mantra is a calling from the Creator, but dismissing the aspect of God that represents law and justice.

> POLITICIANS CONSTANTLY TALK OUT OF BOTH SIDES OF THEIR MOUTHS, TRYING TO GUILT AMERICANS INTO BELIEVING AN OPEN BORDER MANTRA IS A CALLING FROM THE CREATOR, BUT DISMISS THE IDEA THAT GOD THAT REPRESENTS LAW AND JUSTICE.

Perhaps nowhere else did the divide between leftist politicians and those of sane, logical mind show wider than the case of Kate Steinle, the thirty-two-year-old woman who was walking along a pier in San Francisco with her father when she was gunned down in broad daylight.[21] As she uttered her last words, "Help me, Dad," her attacker—an illegal immigrant named Juan Francisco Lopez-Sanchez, who first admitted to police he committed the killing but then pleaded not guilty at his arraignment—fled.[22] Turns out, Sanchez already had a voluminous US criminal record that included the use of thirty aliases and at least three lengthy prison sentences and prior deportations, and he shouldn't have been in America in the first place.[23] In fact, he was in San Francisco only because it was a sanctuary city and he knew he wouldn't be deported.[24] But the Left's response to those who demanded justice—to those who called for a clamp on the border, an overturn of sanctuary city policy, a recognition that existing policy wasn't working but rather endangering the lives of innocent Americans?

There was this, from Minority Speaker Nancy Pelosi: "The fact that San Francisco is a sanctuary city—and there are many sanctuary cities; many people live in sanctuary cities across the country—that has nothing to do with what happened in San Francisco [with Steinle]. . . . What we also have to look at is, how did this person come into possession of a gun in a state where his having a gun as a convicted felon would raise serious questions."[25]

And this, from the sanctuary cities: *We're not changing.* Even in the face of Steinle's murder, neither San Francisco nor the two hundred or so other sanctuary cities around the nation apparently saw any immediate need to roll back their welcome mats to illegals.[26]

No wonder Donald Trump's poll numbers in the early part of his presidential campaign hit such high notes, besting at most points all the other Republican candidates in the field by several percentage points. At the same time Steinle's body was being buried, Trump was aggressively and bluntly tapping into voter anger and exposing the real disconnect between politicians and the rest of America on an issue that seems so easy to understand: if border policies were enforced, those with criminal intent couldn't be here in the first place to commit more crimes.

The long-term ramification of letting emotion, sympathy,

and political agenda rather than the rule of law drive immigration policy and regulation is the loss of the republic our early patriots fought so hard to win. It's the loss of respect for the legal and judicial systems that are supposed to be blind to the political winds of the day. It's the demise of our society, as it was established and forged.

Steinle's dire fate, sadly, was just one of many similar tales. Police in May 2014 arrested a man named Oscar Ayala-Arizmendi, a thirty-six-year-old illegal immigrant who was accused of abducting and keeping a twenty-seven-year-old woman as a sex slave in his Idaho home for eighteen months.[27] He also allegedly beat her with a hammer, forced her to take drugs, and booby-trapped the house so she could not leave.[28] As one perceptive blogger opined, "The next time a liberal tells you that illegals are poor, oppressed victims of capitalism who are just coming here to work hard, remember the name Oscar Ayala-Arizmendi."[29]

In another case, an investigation by the western Washington–based KING 5 news found that an illegal immigrant named Jose Lopez Madrigal, who was arrested and accused of raping a woman in 2010, had actually been deported nine times, the first in 1989, after he was convicted of theft using a firearm during a California incident.[30]

Madrigal, from Mexico, was then deported for drug sales, sexual assault, and various other incidents between 1989 and 2003. He was deported three times in 1999 alone, and another three times in 2003. Immigrations and Customs Enforcement wouldn't comment on his case. But KING 5 pieced together his past via various source interviews, leading those in the community, and around the nation, to wonder, *How could someone so violent fall through the cracks of immigration law?* As KING 5 put it, "One criminal justice source says Madrigal is a poster boy for the federal government's ineffectiveness at keeping the most serious criminal aliens—illegals who commit crimes—out of the United States."[31]

In yet another case, police in Princeton, New Jersey, in May 2014 were finally able to bring to justice an illegal alien, Humberto Gonzalez, for the sexual assault of a fifty-three-year-old woman. The incident occurred in 2005, but at that time police could only collect his DNA from the victim; Gonzalez fled.

THE LONG-TERM RAMIFICATION OF LETTING EMOTION, SYMPATHY AND POLITICAL AGENDA RATHER THAN THE RULE OF LAW DRIVE IMMIGRATION POLICY AND REGULATION IS THE LOSS OF THE REPUBLIC OUR EARLY PATRIOTS FOUGHT SO HARD TO WIN.

In 2012, authorities caught a break when Gonzalez was booked into a Texas jail for aggravated assault with a deadly weapon for a separate case, and his DNA flagged in the system for the 2005 rape. Finally, in mid-2014, Gonzalez was found guilty of kidnapping, criminal restraint, and assault, and faced up to fifty years in prison.[32] The victim and victim's family cheered. But a more cynical comment is, Gonzalez shouldn't have been in the country in the first place.

That's what makes crime by illegal immigrants so infuriating:

legally, they shouldn't even be here. Meanwhile, our president and complicit Congress bend over backwards to encourage more to come.

In a November 2014 address at the White House, Obama vowed to use his executive power to defer the deportations of about five million undocumented immigrants, based in part on their family ties to the United States. At the same time, he spun truths and twisted commonly accepted definitions, outright denying he was even pressing for amnesty.

"Now, let's be clear about [this deal]. . . . All we're saying is we're not going to deport you. I know some of the critics of this action call it amnesty. Well, it's not," he said then, before turning his voice toward Capitol Hill and his Republican opposition: "To those members of Congress who question my authority to make our immigration system work better, or question the wisdom of me acting where Congress has failed, I have one answer: Pass a bill."[33]

His bully tactics worked. A few months later, Republicans in Congress, under the leadership of Speaker John Boehner, passed through a clean funding bill for the Department of Homeland Security—the same funding that Tea Party types wanted to use to barter with Obama and stop his amnesty.[34]

So what's a concerned American supposed to do? Write a member of Congress? Take vengeance at the polls? That doesn't seem to be working.

In June 2012, the Obama administration announced its "deferred action for childhood arrivals," the so-dubbed DREAMers program, to give temporary legal status to certain illegals who entered the United States as minors and delay their deportations for a minimum of two years.[35] In November 2014, President

Obama announced an expansion to the DREAMers program, as well as a new Deferred Action for Parental Accountability, or DAPA, program. DAPA grants for a period of three years a shelter from deportation to illegal immigrants who are parents of US citizens and lawful permanent residents.[36]

It didn't take long for word to get out around the world: *Hey, come to America. You won't be deported.*

IT DIDN'T TAKE LONG FOR WORD TO GET OUT AROUND THE WORLD:

HEY, COME TO AMERICA. YOU WON'T BE DEPORTED.

In mid-2014, newspapers in El Salvador, such as the *Diario el Mundo*, and others in Honduras began writing of the Obama administration's deferred deportation program—and coincidentally, thousands of minor-aged children from south of the Mexican border began showing up at America's boundaries.[37] In fairness, Obama never explicitly told illegals to come to the United States. But he may as well have.

In June 2014, hundreds of unaccompanied illegal children were transported from southern Texas to a way station overseen by Border Patrol agents in Nogales, Arizona, part of the federal government's attempt to deal with the thousands crossing over the border from Mexico into the Rio Grande Valley.[38] By August 2014, media outlets were reporting that more than thirty thousand unaccompanied children who had crossed illegally into the United States had been shipped to sponsor families in various states, including Alaska, Hawaii, Texas, California,

Florida, Georgia, New York, North Carolina, and Virginia. Who paid for this transportation? Taxpayers, of course.[39] It didn't take long for the situation to turn chaotic.

In June 2014, Hector Garza, a Border Patrol agent and spokesperson for the National Border Patrol Council Local 2455 described a Laredo, Texas, immigrant processing scene at one Greyhound bus station: "The majority of these people crossed the border illegally and were then dropped off here at the bus station, so they could continue to their final destination. And that destination is an American city near you. This right here is border insecurity at its best. . . . Our federal government is releasing thousands and thousands of illegal aliens into our communities."[40]

Communities rose up in opposition. In July 2014, protesters in Murrieta, California, waving American flags and signs that read, "Stop illegal immigration," were able to prevent a Homeland Security bus carrying dozens of minor-aged illegal immigrants from unloading its passengers. The bus was rerouted to a San Diego facility instead.[41]

But the chaos only ratcheted up. By September 2014, media outlets around the nation were reporting an uptick in diseases and viruses. Just months after the tally of illegals crossing into the United States hit forty thousand, more than a thousand children in ten different states were found to be infected with a mysterious virus, the enterovirus EV-D68.[42] Hospitals in Missouri, Colorado, Kansas, Utah, and several other states struggled to treat the victims. Dr. Mary Anne Jackson, the division director for Infectious Diseases at Children's Mercy Hospital in Kansas City, remarked to CNN of the 450 children who were treated for EV-D68 at the facility in the span of just a few months, "I've practiced for 30 years in pediatrics and I've never seen anything quite like this."[43]

THE INFLUX OF ILLEGAL IMMIGRANT CHILDREN HAPPENING

AROUND THE SAME TIME AS THE UNCHARACTERISTIC UPTICK IN

THE EV-D68 VIRUS IS CURIOUS.

Perhaps it's not fair to blame the influx of illegal immigrant children for the uncharacteristic uptick in the EV-D68 virus. But the timing is curious—curious enough that even Rep. Phil Gingrey, a Georgia lawmaker with thirty-plus years as a medical doctor, penned a letter to the Centers for Disease Control and Prevention's Thomas Frieden to request intervention.

> As you know, the United States is currently experiencing a crisis at our southern border. The influx of families and unaccompanied children at the border poses many risks, including grave public health threats. . . .
>
> [R]eports of illegal migrants carrying deadly diseases such as swine flu, dengue fever, Ebola virus, and tuberculosis are particularly concerning. Many of the children who are coming across the border also lack basic vaccinations such as those to prevent chicken pox or measles. This makes those Americans that are not vaccinated—and especially young children and the elderly—particularly susceptible.

Reports have indicated that several border agents have contracted diseases through contact with the unaccompanied minors. As the unaccompanied children continue to be transported to shelters around the country on commercial airlines and other forms of transportation, I have serious concerns that the diseases carried by these children may begin to spread too rapidly to control. . . .

I request that the CDC take immediate action to assess the public risk posed by the influx of unaccompanied children and their subsequent transfer to different parts of the country.[44]

The White House, however, turned a blind eye. So did Congress. The attitudes of our nations' leaders, in fact, could be aptly summarized by Pelosi's visit to the border and widely reported statement: "This crisis that some call a crisis, we have to view as an opportunity. If you believe as we do that every child, every person has a spark of divinity in them, and is therefore worthy of respect—what we saw in those [immigrant holding] rooms was a dazzling, sparkling array of God's children, deserving of respect."[45] In a separate media interview on MSNBC's *Morning Joe* shortly after that border visit, Pelosi then described these illegal children as children of God, no different from anybody, who should be regarded as akin to "baby Jesus" fleeing Bethlehem to escape violence.[46]

Again with the biblical call to break law.

Here's the response America should have given Pelosi: If you find these children so endearing, adopt them. Adopt them and bring them into your home. Become a sponsor for them. Not all—just one or two. Just enough to become the example of what you expect other American citizens to do without choice, without voice.

Politicians who push amnesty ought not to be allowed to mount their soapboxes, wag their disapproving fingers at those who oppose illegal immigration, and then go home to their million-dollar mansions and armed security-guarded residences and congratulate themselves for compassionate governance, entirely ignorant or dismissive of the chaos they've created in average American communities. They should have to deal with their messes, up close and personal.

> POLITICIANS WHO PUSH AMNESTY OUGHT NOT TO BE ALLOWED TO MOUNT THEIR SOAPBOXES, WAG THEIR DISAPPROVING FINGERS AT THOSE WHO OPPOSE ILLEGAL IMMIGRATION, AND THEN GO HOME TO THEIR MILLION-DOLLAR MANSIONS ARMED WITH SECURITY GUARDS.

But this state of hypocritical governance combined with political push to dismiss the rule of law is what happens when we, as a nation, fail to recognize our freedoms and our country as a gift from God.

Here are some quick-fix campaigns we can launch:

- Press government for punitive measures on businesses that knowingly hire illegal immigrants.

- Press legislators to hire more border control agents.

- Press representatives to install more surveillance technology, including drones, at the border to monitor, track, and report illegal crossings.

- Press for the widespread implementation of the 287(g) program, which even in its 2013 revised form allows local police departments to work in tandem with federal immigration officials and sweep criminal illegal immigrants off the streets.[47]

- Press the powers that be in political offices to outright reject amnesty.

Those all sound simple, right? But unfortunately, they're all a case of been there, done that—little more than lessons in futility. Just look at what the government's already done to oppose any efforts to punish businesses for hiring illegals.

In late 2014, media revealed a little-known kink in Obamacare that opened the doors for businesses to receive a three-thousand-dollar-per-person hiring incentive—for illegals.[48] PolitiFact reported the incentive would work only for a "small subset of businesses."[49] But is that caveat really a comfort?

The incentive comes on the heels of watery statements from the US Chamber of Commerce, the business sector's major Capitol Hill lobby, about the effect of illegal immigration on the nation's economy. The nonprofit may argue that its chief, Tom Donohue, does not support amnesty and never has.[50] But at the same time, the Chamber in 2013 spent more than $50 million on various lobby campaigns, some aimed at passing immigration reforms, and others, simultaneously, fighting the Tea Party.

Chamber CEO and president Donohue said to national

media in January 2014, "We're determined to make 2014 the year that immigration reform is finally enacted," vowing to "pull out all the stops" to bring legislation to President Obama by the end of the year.[51]

How to wage war against such forces?

The solution isn't easy, and it's definitely not overnight. But it starts with realizing and embracing what God envisioned for our nation. Here's a biblical passage from Romans that Christians often use to justify their reluctance to involve themselves in political matters; it ought to instead be applied to the illegals who seek to cross borders without permission:

> Let everyone be subject to the governing authorities, for there is no authority except that which God has established. The authorities that exist have been established by God. Consequently, whoever rebels against the authority is rebelling against what God has instituted, and those who do so will bring judgment on themselves. (Rom. 13:1–2 NIV)

With a clear mind and conscience, then, we each should fight against illegal immigration, no matter how hopeless the battle seems. Our nation is a gift from God, one to cherish, one built on the rule of law. When it comes to immigration and the fate of our nation, we can't let that reality die. We have to fight and vote and campaign and legislate and policy-make—and then fight some more.

Rev. Franklin Graham, one of Christianity's leading evangelists and the president of the nonprofit Samaritan's Purse, isn't afraid of the battle. Responding via Twitter in mid-April 2015 to a string of ISIS terror atrocities and video warnings of more to come, Graham wrote, "Our govt needs to halt all immigration of Muslims from countries that have active terrorist cells & take military action to defeat ISIS."[52]

We should be so bold.

FIVE

DEBT IS A DEVICE OF THE DEVIL

There are two ways to conquer and enslave a nation. One is by the sword. The other is by debt. —JOHN ADAMS

The National Center for Constitutional Studies details on its website the two ways of interpreting the Constitution: first, by trying to discern the intent of the Founding Fathers, and second, by making up something out of thin air. And on the issue of US monetary policy, the NCCS is clear. The Founders' intent was that Congress was "to establish and control our money system based on [a] gold and silver standard to prevent manipulation," the organization stated, on its website. Option B?

That's the made-up intent, the NCCS opined, which is to "give control of [the] monetary system to private bankers who issue fiat money which lets them make money out of nothing—money on which we then pay them interest."[1]

So on monetary policy, where does America now stand?

Option B. Firmly in the camp of the fiat system. President

Franklin Delano Roosevelt—in a series of quiet steps that began with a March 4, 1933, private announcement to advisers about his closing of the nation's banks, and finished several months later with the government-pressed collection of gold from the hands of the private sector—basically removed America from the gold standard of monetary policy. Media accounts of Roosevelt's role in the Federal Reserve's collection of gold from the private sector indicate he was reluctant to admit to the public his true intent—to remove America from a gold-based monetary system—because he was worried about fueling a run on banks.[2] But his policies spoke volumes. Within weeks of his inauguration, Roosevelt announced that paper money could no longer be converted into gold by the banks, and that gold could no longer lawfully be exported. Then, in an April 5, 1933, executive order, he boldly pronounced that no citizen could own more than one hundred dollars in gold coins, except certain collectors, and publicly labeled those who refused to turn over their stashes to the government as unpatriotic "hoarders."[3]

He justified his demands by saying the flailing economy required his immediate monetary policy intervention—though other historians and political watchers say it was the other way around, that Roosevelt's ban on private ownership of gold actually created a national financial panic in the banking sector. Regardless, he rammed through his gold confiscation campaign with an appeal to the patriotism of American citizens, laced with a scolding: "Many persons throughout the US have hastened to turn in gold in their possession as an expression of their faith in the government and as a result of their desire to be helpful in the emergency. There are others, however, who have waited for the government to issue a formal order for the return of gold in their possession," he said.[4]

Within weeks, the government had collected a cool $300 million in gold coins and another $470 million in gold certificates. And just a few months after that, the government set the price of gold at $35 per ounce, a significant jump from the $20.71 per ounce it was going for during the collection period and one that effectively bolstered the value of the Federal Reserve's coffers by 69 percent.[5]

Magic money.

Roosevelt's executive dictates on this new shift in American monetary policy were codified by Congress in the January 30, 1934, Gold Reserve Act, which awarded to the Federal Reserve the legal title to all the gold that had been collected from private citizens.[6]

But it was President Richard Nixon who sounded the death knell on America's gold standard. He emerged from an August 1971 secret meeting at Camp David to announce that America would no longer allow foreign nations the ability to exchange US paper currencies for US gold, as stipulated by the 1944 Bretton Woods agreement. Instead, he said, foreign nations would be allowed to convert their US currencies only into the US dollar—that the US dollar would "no longer be 'convertible' to anything other than itself," as one media outlet put it.[7] Why? In part, because Great Britain had tried to turn in currency for $3 billion worth of US gold, creating a panic in the market.[8] So Nixon wanted to act fast to stem what he saw as a financial disaster—the exposure of America's inability to actually back all its currency with gold.

He also, as part of this so-called Nixon Shock of monetary policy, implemented new wage and price controls aimed at curbing inflation.[9] It didn't work. The *Wall Street Journal* reported Nixon's failure: "The 'Nixon Shock' was followed by a decade of one of the worst inflations of American history and the most stagnant economy since the Great Depression. The price of gold rose to $800 from $35."[10]

So the takeaway?

The government will go to great lengths—holding secret meetings, issuing executive orders, masking true political intents—to control the nation's monetary system. It's not difficult to understand why. A fiat system that wipes out the intrinsic value of money and lets the powers that be—the government and banks—determine and dictate the value of currency is a heady perk for those select few already atop the pyramid of wealth. He who controls the purse strings holds the power. But for the rest of us, average Americans, the benefits of a fiat system are few.

THE GOVERNMENT WILL GO TO GREAT LENGTHS—HOLDING SECRET MEETINGS, ISSUING EXECUTIVE ORDERS, MASKING TRUE POLITICAL INTENTS—TO CONTROL THE NATION'S MONETARY SYSTEM.

Probably the best-known modern-day detractor of the system is former Texas representative Ron Paul, who has used his public speaking podium for years to warn about the takeover of the US monetary system by the Federal Reserve, the central banking system created in December 1913, and about the advent of fiat money. As a post at RonPaul.com states:

> Nowadays, most dollars are just blips on a computer screen and it's extremely easy for the Federal Reserve to create money out of thin air whenever they want to.
>
> If our money were backed by gold and silver, people couldn't just sit in some fancy building and push a button to create new money. They would have to engage in honest trade with another party that already has some gold in their possession. Alternatively, they would have to risk their lives and assets to find a suitable spot to build a gold mine, then get dirty and sweaty and actually dig up the gold. Not something I can imagine our "money elves" at the Fed getting down to whenever they feel like playing God with the economy."[11]

Paul also wrote in his 2009 book *End the Fed* that the Federal Reserve has become little more than a bailout for big banks—so much so that "the modern system of money and banking is not a free-market system," but rather "half socialized" by the government.[12] His overall view is that a return to the gold standard would moot the necessity for a centralized banking system and give Americans—not banks and government—more control of the economy. Think that's crazy? Consider this: Communist revolutionary Vladimir Lenin wrote shortly before Russia's October Revolution: "Without big banks, socialism would be impossible."[13] If Lenin was for it, maybe America shouldn't be.

But the larger issue is how this fiat system plays into our national debt—and how debt, both on the national scale and personal level, steals our freedoms and independence.

It's basic Bible teaching. As Proverbs 22:7 states, "The rich rule over the poor and the borrower is slave to the lender" (NIV). That bit of wisdom is applicable on the individual level, as well as on the national level. A couple with kids, who rack up their credit cards on family vacations, high-priced clothing, and frequent dinners at restaurants and then face mounting and crushing debt has only a couple of choices, neither very palatable: Dodge the debt, and accept the financial and moral repercussions that come with that cop-out; or pay the debt, and do whatever it takes to clear the incurred obligations, even giving up free time to take on multiple jobs. Either way, the couple is going to lose some independence and freedom. They're going to live with self-imposed chains for a little while.

If only our politicians were forced to make such difficult decisions. But they aren't. The idea of "spend only what you have" economics is almost an anathema on Capitol Hill. And truly, politicians like nothing better than to complicate the issues of taxes, budgets, and the economy because it allows them to spend freely without oversight and accountability—to award supporters and dole out financial favors in a semisecretive way.

Just look at the ever-growing federal tax code as proof. In 1913, federal tax law spanned 400 pages. In 1939, it had grown to only 504 pages. But between 1940 and 1945, the federal tax laws took 8,200 pages to explain, and by 1995, they were 40,500 pages. Go forward a few short years to 2013, and the tax law manuals were 73,954 pages in length.[14]

It doesn't have to be this way. As a matter of fact, in a free society, it really shouldn't be this way.

It also doesn't have to be that members of Congress take taxpayers' hard-earned money and spend it frivolously, in ways that aren't in line with the limited government principles of the Constitution. But they do. Just look at a recent copy of the Citizens Against Government Waste's near-annual *Congressional Pig Book*, which tracks egregious pork-barrel spending in appropriations bills.

> POLITICIANS LIKE NOTHING BETTER THAN TO COMPLICATE THE ISSUES OF TAXES, BUDGETS, AND THE ECONOMY BECAUSE IT ALLOWS THEM TO SPEND FREELY WITHOUT OVERSIGHT.

The summary section of the 2014 CAGW report states Congress spent $90 million that year on upgrades to an M1 Abrams tank, something that the Pentagon didn't even want; $15 million for a Pacific Coastal Salmon Recovery Fund; $5.9 million for an East-West Center long-sought by Hawaii's Sen. Brian Schatz; and $150,000 for the Christopher Columbus Fellowship Foundation, a pet project of Mississippi senator Thad Cochran.[15]

That's just a drop in the bucket of what the nonprofit regularly finds as congressional pork, of course.

If politicians could spend only what the United States actually had in its coffers, as the gold standard once demanded—and as a moral American people once intuitively understood—then our national debt, as of October 2015, wouldn't be pushing $18.2 trillion. But the fiat system allows the easy printing of paper money, and by extension, the easy distribution of cash and tax-paid benefits and pork projects by politicians toward their favored masses. The national debt is at the level now where Proverbs 22:7 is knocking at the door of each and every home owner and renter in America and leaving behind this notice: Your household's portion of the national debt is more than $146,000.[16]

How is that not a form of slavery? Our politicians can't rein in spending—and now every home in America is in the red for more money than most even earn in a year. Think of the bondage our children face in the coming years from this crushing debt. What's worse, we can't even get a true accounting of the numbers.

To cover their tracks and downplay the financial distress this nation is facing with its ever-growing tab, politicians play clever hide-and-seek games with America's money. *Forbes* gives an example: "The largest owner of US debt is Social Security [with 16 percent]. Since the Social Security system is a government entity, how can the government own its own debt? Good question. This is where the 'house of cards' theory resides. Some believe the federal government is merely moving the IOUs from one shell to another, hoping to escape the watchful eye of its citizens."[17]

Isn't that something—the Social Security Act was signed into law in 1935, mandating the government collection of American workers' payroll taxes. Then the government misuses and misspends these funds, and tosses some IOUs back into the fund—IOUs that will either go unpaid or be thrown on the backs of taxpayers to repay what they're already paid. What a racket. In the private corporate world, that'd be called embezzlement. To put some numbers on it, the Government Accountability Office found in March 2015 an estimated $5.1 billion of questionable payments had been disbursed from

Supplemental Security Income coffers, a program of Social Security. Our hard-earned tax dollars at work. That's just a slice of the federal misappropriating life, though. The GAO discovered further that "improper payment estimates totaled $124.7 billion in fiscal year 2014," across twenty-two federal agencies.[18]

But debt can get really dangerous when foreign entities—some of them hostile to America—get involved.

DEBT CAN GET REALLY DANGEROUS WHEN HOSTILE FOREIGN

ENTITIES GET INVOLVED.

Nearly 35 percent of US debt at the end of 2014 was owned by foreign nations—China being the largest, followed closely by Japan. And roughly 10 percent of that 35 percent foreign-held debt, which is in the form of Treasury securities, is actually owned by nations that aren't exactly friendly to the United States, including Iran, Iraq, and Libya.[19] Why care?

As the libertarian Cato Institute reported way back in 2008, "The rise in foreign-held US Treasury debt and the overall increase in claims against the United States are causing concern that the United States may end up being heavily indebted to oil-rich nations and to non-democratic countries like China, and that foreigners may end up owning a large chuck of the United States."[20]

The conservative Heritage Foundation warned of our reliance on overseas governments to take up our debt, too, saying in a 2013 report that even the slightest shift in global perceptions of the US economy, or confidence in our markets, could have devastating impacts on the average American: "Central banks have been both largely independent of national fiscal authorities and credibly opposed to high inflation . . . ," Heritage reported. "However, if global bond buyers ever lost confidence in a central bank's independence, its resolve regarding price stability, or its ability to contain inflation, then interest rates would likely jump substantially and very quickly."[21]

All of sudden, the cost of borrowing to buy that new home or car just jumped a lot higher.

> THE SIMPLE FACT IS WE'RE LIVING ABOVE OUR MEANS, AS INDIVIDUALS AND AS A NATION. UNFORTUNATELY, THE POLITICAL CLIMATE SHOWS LITTLE STOMACH FOR STOPPING THE SPENDING.

The simple fact is we're living above our means, as individuals and as a nation. Unfortunately, the political climate shows little stomach for stopping the spending. Think about it. When times get financially tough and budget hawks squawk, what do our leaders on Capitol Hill do?

First, what they don't do: cut spending.

Now, what they do: Raise the debt limit. Print more money. And hike taxes and fees, when politically expedient. As the Congressional Research Service explains, the debt limit "provides Congress with the strings to control the federal purse, allowing Congress to assert its constitutional prerogatives to control spending."[22] But when's the last time in recent history that Congress used the power of the purse strings to rein in government spending? As the CRS also found, Congress modified the debt limit fourteen times between 2001 and 2014, either outright raising it—three times between July 2008 and February 2009, by the way—or standing by as the Treasury secretary invoked certain privileges that allowed for an extension of borrowing ability.[23]

How many times did Congress, conversely, cut spending during this time frame?

Twice, found one professor of political science, who grew curious about a campaigning Republican who claimed during the 2014 election season that Congress had actually scaled back spending in the previous two years. So he researched the claim. And professor Paul Kengor, who also serves as executive director of the Center for Vision and Values at Grove City College, found that Congress did indeed cut spending from $3.6 trillion in 2011 to $3.53 trillion in 2012, and then again to $3.45 trillion in 2013. At the same time, he said he was shocked by his findings. Why? Because that was "the first time since 1953–55 that spending was cut in consecutive years—in literally over a half century," he wrote, in a widely published article.[24]

It's easy to overspend when money, in essence, comes from thin air.

The government doesn't call it printing money, but rather "quantitative easing." But what this fancy term describes is a manipulation of values and worth. The *Economist* gives a good definition of it:

To carry out QE, central banks create money by buying securities, such as government bonds, from banks, with electronic cash that did not exist before. The new money swells the size of bank reserves in the economy by the quantity of assets purchased—hence "quantitative" easing. Like lowering interest rates, QE is supposed to stimulate the economy by encouraging banks to make more loans. The idea is that banks take the new money and buy assets to replace the ones they have sold to the central bank. That raises stock prices and lowers interest rates, which in turn boosts investment.[25]

It's such a popular financial strategy that the Federal Reserve has been able to bolster its holdings, at least in its record books, from less than $1 trillion in 2007 to more than $4 trillion in 2014, simply through several rounds of quantitative easing.[26]

Once again, magic money. Beneficial for the few at the top of the wealth and power structures. Not so beneficial for the average, hardworking citizen who's likely still laboring under the delusion that it's the free market, not government and banking interests, that control America's economy.

So what's the solution to this cyclical spend-and-print deception that Financial America 2015 finds itself facing?

Some would say returning to the gold standard, and forcing government to only spend what it can back by bullion, would force feds to behave more prudently with taxpayer dollars. Agreed—but this just isn't going to happen anytime soon. Government has tasted at the trough of fiat currency and found it to its liking, and to its self-interest. Same with quantitative easing—why wait for revenues to increase or make the politically difficult decisions that go with cutting programs and budgets, when one can simply let the banks do a little bond buying, a little electronic inputting, and—voilà—money is born?

The real solution to our national debt crisis must begin at the individual level. Parents must teach their children to live within their means; families must confine most of their expenditures to that which can be bought with cash. Communities must restrict their local governments from offering costly services that aren't in line with the Constitution, anyway, and that require higher and higher tax collections from citizens in order to maintain. And local governments must compel their state officials to stop burdening them with unfunded mandates—as near impossible as that might be.

> THE REAL SOLUTION TO OUR NATIONAL DEBT CRISIS MUST BEGIN AT THE INDIVIDUAL LEVEL. PARENTS MUST TEACH THEIR CHILDREN TO LIVE WITHIN THEIR MEANS; FAMILIES MUST CONFINE MOST OF THEIR EXPENDITURES TO THAT WHICH CAN BE BOUGHT WITH CASH.

But it all starts within the home.

Cut up the credit cards. Save a portion of income each payday. Consider, very seriously, the tithe.

Regarding tithes and offerings, Malachi 3:9–10 says, "'You are under a curse—your whole nation—because you are robbing me. Bring the whole tithe into the storehouse, that there may be food in my house. Test me in this,' says the Lord Almighty, 'and see if I will not throw open the floodgates of heaven and pour out so much blessing that there will not be room enough to store it'" (NIV).

Pushing for a constitutional amendment to force Congress to balance its budgets is a good idea. So is fighting for a return to the limited-government principles—and to a less expansive and expensive entitlement system—that helped fuel this nation's economic might. But the root problem with the US economy is the mind-set and morals of America's citizenry. To address that, we need God. And toward that He speaks clearly—first, in Psalm 37:21: "The wicked borrow and do not repay" (NIV); and again, in Deuteronomy 28:12, intimating that the blessed are those with no debt: "You will lend to many nations but will borrow from none" (NIV).

THE ROOT PROBLEM WITH THE US ECONOMY IS THE MIND-SET

AND MORALS OF AMERICA'S CITIZENRY. TO ADDRESS THAT, WE

NEED GOD.

Wise words to consider for a nation that's facing what one former financial adviser to President Ronald Reagan described as near utter collapse.

Paul Craig Roberts, who served as assistant secretary of the Treasury for Economic Policy, predicted in 2015: "At any time, the Western house of cards could collapse. It (the financial system) is a house of cards. There are no economic fundamentals that support stock prices—the Dow Jones. There are no economic fundamentals that support the strong dollar."[27]

Why is this?

Our economy is not real—it's largely a fantasy of the government. And when they're done playing, the cards will collapse, and with them, the whole of America's house. The trick for the individual is to make sure personal financial ducks are in a row so the collapse isn't as personally devastating. Put God at the helm, not the government-backed banks: tithe, pay off debt, use more cash and fewer cards, and teach those in your family and immediate community to do the same.

SIX

BE BOLD: WE ARE BOSSES OF PRESIDENTS, POLITICIANS, AND POLICE

For you were called to freedom, brothers. Only do not use your freedom as an opportunity for the flesh, but through love serve one another. —GALATIANS 5:13

It's worthwhile at this point to take a long, lingering look at the opening lines of the Declaration of Independence:

> When in the Course of human events, it becomes necessary for one people to dissolve the political bands which have connected them with another, and to assume among the powers of the earth, the separate and equal station to which the Laws of Nature and of Nature's God entitle them, a decent respect to the opinions of mankind requires that they should declare the causes which impel them to the separation. We hold these truths to be self-evident, that all men are created equal, that they are endowed by their

Creator with certain unalienable Rights, that among these are Life, Liberty and the pursuit of Happiness—That to secure these rights, Governments are instituted among Men, deriving their just powers from the consent of the governed,—That whenever any Form of Government becomes destructive of these ends, it is the Right of the People to alter or to abolish it, and to institute new Government.

A few points to note: One, atheists ought to hold their tongues about the basic principles that shaped our nation. It's clear our Founders believed in the existence of a higher power, a Creator. Two, the Founding Fathers recognized we're all equal in God's eyes. Three, the government's interests are subservient to the God-given rights of the people. And four, governments that stray from these principles might be abolished and replaced with another.

Now take a look at what's going on in Congress, in the White House, in government offices around the nation, and reflect: Are these politicians really abiding by these basic principles? Are they even working for us, their constituents?

Or have the government bodies in the United States become a sort of separate society, a segment of workers who receive special privileges, above and beyond what the average American citizens—the taxpayers—receive?

We're the employer. This is the premise of our governmental system. The president of the United States is the employee. So are all the lawmakers and staffers on Capitol Hill, the officials who work at the myriad of government agencies, the tellers at the local Department of Motor Vehicles, the clerks at the state courthouse, the teachers, lunch ladies, and administrators in the county school system—even the librarians in the community libraries. So as we go about trying to reclaim this nation of ours and put it back under the protection and leadership of God, and such biblical principles come to mind as Hebrews 13:17, commanding us to "obey your leaders and submit to them," let's remember that in America the real leaders and bosses in our government are the people, you and me. All those named above—they're servants of the people.

Still, there sure are a lot of them.

The US Census Bureau, which produces a report on the state of the nation's governments every five years, found 2.5 million full-time federal employees in the United States in 2013—and that total went up to 2.7 million if you factored in part-timers. That includes the nearly 776,000 who worked then in national defense; the nearly 200,000 for Homeland Security, the agency created in 2003; the combined 380,000-plus in health and hospital sectors; and the estimated 580,000 for the Postal Service.[1]

But don't forget the state and local governments.

ACCORDING TO THE US CENSUS BUREAU, THERE ARE MORE THAN NINETY THOUSAND STATE AND LOCAL BODIES OF GOVERNMENTS ACROSS THE UNITED STATES.

According to the US Census Bureau, there are more than ninety thousand state and local bodies of governments across the

United States. The Census Bureau puts these bodies into two distinct categories: general purpose governments, like counties and municipalities, which provide basic police, education, road maintenance, and related services; and special purpose entities, such as water and sewer districts and transit authorities.[2]

- As of March 2013, about 3.7 million worked full-time in various capacities of state-level governments across the nation, and another nearly 1.6 million on a part-time basis.[3]

- Another 14 million or so worked in various local government roles across the nation during that same time frame, about 10.6 million of whom were considered full-time.[4]

And their payrolls? Combine federal, state, and local governments, and the price taxpayers are paying is mind-boggling.

A Census Bureau chart entitled "Total Payroll for the Month of March for Federal, State and Local Governments, 2004–2013" included this summary: "In March 2013, the three levels of government in the United States paid their employees a total of $87.9 billion."[5]

"During the month of March 2013, full-time state employees received $18.3 billion, while local employees earned $47.2 billion. Part-time state employees earned $2.2 billion, while local government part-time employees received $3.7 billion," the Census Bureau reported.[6]

Education takes the largest pot, with "nearly half of the total federal, state and local government workforce" serving in this field, the report stated.[7]

TOTAL PAYROLL FOR THE MONTH OF MARCH FOR FEDERAL, STATE, AND LOCAL GOVERNMENTS: 2004-2013

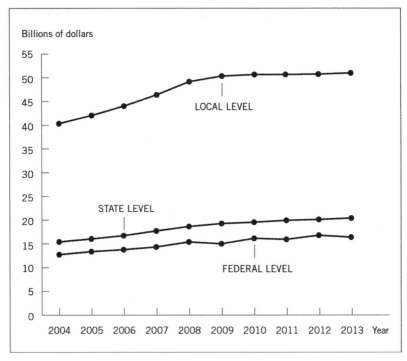

U.S. Census Bureau, 2013 Annual Survey of Public Employment & Payroll and Historical Tables.

But holy cow. Nearly $88 billion paid in one month for government services in this country? Yes, you read that right. One month.

Unfortunately, the services we're getting in return are often inadequate. How many taxpayers have felt the sting of a surly government employee who just wasn't quite up to par on the customer service front? Or, been treated to the rude response of a court clerk who just didn't feel it his or her job to assist an individual fill out a required document? How about the treatment many complain they've received from the Internal Revenue Service? These officials are paid by tax dollars; their paychecks are provided courtesy of you and me. Yet, try and get one to answer a tax-related question on the telephone in a timely, courteous, and informative manner. The IRS won't even help the elderly and low-income fill out their tax forms anymore. Citing budget cuts, the agency announced in fiscal 2014 an end to its "longstanding practice of preparing tax returns for low income, elderly and disabled taxpayers who seek help."[8]

These aren't petty complaints. They are examples of how the rightful employer-employee relationship between the taxpayer and the government worker has been reversed. Public employees have become the managers, claiming they have a right to their jobs, and as such, demand their annual budget proposals be fulfilled. Taxpayers have become little more than the source providing these budget dollars. And after the bills have been paid—after the budgets have been approved and the tax dollars appropriated—we're just the petty nuisances who interrupt the government employees from doing their jobs.

NEARLY $88 BILLION IS PAID IN ONE MONTH FOR GOVERNMENT

SERVICES IN THIS COUNTRY.

Think about it. Isn't that the attitude, more often than not, that emanates from our public officials?

The root is arrogance. Our government officials have forgotten who works for whom.

George Washington has been widely, albeit wrongly, credited with making this statement: "Government is not reason, it is not eloquence, it is force; like fire, a troublesome servant and a fearful master." The Fred W. Smith National Library for the Study of George Washington says Washington never uttered that line—that "the library has yet to find an explanation for this misquote, locate another individual who said this statement," or find a similar remark the former president actually said that could have been misconstrued as this statement.[9] But the sentiment still fits. Government, once established, becomes a force unto itself, a living, breathing entity with a pressing desire to not only live, but grow. Unfortunately, when government grows, individual freedoms suffer.

> GOVERNMENT, ONCE ESTABLISHED, BECOMES A FORCE UNTO ITSELF, A LIVING, BREATHING ENTITY WITH A PRESSING DESIRE TO NOT ONLY LIVE, BUT GROW. UNFORTUNATELY, WHEN GOVERNMENT GROWS, INDIVIDUAL FREEDOMS SUFFER.

The Bible speaks to this truth as well.

Samuel was chosen by God to become a great prophet and judge to the Israeli people. In his old age, he appointed his sons, Joel and Abijah, to take his place and serve as the new judges. But they ruled corruptly, and the elders demanded a king instead. This was shocking; God had intended that His people cleave to Him, not to a king, and He wanted them to remain separate and different from the other nations. So Samuel, when presented with their demand, turned to God for an answer. And 1 Samuel 8 gives God's reply: "The Lord said to Samuel, 'Do everything the people request of you. For it is not you that they have rejected, but it is me that they have rejected as their king. . . . So now do as they say. But seriously warn them and make them aware of the policies of the king who will rule over them'" (vv. 7, 9 NET).

So Samuel did as he was told and warned the people what they could expect by putting a king, not God, as their leader. He said:

> Here are the policies of the king who will rule over you: He will conscript your sons and put them in his chariot forces and in his cavalry; they will run in front of his chariot. He will appoint for himself leaders of thousands and leaders of fifties, as well as those who plow his ground, reap his harvest, and make his weapons of war and his chariot equipment. He will take your daughters to be ointment makers, cooks, and bakers. He will take your best fields and vineyards and give them to his own servants. He will demand a tenth of your seed and of the produce of your vineyards and give it to his administrators and his servants. He will take your male and female servants, as well as your best cattle and your donkeys, and assign them for his own use. He will demand a tenth of your flocks, and you yourselves will be his servants. (vv. 11–17 NET)

Our leaders aren't taking a tenth of our flocks. But they are displaying an attitude that's similar to what God warned would happen if He's placed as second fiddle to a king.

In 2015, congressional members received $174,000 per year as base salary. The speaker of the House—that year, John Boehner—received $223,500. Members of Congress also see an annual cost-of-living increase that goes through automatically, unless they vote not to accept it.[10]

Since 2001, the president of the United States has received an annual pay of $400,000, plus another $50,000 for expenses. The vice president, meanwhile, gets $230,700.[11]

Compare that to the average American worker's salary, which came in at $24.57 per hour, according to December 2014 Census Bureau figures—about $850 pay per week, just under $45,000 a year.[12]

IN 2005, ONLY 33 PERCENT OF PRIVATE SECTOR EMPLOYEES WITH WORKPLACE RETIREMENT PLANS HAD PENSIONS, YET COVERAGE WAS AT 85 PERCENT IN 1975.

Expecting the well-paid on Capitol Hill to understand the hopes, struggles, and realities of the average, common-folk American is fast becoming a lesson in futility. But pay tells only part of the story.

The president, vice president, and their families have at their disposal a full-time team of physicians who work right at the White House, and who travel with the first family to tend to any on-road medical needs. All presidents, even those who serve only one term, are given a lifetime pension that pretty much guarantees they'll never have to worry about money again. And, of course, presidents and their wives all have the option of having full-time Secret Service agents protect them for the rest of their lives, at taxpayer expense.[13]

In Congress, members may start collecting a pension at age sixty-two if they've completed at least five years of service. That means a senator serving only one term is eligible for a pension; in the House, where members serve two-year terms, the member must finish nearly three terms before collecting a pension. But that's not really a long time to work to earn a pension for life. On top of that, members who are only fifty are eligible to take a pension after they've completed twenty years of service—and there are no age limits at all for those who've served twenty-five years. As for the private sector?

Private-sector pensions have been on a downward trend that began in the mid-1980s. In just a three-decade period, the level of pensions supplied by private businesses for their employees dropped by nearly 50 percentage points.

"In 2005, only 33 percent of private sector employees with workplace retirement plans had pensions, yet coverage was at 85 percent in 1975," the National Institute on Retirement Security found.[14]

And by 2014, *U.S. News and World Report* analyzed the investment consulting firm NECP, LLC's corporate trends survey and reported: "Among 117 corporate-sponsored plans, just 28 percent remained open. A third were closed to new entrants (while allowing current participants to earn benefits) and 39 percent were frozen – allowing neither new entrants nor accruals."

One takeaway? More and more employers were outright eliminating pensions, a twenty-first-century business reality that doesn't appear destined to change. The public sector, however, breeds a different beast.[15]

As of October 2014, there were 601 retired congressional members—351 of whom who had left office under the terms of the Civil Service Retirement System, and 250 under the Federal Employees' Retirement System that took effect in 1984. The CSRS retired members received in 2014 an annual average pension amount of $72,660; the FERS members, an average of $41,652 per year.[16] Until 1984, congressional members didn't even pay into Social Security—the same retirement system the average US worker is forced to participate in via automatic paycheck deductions (the same retirement program these once-exempted members of Congress then raided and filled with "IOUs").

Not a bad haul for a few years as a servant to the people.

McClatchy Washington Bureau found Rep. George Miller, who served forty years as a California Democrat, was eligible to collect a yearly pension of $125,500. Sen. Saxby Chambliss, a Georgia Republican, could collect an annual pension of $53,000, under the terms of his twenty years of service. Even losing members of Congress take home quite a consolation prize. Sen. Kay Hagan (D-NC) didn't win her bid for a second term. But she was still eligible under federal laws to collect an annual pension of $16,000.[17]

How very generous of the taxpayers.

That's just the tip.

How many private-sector employees finding their work productivity hampered by an oncoming cold or illness can take a short walk down the hall of their place of business and ask the on-premise doctor for a quick checkup and prescription?

Not many. Most people have to call in sick, make a doctor's appointment, and slog their sick selves to the waiting rooms of the medical offices that are preapproved by their insurance companies.

Not members of Congress. "Current members are eligible to receive limited services from the Office of the Attending Physician in the US Capitol for an annual fee," the Congressional Research Service reported. "Service includes routine exams, consultations, and certain diagnostic tests."[18]

The annual fee in 2015 was $596, a price that many private-sector Americans might gladly pay, as a matter of saving time and convenience.[19] But most businesses don't offer that perk.

Most Americans aren't eligible for this one, either: "Current members [of Congress] are also authorized to receive medical and emergency dental care at military treatment facilities. There is no charge for outpatient care if it is provided in the National Capital Region," said the Congressional Research Service.[20]

Here are a few more:

- Members of Congress, both present and former, are given special parking places on Capitol Hill—a premium perk in a city known far and wide for aggressively ticketing parking violators—as well as private office elevators, dining areas, and exercise facilities in their tax-paid places of work.[21]

- Members of Congress have an enviable days-off schedule. In 2014, they were scheduled to work 133 days in Washington, DC. By comparison, the average American worker, with two weeks of vacation each year, spends about 240 days at the office annually.[22]

- Members of Congress are also afforded special treatment from some airlines and airports—they're given access to private, designated telephone lines for calling in reservations, they're granted free parking at a couple of select airports, and they're even allowed to make multiple travel reservations at once but only required to pay for the flights they actually take.[23] The common American, by contrast, deals with automated and delayed telephone service; parking lots that are crowded and costly; and prohibitive cancellation policies.

- Those in Congress have an even better death benefit for their spouses and surviving family members than US soldiers and Marines killed in the course of military duty. If a member of Congress dies during legislative service, the surviving family members are entitled to receive at least a full year's pay of the deceased—at least $174,000. By contrast, the families of military members killed during duty receive a payment of $100,000.[24]

- Members of Congress are able to engage in some serious insider trading—despite strict regulations against average Americans doing the same. Congress passed the Stop Trading on Congressional Knowledge Act, or STOCK Act, in 2012, which was supposed to address this very conflict of interest. But members turned around a few months later and gutted the accountability portion of the law.[25] They're still supposedly barred from trading on knowledge gained on the job while serving in Congress. But the law doesn't require them to publicly disclose their trades any longer. The US Securities and Exchange Commission is clear on what happens to the average American caught engaging in insider trading, however: "Violation of the prohibition on insider trading can result in a prison sentence and civil and criminal fines for the individuals who commit the violation."[26]

No wonder members of Congress are among some of America's wealthiest. The median net worth of a congressional member in 2013 was nearly $1.03 million. The average American's net worth that same year, meanwhile, was little more than $56,000.[27] Also in 2013: More than 50 percent—271 of the 533—of the members of Congress were millionaires.

"It would take the combined wealth of more than 18 American households to equal the value of a single federal lawmaker's household," the Center for Responsive Politics found.

"IT WOULD TAKE THE COMBINED WEALTH OF MORE THAN 18 AMERICAN HOUSEHOLDS TO EQUAL THE VALUE OF A SINGLE FEDERAL LAWMAKER'S HOUSEHOLD." –CENTER FOR RESPONSIVE POLITICS

A year later, and the financial perks for members of Congress continued.

Roll Call reported in its annual survey of congressional wealth, published in October 2014, that the "combined minimum net worth of Congress jumped—up more than $150 million to $2.1 billion—according to a CQ *Roll Call* analysis of the financial disclosure forms for every member of Congress and delegate who filed one for 2013. That's an increase of about $300,000 to $3.9 million per lawmaker."[28]

Shocked? Angry?

We ought to be—angry and outraged, and ready to demand change. Sadly, politicians get away only with what the people allow, which puts the onus on the people to bring about that change.

REPEAT WHEN NECESSARY: THEY DON'T DESERVE IT, AND THEY'RE

NOT ENTITLED TO IT.

The first step to reversing this trend of elitism and special class we've bestowed upon our elected servants is to realize and repeat when necessary: They don't deserve it and they're not entitled to it. Why would they be? Members of the government are in those roles only because the taxpayers have allowed them those positions. If they can't serve humbly, with gratitude and with a servant's heart, then they should be removed.

That's the spirit of our nation's founding.

The next step is to pay attention to what our politicians and government workers do. A campaign promise is just that—some spoken words. But when the election's ended and the ballot boxes are put away, that's the time of real busyness for the voter—the time to make sure the elected stand fast and firm and deliver on promises. Tracking their votes, calling their offices, e-mailing their staffers, and kicking off letter campaigns and petition drives when necessary—these should be run-of-the-mill occurrences for all voters. We can't just elect them and let them govern. That's an abdication of the duties we were given by our Founding Fathers as well as by those who followed and who saw this nation as a shining city on a hill.

Want to give a government body a quick wake-up lesson on who's the boss? FOIA the public workers' salaries and post them to a local blog, or send them in to a local newspaper for publication. The Freedom of Information Act is a friend in this. It's a hearty reminder of who is paying whom and how much—a speedy lesson about the authority of the taxpayer over the tax paid. Hey, it's watchdogging—what we've been commissioned to do.

As Andrew Jackson said during his farewell address in 1837, "Eternal vigilance by the people is the price of liberty, and . . . you must pay the price if you wish to secure the blessing. It behooves you, therefore, to be watchful in your States as well as in the Federal Government."[29]

It's part of the responsibility of being an American. To shirk is to degrade our greatness.

But really, the outline for good governance goes further back in time than 1837—further back then the signing of the Declaration of Independence and the US Constitution. God gave us a blueprint of what a well-governed nation should look like, and what a proper leader ought to do and not do. It's up to us to take these biblical principles and make sure they're implemented and upheld.

In Deuteronomy, God spoke to Moses, who in turn told all of Israel, to "be sure to appoint over you a king the Lord your God chooses" (17:15 NIV). Among the warnings: Don't choose a foreigner. Don't choose one who isn't an Israelite. And more:

> The king, moreover, must not acquire great numbers of horses for
> himself or make the people return to Egypt to get more of them . . .
> He must not take many wives, or his heart will be led astray. He
> must not accumulate large amounts of silver and gold. When he
> takes the throne of his kingdom, he is to write for himself on a
> scroll a copy of this law, taken from that of the Levitical priests. It
> is to be with him, and he is to read it all the days of his life so that
> he may learn to revere the Lord his God and follow carefully all
> the words of this law and these decrees and not consider himself
> better than his fellow Israelites and turn from the law to the right
> or to the left (vv. 16–20 NIV).

The symbolism of this passage may be a bit different today
than in the time of Moses. But the message certainly hasn't
changed.

If we want leaders who serve with pure hearts for the
people—if we want politicians and government officials of
humble attitudes and proper perspectives of their roles and
positions—we need to choose leaders, politicians, and government representatives who follow paths forged by God, who keep
themselves in check to a higher power. A little more spiritual
discernment—and a little less concern about the "R" or "D," the
lofty campaign rhetoric, and the meaningless political promises.

SEVEN

DUST OFF THE CONSTITUTION—
READ IT, LEARN IT, TEACH IT, LIVE IT

For the Lord is our judge; the Lord is our lawgiver; the Lord is our king; he will save us. —ISAIAH 33:22

In late 2014, national media exposed a teacher at a Tennessee elementary school who had allegedly given her eight-year-old student a handout from the Nation of Islam. The document asked, "What does it take to be on Mount Rushmore?" It then went on to describe George Washington as a "prime breeder of black people" and Theodore Roosevelt as a racist who labeled blacks "ape-like."[1] The teacher and school administrators explained away the ensuing national furor by saying the document had never been intended for the student's eyes—that he had wrongly snatched it off the desk.[2] But the question remained: why was it in the classroom in the first place?

A couple of years earlier, schools in Texas came under fire

for a lesson plan that presented the patriots who staged the 1773 Boston Tea Party uprisings—the protests against taxation without representation—in a negative light. Teachers using this particular world history and social studies lesson plan were directed to read a summary of the American patriots' protests as if it were a late-breaking, modern-day news report.[3] This is an excerpt of the so-called breaking news story:

> A local militia, believed to be a terrorist organization, attacked the property of private citizens today at the port. Although no one was injured in the attack, a large quantity of merchandise, considered to be valuable to its owners and loathsome to the perpetrators, was destroyed. The terrorists, dressed as natives and apparently intoxicated, were able to escape into the night with the help of local citizens who harbor these fugitives and conceal their identities from the authorities. It is believed that the terrorist attack was a response to the policies enacted by the occupying country's government.[4]

The directions then call for students to discuss the situation, after which the teacher reveals the shocker: the "terrorist attack" just described was the Boston Tea Party.[5]

In mid-2014, the media began reporting on some curious questions being posed for use in classrooms around the United States. Among these questions, written by Grant Wiggins, a Pearson Education author and a professional development trainer for the Common Core educational program, were: "Was George Washington any different from Palestinian terrorists trying to protect their country?" "Was Jefferson a hypocrite? Did he really think of a slave as a sub-human while writing the Declaration of Independence?"[6]

In late 2014, students in Madison, Wisconsin, were given classroom instruction about the similarities between the Ferguson, Missouri, riots and "hands up, don't shoot" protests that came on the heels of a white police officer's shooting of a black teenager, and the Boston Tea Party. The school district distributed a guide encouraging teachers to use the Ferguson protests as a teachable moment, and provided a list of recommended resources.[7] Among them was a link to a blog post from Mike Kaechele, a self-identified social studies teacher in Michigan, whose "Ferguson vs. Boston" piece included a side-by-side photo of a black man looting a Ferguson-area store and an image of Boston tea partiers in the throes of their rebellion. Superimposed on the picture was this question: "When is rioting justified?"[8]

Kaechele's post also included several sample questions teachers could use to get the class conversations rolling, including a discussion of the "similarities between the events," the "stereotypes" the Boston protesters displayed by dressing as Native Americans during the dumping of the tea, and whether those portrayed in the Boston event deserve to be considered heroes, rather than criminals.[9]

What we teach our children matters. We cannot stand quiet and allow the history of our nation to become so badly skewed.

If parents don't take it upon themselves to teach their children the Constitution, and the history that went into its forging, the upcoming generation is going to be brainwashed to believe the Founding Fathers and early American patriots were little more than racist and rogue rebels on a violent, thuggish quest for British blood—no different from today's average street criminal committing a robbery.

WE NEED TO TEACH OUR CHILDREN THE CONSTITUTION AND THE

HISTORY THAT WENT INTO ITS FORGING, OR THEY MAY END UP

BELIEVING THE FOUNDING FATHERS WERE LITTLE MORE THAN

RACIST STREET CRIMINALS.

Proverbs 16:12 says, "It is an abomination for kings to commit wicked acts, for a throne is established on righteousness" (NASB). But what's being taught in today's schools completely obliterates that principle. The upcoming generation, ingrained with the idea that our nation's Founders were bigoted slave supporters and its founding was based on acts of terrorism, won't recognize the exceptionalism of America—and won't appreciate the throne of righteousness that was established during our early years.

How will the upcoming generation govern without this compass?

It's not just the schools that are guilty of imposing these views. In July 2014, the National Consortium for the Study of Terrorism and Responses to Terrorism (START) project—a study funded in part by the Department of Homeland Science and Technology Directorate's Office of University—found that most law enforcement in the United States expressed more concern about "sovereign citizens" than about Islamic extremists and jihadists.[10]

"Sovereign citizen" is the term given to those in America who rebel against the idea of any type of government—federal, state, or local—telling them what to do, particularly when it comes to paying taxes. Granted, some in this segment of society have committed acts of violence against police, but the Department of Homeland Security itself has given the movement a peace star. In a 2015 report on the sovereign citizen movement, conducted by its Office of Intelligence and Analysis, federal authorities drew a distinction between "sovereign citizen extremists" and "sovereign citizens" and wrote, "Most sovereign citizens are nonviolent and this assessment applies only to those that use violence to advance their goals."[11]

So why do law enforcement officials who took part in the 2014 START project consider those with antigovernment views such a personal and public threat?

Between 2006 and 2007, START found officers cared most about jihadists, neo-Nazis and racist skinheads, in that order. Members of the militia and patriot groups, as well as those in the sovereign citizens movement, came in only sixth and seventh on the 2006–07 list, respectively, in terms of raising law enforcement's red flags.

But by 2013–14, perceptions had changed, and sovereign citizens were listed as Perceived Threat No. 1, followed by Islamic extremists and jihadists, and by members of the militia and self-described patriots.

It's significant to note this civilian law enforcement mindset, especially when you consider that our nation was founded by those with sincere suspicions of government and an understandable reluctance to fall in line with the established powers that be.

Around the same time this START report was making a splash, the government watchdog Judicial Watch found that the

PERCEIVED THREAT OF EXTREMIST GROUPS BY TYPE OF GROUP[12]

TYPE OF GROUP	POTENTIAL THREAT (2013–14)	POTENTIAL THREAT (2006–07)
SOVEREIGN CITIZENS	3.20 (1)	2.49 (7)
ISLAMIC EXTREMISTS/JIHADISTS	2.89 (2)	3.13 (1)
MILITIA/PATRIOT	2.67 (3)	2.61 (6)
RACIST SKINHEADS	2.58 (4)	2.82 (3)
NEO-NAZIS	2.56 (5)	2.94 (2)
EXTREME ANIMAL RIGHTISTS	2.54 (6)	2.79 (4)
EXTREME ENVIRONMENTALISTS	2.51 (7)	2.74 (5)
KLUX KLUX KLAN	2.38 (8)	2.47 (8)
LEFT-WING REVOLUTIONARIES	2.36 (9)	2.04 (13)
EXTREME ANTI-ABORTION	2.36 (9)	2.30 (11)
BLACK NATIONALISTS	2.34 (11)	2.35 (10)
EXTREME ANTI-TAX	2.33 (12)	2.47 (8)
EXTREME ANTI-IMMIGRATION	2.33 (12)	2.41 (9)
CHRISTIAN IDENTITY	2.19 (13)	2.59 (8)
IDIOSYNCRATIC SECTARIANS	2.19 (13)	2.13 (12)
MILLENNIAL/DOOMSDAY CULTS	2.17 (15)	1.93 (14)
RECONSTRUCTED TRADITIONS	2.13 (16)	2.04 (13)

Department of Defense was training its students to be on alert for conservative organizations, described as frequent fronts for "hate groups," and to watch out for those who talk openly and persistently of individual rights.[13]

Judicial Watch uncovered the matter via a Freedom of Information Act request seeking "any and all records concerning, regarding, or related to the preparation and presentation of training materials on hate groups or hate crimes distributed or used by the Air Force."[14] They received in response 133 pages of lesson plans on extremism used by the Defense Equal Opportunity Management Institute, an organization created in 1971 in response to the 1960s civil rights movement to instruct active and reserve members of the military, as well as civilians.[15]

Some of the documents' claims were startling, including these:

- An extremist is "a person who advocates the use of force or violence [or] advocates supremacist causes based on race, ethnicity, religion, gender, or national origin."[16]

- "Nowadays, instead of dressing in sheets or publically espousing hate messages, many extremists will talk of individual liberties, states' rights, and how to make the world a better place."[17]

- "In U.S. history, there are many examples of extremist ideologies and movements. The colonists who sought to free themselves from British rule and the Confederate states who sought to secede from the Northern states are just two examples."[18]

Once again, Americans are being inundated with the idea that the patriots who started this great nation of ours were little more than radical thugs, unworthy of a label of freedom-seekers.

But that wasn't the first time the Department of Defense was outed for making such claims. In a 2009 letter to Gail McGinn, acting undersecretary of defense for personnel and readiness, the American Civil Liberties Union raised doubts about the "DOD's Level I Antiterrorism Awareness Training" and its adherence to the First Amendment. An excerpt:

We have been informed that the current web-based instruction course asks, as one of its multiple-choice questions, "which of the following is an example of low-level terrorism activity?" To answer correctly, the examinee must select "protests."

For the DoD to instruct its employees that lawful protest activities should be treated as "low-level terrorism" is deeply disturbing . . .

Policing ideas, rather than criminal activities, runs counter to our nation's core principles, undermining the very foundations the Department of Defense is dedicated to preserving. Peaceful protest is not terrorist activity.[19]

If we keep watering down and skewing the truth about how we began and what we stand for, we will no longer be the America our Founders envisioned or that God graced.

Truth be told, we've already got one foot in the grave on that point. Consider Galatians 5:1: "It is for freedom that Christ has set us free. Stand firm, then, and do not let yourselves be burdened again by a yoke of slavery" (NIV). But aren't we doing that very thing—allowing ourselves to be yoked by the government—when we allow those with skewed interpretations of the Constitution to pass massive entitlement measures? If not—where did Obamacare come from? Or, the Medicare Prescription Drug Modernization Act? One, the Patient Protection Affordable Care Act, was passed under a Democratic administration; the other, the massive, $400 billion prescription giveaway, under a Republican administration. Both were billed as must-haves for the welfare of the citizens.

Former president George W. Bush, speaking in 2003 at DAR Constitution Hall in Washington while signing his landmark legislation into law, called it "the greatest advance in health care coverage for America's seniors since the founding of Medicare," and credited "our government [for] finally bringing prescription drug coverage to the seniors of America."[20]

IF WE KEEP WATERING DOWN AND SKEWING THE TRUTH ABOUT HOW WE BEGAN AND WHAT WE STAND FOR, WE WILL NO LONGER BE THE AMERICA OUR FOUNDERS ENVISIONED OR THAT GOD GRACED.

In March 2010, President Obama took pen to paper—twenty-two pens, actually—and with a ceremonious sign-off, brought into law his landmark health care reform, Obamacare. His last-minute words? "[This enshrines] the core principle that everybody should have some basic security when it comes to their health care . . . The bill I'm signing will set in motion reforms that generations of Americans have fought for and marched for and hungered to see."[21]

The commonalities of these two measures and the presidents' statements? They were both brought to fruition based on the idea that government should provide for the general welfare of the people. They're also both antithetical to the Founding Fathers' visions for this nation, pushing God to the side and government to the forefront. We were never supposed to be a nanny-state government, where public servants provide cradle-to-grave care for every individual. Just because health care for all sounds like a good and godly plan doesn't mean it's the role of our government to provide it.

WE WERE NEVER SUPPOSED TO BE A NANNY-STATE GOVERNMENT

WITH CRADLE-TO-GRAVE CARE FOR EVERY INDIVIDUAL.

This is the difference between a government constrained by individuals who recognize a higher power as their provider, and one that's been unchained to intrude on all areas of private life—even if that intrusion is sold as a "for the good of the people" idea—because citizens have turned from God and doubted His ability to provide.

But a citizenry who doesn't read the Constitution or the Founding Father documents and writings wouldn't know this.

"If once [the people] become inattentive to the public affairs, you and I, & Congress & Assemblies, judges & governors shall all become wolves," wrote Thomas Jefferson in 1787. "It seems to be the law of our general nature, in spite of individual exceptions."[22]

Read. The. Constitution. And teach it to your children—don't depend on the schools to do it.

While you're at it, take a peek through some early American history to get a real feel for how far down the path of socialism we've gone. We've developed an entitlement mind-set and fallen into cultural and moral degradation. The silence of an unaware and apathetic population has fueled this morphing. This is not progress; it is demise.

Questioning lawmakers, holding them accountable, securing the legislative and judicial processes, and properly petitioning courts, Congress, and government entities for redress of abuses and overreaches—these are all things that start with knowledge of the Founding Fathers' intents and of America's early history.

Those who can't be bothered to educate themselves don't deserve to wear the banner of "proud American."

So again, read the full Constitution, cover to cover, along with the Declaration of Independence. It takes only an hour or so for both—shockingly short, given the amount of time and paper it's taken to write some of the laws that supposedly stem from these documents. Obamacare, for example, spawned thirty-three thousand pages of regulations that stood an estimated seven feet tall and required the creation of more than a hundred new government agencies to implement.[23] Perhaps if more lawmakers read, understood, and respected the limited-government aspects of the Constitution, we wouldn't be saddled with such ridiculously long pieces of legislation.

But it takes educated citizens to press that point. So after reading the Constitution, look for ways to apply its principles to modern-day politics and news, enhancing your learning. Several organizations offer free courses on the Constitution.

- The nonprofit Constitution Center is a sort of one-stop shopping center for all things Constitution, providing resources for all ages, from elementary school to adult. The online site also provides links to the founding documents, the National Archives, and even videos of American naturalization ceremonies. The site further offers fun quizzes—like "Which Founder Are You?"— and offers a Constitution Day Kit to help users learn about and teach the significance of September 17, 1787.[24]

- The National Archives, aside from being a valuable resource for viewing original and first-person historical documents, offers several important lessons about the Constitution in its Center for Legislative Archives. Foremost for beginners is the course titled "Teaching Six Big Ideas in the Constitution." What are they? Limited government, republicanism, checks and balances, federalism, separation of powers, and popular sovereignty.[25]

• Want a different viewpoint? PBS offers a "Constitution USA with Peter Sagal" instructional video and text course for middle schoolers, high schoolers, and adults. Here's a blurb from the website: "Over the course of the four-hour series, Sagal hits the road, traveling cross-country on a customized red, white and blue Harley-Davidson, to find out how the Constitution lives, how it works, and how it unites us as a nation. From New York to San Francisco . . . Sagal visits dozens of cities and small towns across America, introducing viewers to some of today's major constitutional debates—free speech in the digital age, same-sex marriage, voting rights, separation of church and state." How does that not sound exciting?[26]

Those are just a handful of easy-access places to learn some basic facts about the Constitution. But individual responsibility for keeping our government in check goes deeper. The Constitution is just one side of the equation; learning, acknowledging, and upholding the Judeo-Christian roots that grew us as a nation is the other.

And schools definitely aren't teaching that any longer.

The Constitution was created by a group of individuals who held a heavenly Creator in highest regard, though contentions have waged for years over the distinct religious personality of each founder—not quite secular but not faithful churchgoer either—and whether deist beliefs, orthodox Christianity, or something in between ultimately guided the development of our government. But the fact remains: our Founders were believers in a supreme being, and He wasn't Muslim in nature, or Buddhist, or Wiccan; nor was He aligned with any other religion outside Christianity. Just look at a few of the signs of Christianity that continue to permeate our nation.

- Our nation's money carries the motto "In God We Trust."

- Our corridors and rooms of Congress bear such inscriptions as "America! God shed his grace on thee"; "In God we trust"; "Annuit coeptis" (Latin for "God has favored our undertakings"); and "Preserve me, O God; for in thee do I put my trust."[27]

- Images of the Ten Commandments appear on the bronzed floor of the National Archives,[28] on a bronze statue of Moses in the Library of Congress,[29] and on the US Supreme Court building.[30]

Critics might say these inscriptions, images, and references to God and the Bible were added to Capitol Hill objects and facilities long after the country was founded, so they can't possibly be taken as our true guiding compass. But these comparatively recent additions only show the lasting impression our Founders have made. Roll back the years and you will find that the signs of Christianity dotted the founding landscape of our country, too.

Our Declaration of Independence affirms that all are "endowed by their Creator with certain unalienable rights." And the Constitution contains references not just to God, but to the Christian God. Its closing endorsement states that the document was completed during a convention of the states on September 17, "in the year of our Lord" 1787.[31]

Article 1, Section 7 contains a clause giving the president ten days—"Sundays excepted"—to decide on a bill before it becomes law. Why were Sundays excluded? Because Sunday is the traditional and biblical day of worship for Christians.

Moreover, enough of the Founding Fathers—and their wives—claimed affiliation with the various Protestant denominations to underscore the fact that religion played a big role in shaping their day-to-day thoughts, morals, values, and actions.

The Jefferson Memorial contains several references to God and His divine influences, as spoken through the mouth of our third American president. The panel of the northeast interior wall, for example, states his absolute belief in the necessity for a free nation to recognize the source of freedom—God: "God who gave us life gave us liberty. Can the liberties of a nation be secure when we have removed a conviction that these liberties are the gift of God?" [32]

And John Jay, who represented New York at the Continental Congress, authored three essays in the *Federalist*, served as secretary of foreign affairs, and was appointed chief justice of the Supreme Court by George Washington, had this to say about God and the religion of our nation: "Providence has given to our people the choice of their rulers, and it is the duty as well as the privilege and interest of our Christian nation to select and prefer Christians for their rulers."[33]

Dig deeper; there are plenty more.

Our nation's history is rife with examples that show the tie between Constitution and Bible, between God and government. But expecting public schools to teach these truths is national suicide. We must take it upon ourselves to learn and teach them to the upcoming generations. The price for our failure? More of what we already see: a nation of souls morally adrift and forgetful of our source of greatness, the Almighty, and unmindful of the hard-won principles of limited governance pressed into the Constitution. We're only a hop and skip from becoming a body of citizens all too willing to be "burdened again by a yoke of slavery" for a false government promise of protection and provision.

EIGHT

EXECUTIVE ORDERS OUGHT TO BE OUTLAWED

An overseer, as God's steward, must be above reproach. He must not be arrogant. —TITUS 1:7

What if executive orders were outlawed in America?

Imagine a bill—it could be entitled the "Reining in President" Act, or RIP Act, for short—that stated something like: "H.R. 5267, expressing the sense of Congress that the various presidents of the United States have overreached their executive authority, circumvented constitutional boundaries, and broadened the powers of the White House office by the steady and frequent issuance of executive orders, executive memos, and presidential proclamations, now finds these powers and acts unconstitutional, unlawful, and subject to repeal and to civil and criminal prosecutions."

That would be a considerable clamp on the White House,

the occupants of which have exerted quite a bit of legislative and policy influence using this congressional bypass, particularly since Teddy Roosevelt's time. What's especially galling about the power is that it's not granted in the Constitution. Not anywhere.

EXECUTIVE ORDERS ARE GHASTLY DEVIATIONS FROM THE LIMITED-GOVERNMENT PRINCIPLES THE FOUNDERS SET IN PLACE, AND THEY'VE DONE A LOT OF MISCHIEF IN RECENT DECADES, TO PUT IT MILDLY.

Executive orders are ghastly deviations from the limited-government principles the Founders set in place, and they've done a lot of mischief in recent decades, to put it mildly. The president has only a handful of authorities, as defined by the Constitution. They are listed in Article II, Sections 2 and 3:

- to serve as the commander-in-chief of the Army, Navy, and state militias;

- to receive, upon request, written opinions from his various department heads;

- to pardon and grant reprieves, except in cases involving impeachment;

- to make treaties, with the advice and consent of the Senate, and the approval of two-thirds of the Senate;

- to nominate, with the advice and consent of the Senate, ambassadors, Supreme Court judges, and individuals to fill other US offices;

- to fill vacancies in the Senate that occur during recesses (those appointments expire at the end of the next session);

- to provide for Congress "from time to time" information about the state of the union, and make recommendations for improvements;

- to convene the Houses of Congress "on extraordinary occasions," and provide recommendations, and adjourn them for a set amount of time;

- to receive ambassadors and other public officials;

- to enforce the nation's laws;

- to issue commissions for all the officers of the United States.[1]

That's it. Just a handful of powers, limited in scope. Notice—nothing in there about executive orders or letting the president bypass Congress to issue policies and laws. It's both interesting and pitiful, then, to realize how far we've strayed from this constitutional compass. Just look at what Cornell University Law School's Legal Information Institute puts out as an executive power on its own website: "The president . . . can issue executive orders, which have the force of law but do not have to be approved by Congress."[2]

That's the mind-set of the next generation of legal minds—and unfortunately, it's an illusion that's been successfully pushed onto the American people for years. We need to remember these simple mantras: The president is a servant. The president works for the people.

The type of leaders we need to seek for America, especially for America's highest office, should meet this standard, from Exodus 18:21: "You shall select out of all the people able men who fear God, men of truth, those who hate dishonest gain; and you shall place these over them as leaders of thousands, or hundreds, of fifties and of tens" (NASB).

Our presidents shouldn't be foisting massive regulatory controls on citizens absent congressional approval, because ours is a government that calls for distinct powers for the three separate branches, and abiding anything less is a grab at power—a dishonest gain.

OURS IS A GOVERNMENT THAT CALLS FOR DISTINCT POWERS FOR THE THREE SEPARATE BRANCHES, AND ABIDING ANYTHING LESS IS A GRAB AT POWER.

Who can forget President Obama's famously arrogant exclamation—"I've got a pen and I've got a phone, and I can use that pen to sign executive orders and take executive actions and administrative actions that move the [legislative] ball forward"[3]—and his absolute dismissiveness of the authorities of Congress?

This is not how a president with humble reverence for his role and for the station granted him by God is supposed to govern.

But look at the statistics on all our presidents:[4]

PRESIDENT	TOTAL ORDERS*	AVERAGE / YEAR	YEARS IN OFFICE
GEORGE WASHINGTON	8	1	7.85
JOHN ADAMS	1	0.25	4.00
THOMAS JEFFERSON	4	1	8.00
JAMES MADISON	1	0.13	8.00
JAMES MONROE	1	0.13	8.00
JOHN QUINCY ADAMS	3	1	4.00
ANDREW JACKSON	12	2	8.00
MARTIN VAN BUREN	10	3	4.00
WILLIAM HENRY HARRISON	0	0	0.08
JOHN TYLER	17	4	3.92
JAMES K. POLK	18	5	4.00
ZACHARY TAYLOR	5	4	1.35
MILLARD FILLMORE	12	5	2.65
FRANKLIN PIERCE	35	9	4.00
JAMES BUCHANAN	16	4	4.00
ABRAHAM LINCOLN	48	12	4.12
ANDREW JOHNSON	79	20	3.89
ULYSSES S. GRANT	217	27	8.00

PRESIDENT	TOTAL ORDERS*	AVERAGE / YEAR	YEARS IN OFFICE
RUTHERFORD B. HAYES	92	23	4.00
JAMES GARFIELD	6	11	0.55
CHESTER ARTHUR	96	28	3.46
GROVER CLEVELAND - I	113	28	4.00
BENJAMIN HARRISON	143	36	4.00
GROVER CLEVELAND - II	140	35	4.00
WILLIAM MCKINLEY	185	41	4.53
THEODORE ROOSEVELT	1,081	145	7.47
WILLIAM HOWARD TAFT	724	181	4.00
WOODROW WILSON	1,803	225	8.00
WARREN G. HARDING	522	217	2.41
CALVIN COOLIDGE	1,203	215	5.59
HERBERT HOOVER	968	242	4.00
FRANKLIN D. ROOSEVELT	3,721	307	12.12
HARRY S. TRUMAN	907	117	7.78
DWIGHT D. EISENHOWER	484	61	8.00
JOHN F. KENNEDY	214	75	2.84
LYNDON B. JOHNSON	325	63	5.17
RICHARD NIXON	346	62	5.55
GERALD R. FORD	169	69	2.45
JIMMY CARTER	320	80	4.00
RONALD REAGAN	381	48	8.00
GEORGE BUSH	166	42	4.00
WILLIAM J. CLINTON	364	46	8.00
GEORGE W. BUSH	291	36	8.00
BARACK OBAMA	213	33	6.50

Note: Obama EO counts are updated monthly following the 20th day of the month to recompute average per year. Orders issued between updates can be accessed here: http://www.presidency.ucsb.edu/executive_orders.php?year=2015

Last Update: Data Through July 20, 2015 (through 6.5 years of the Obama Administration)

Notes:
* 1789 to 1945 (Roosevelt) data include "numbered" and "unnumbered" executive orders. 1945 (Truman) & 1967 (Johnson) data include only numbered executive orders including those with letter designations (ex. Executive Order 9577-A).

Data Sources:
1789–1945 (Roosevelt) data from Lyn Ragsdale, "Vital Statistics on the Presidency: Washington to Clinton." rev. ed. (Washington, D.C.: CQ Press, 1998); data compiled by John Woolley, The American Presidency Project; and figures from the National Archives and Records Administration.
1945 (Truman)—present data compiled by Gerhard Peters, The American Presidency Project, from documents contained in the Federal Register.

But the numbers tell only one side of the story. These statistics may show which president tapped into his executive power with the greatest frequency, but what they don't tell is which orders exerted the greatest level of legislative influence— or inflicted the greatest amount of policy damage—onto the American people. Obama, for instance, issued only 206 orders by April 2015. But that comparatively small number doesn't reveal that his actions threw the legal system into chaos, as courts were forced to confront lawsuits from states over his immigration amnesty orders.[5]

It also doesn't reveal the trickle-down devastations that can occur from such executive actions, like another one Obama issued requiring federal offices and agencies to cut greenhouse gas emissions by 40 percent of 2008 levels and to derive 25 percent of their total energy use from "clean sources," all by 2025.[6]

That order also stated:

> In addition to setting aggressive new efficiency standards for federal agencies, the administration is engaging with major federal suppliers to encourage them to adopt similar practices. Today, the administration is hosting a roundtable that will bring some of the largest federal suppliers together to discuss the benefits of the [greenhouse gas emission] reduction targets or to make their first-ever corporate commitments to disclose emissions and set new reduction goals.[7]

IBM voluntarily vowed to reduce carbon dioxide emissions by 35 percent by 2020. GE promised to invest $25 billion in research and development of "environmentally responsible products" and reduce greenhouse gas emissions by 20 percent from a 2011 baseline. Humana, Inc., committed to greenhouse gas emission cuts of 5 percent of a 2013 baseline between 2015 and 2017. Northrop Grumman agreed to a 30 percent reduction of greenhouse gas emissions from 2010 levels and a drop in water consumption by 20 percent of 2014 levels.[8]

That's just a handful of the businesses Obama's executive order "encourage[d]" to the point of action. The problem with such encouragement, however, is that it reeks of crony capitalism. What are these businesses getting in return?

Another problem—and this goes to the heart of what ails our country—is that using executive orders as a jumping point to bring about private-sector change is shady constitutional business. Obama couldn't get Congress, even when dominated by Democrats, to agree to his drastic and dramatic emission control desires or his cap-and-trade program. So he bypassed

Congress with his pen, ordered the federal agencies to enact the cuts he wanted for the entire nation, and then pulled in some of the nation's biggest businesses and largest revenue makers to "encourage" them to follow suit. Some might call that smart politicking.

What it's really called is arrogance. And the Bible has a story that illuminates.

> Now Naboth the Jezreelite had a vineyard in Jezreel, beside the palace of Ahab king of Samaria. And after this Ahab said to Naboth, "Give me your vineyard, that I may have it for a vegetable garden, because it is near my house, and I will give you a better vineyard for it; or, if it seems good to you, I will give you its value in money." But Naboth said to Ahab, "The LORD forbid that I should give you the inheritance of my fathers." (I Kings 21:1–3)

So Ahab went home and lay in his bed, downtrodden and displeased, refusing to eat food, until his wife, Jezebel, came to inquire. Ahab explained how Naboth turned away his offer, and she responded:

> Do you now govern Israel? Arise, and eat bread, and let your heart be cheerful; I will give you the vineyard of Naboth the Jezreelite." So she wrote letters in Ahab's name and sealed them with his seal, and she sent the letters to the elders and the nobles who dwelt with Naboth in his city. And she wrote in the letters, "Proclaim a fast, and set Naboth on high among the people; and set two base worthless men opposite him, and let them bring a charge against him, saying, 'You have cursed God and the king. Then take him out, and stone him to death.'" And the men of his city, the elders and the elders

and the leaders who lived in his city, did as Jezebel had sent word to them. As it was written in the letters that she had sent to them, they proclaimed a fast, and set Naboth at the head of the people. And the two worthless men came in and sat opposite him. And the worthless man brought a charge against Naboth, in the presence of the people, saying, "Naboth cursed God and the king." So they took him outside the city, and stoned him to death with stones. Then they sent to Jezebel, saying, "Naboth has been stoned; he is dead." As soon as Jezebel heard that Naboth had been stoned and was dead, Jezebel said to Ahab, "Arise, take possession of the vineyard of Naboth the Jezreelite, which he refused to give you for money; for Naboth is not alive, but dead." And as soon as Ahab heard that Naboth was dead, Ahab arose to go down to the vineyard of Naboth the Jezreelite, to take possession of it. (I Kings 21:7–16)

When Obama pushed aside the will of Congress—the members of which are put in that position to represent the will of the people—and plowed self-righteously ahead with his own environmental agenda, enticing some of the nation's biggest businesses to follow, he displayed an attitude of contempt for the voters, the elected, and the constitutional principles he swore to uphold. In America, that's not how we do business. He first behaved like the spoiled and pouty child—a la Ahab, who took to bed and turned away food. He then steamrolled his will over the freedoms of others—a la Jezebel, master orchestrator of murder. Obama's methods may be different, but his executive attitude sure is similar.

If we wanted a king, we never would have fought the British.

But that passage doesn't apply just to Obama—it applies to the whole system of executive orders.

IF WE WANTED A KING, WE NEVER WOULD HAVE FOUGHT

THE BRITISH.

This power of the presidency, derived from a skewed interpretation of the Article II constitutional instruction for White House chiefs to "take care that the laws be faithfully executed," is supposed to be limited in scope, applicable only to the federal offices and agencies and confined to guiding and managing these agencies' operations. But Congress, through the years, has allowed the president to flex his executive muscle and piggyback executive orders off legislative actions, and in so doing, exert greater influence on the American citizenry.

That's how we get, for instance, massive national monument declarations setting aside huge swaths of land for federal control and management. Or, US military strikes against countries without congressional declaration of war. Former president Bill Clinton's guilty of both of these actions.

In March 1999, Clinton ordered air and missile strikes over Kosovo to beat back what he called a "mounting military offensive" from Serbia's president Slobodan Milosevic, to protect America's interests and to "prevent a wider war [and] to diffuse a powder key at the heart of Europe."[9] In April 1999, Clinton signed an executive order designating Yugoslavia, Albania, and adjacent ocean waters and airspace a "combat zone."[10]

Citing his commander-in-chief role over the US military and his chief executive status in the White House, Clinton claimed authority to bypass Congress for permission to strike—despite the Constitution's stipulation that only this branch of government has the power to declare war. California Rep. Tom Campbell shortly after invoked the War Powers Act to force Congress to vote yea or nay to the war. The House voted against a declaration of war. The House also failed to pass a separate resolution that would have given the thumbs-up for the president to continue airstrikes. Sixty days passed, and Clinton's lone-wolf air war over Kosovo continued, violating the time limit contained in the War Powers Act for a president to seek congressional approval for war or to stop strikes.[11]

Campbell ultimately filed suit, accusing Clinton of both violating the Constitution, by unilaterally attacking a country that wasn't even doing harm to the United States, and of breaking the sixty-day deadline in the War Powers Act that requires that a president go back to Congress for approval for continued attacks.[12] Clinton's strikes over Kosovo lasted seventy-eight days.[13] The courts dismissed the suit, saying Congress didn't have standing to bring the claim.[14]

The end result?

Clinton degraded the Constitution for what even his administration "tacitly admitted [was a] situation in Kosovo [that] did not threaten vital US security interests," the Heritage Foundation found.[15]

He managed to push the powers of the presidency just a little bit further, encroach into congressional territory a little bit more.

A couple of years earlier, Clinton had acted similarly unilaterally to declare the nation's largest national monument, the 1.7 million–acre Grand Staircase-Escalante National Monument. In a 1996 proclamation and with the swoop of a pen, Clinton set

aside a twenty-seven-hundred-square-mile parcel of property—
about the combined size of Delaware and Rhode Island—for
federal control and management.[16] Utah senator Orrin Hatch
described the intrusion into his state as "the mother of all land
grabs."[17] The Utah-based *Spokesman-Review* shot out a stinging
critique of Clinton's executive action, calling it economi-
cally damaging to the state—and arrogant. In an op-ed titled
"Clinton Land Grab Concerns Us All: Pure Arrogance," the
newspaper reported a loss from the proclamation of $1 trillion
in coal reserves, as well as untold numbers of mining jobs.

The writer went on: "It should take an act of Congress to
create a national monument—not a vote-hungry politician.
And states and communities affected by proposals to lock up
natural resources should have a say in the matter—not just the
environmentalists."[18]

Far too many times, our nation's highest executive has
exercised an air of independence while governing, rather than
adopting our republic's rule-of-law approach or abiding by our
constitutional checks and balances system.

Put another way: "An elective despotism was not the
government we fought for, but one which should not only be
founded on true free principles, but in which the powers of
government should be so divided and balanced among general
bodies of magistracy, as that no one could transcend their legal
limits without being effectually checked and restrained by the
others."[19]

That's how Thomas Jefferson saw it—and so do I.

Yet we're far from that ideal, aren't we?

Look at where executive orders and an arrogant presidency
have taken us:[20]

- Jimmy Carter created the Federal Emergency Management Agency.

- Franklin Roosevelt set up internment camps and relocated thousands of Japanese-Americans, German-Americans, and Italian-Americans for the duration of World War II.

- Harry Truman seized control of all the nation's steel mills—until the Supreme Court reeled him in and declared his action unconstitutional.

- Dwight Eisenhower desegregated public schools.

- Abraham Lincoln suspended the writ of habeus corpus, allowing for authorities to arrest and detain suspects indefinitely.[21]

- Franklin Roosevelt created the Works Progress Administration to employ millions of Americans and lift them from Depression-era poverty.[22]

- George W. Bush established the Office of Homeland Security, a massive bureaucracy that now employs more than 240,000.[23]

IF CONGRESS WON'T ACT TO REIN IN PRESIDENTS AND CURTAIL THEIR EXECUTIVE OVERREACHES, THEN "WE THE PEOPLE" NEED TO STEP UP TO THE PLATE.

There are thousands more—thousands. And the point isn't whether the executive order is beneficial for our nation or not. Many would argue Lincoln's Emancipation Proclamation was a clear step in the right direction of civil rights even though it freed slaves only in states that had seceded from the Union.[24]

The larger issue is the state of our Constitution, and whether allowing presidents to exercise monarch-like powers degrades our freedoms—and whether doing so sets up a system of government run by dismissive, arrogant leaders. Toward that end, executive orders certainly do.

If Congress won't act to rein in presidents and curtail their executive overreaches, then "we the people" need to step up to the plate. We need to force lawmakers to remember the power of the purse, to defund any executive orders that require taxpayer infusions. We also need to petition our legislators to override executive orders that aren't part of powers already granted by Congress or the Constitution. The Congressional Research Service reported in 2011 that "as long as it is not constitutionally based, Congress may repeal a presidential order, or terminate the underlying authority upon which the action is predicated."[25]

Legislators did it before, with former president George H. W. Bush's order to the Department of Health and Human Services secretary to set up a human fetal tissue bank for research. "To effectuate this repeal," the CRS reported, "Congress simply directed that the 'provisions of Executive Order 12806 shall not have any legal effect.'"[26]

Presidents can also revoke orders put in place by previous presidents. President Gerald Ford issued an order for federal agencies to incorporate inflation impact statements into proposed legislation; President Jimmy Carter amended that practice and instead required agencies to include potential economic impacts of certain rules. President Ronald Reagan then amended Carter's order and directed agencies to implement new rules only if "the potential benefits to society for the regulation outweigh the potential costs to society."[27]

Executive orders aren't set in stone. As a matter of fact, they shouldn't even have been laid into stone, given their complete lack of constitutional basis. It's only by the arrogance of government and the human nature quest for power, combined with an unaware and complicit public, that they're allowed to exist in America at all. Beating these back is crucial to reining in the federal government and reminding the nation's highest-ranking politician, "Hey, you may be leader of the free world, but in America, you work for me. In God's eyes, you're no better than I."

A rightful role of a leader is to lead by example; a proper leadership attitude is to serve with a humble heart.

"IF I THEN, YOUR LORD AND TEACHER, HAVE WASHED YOUR FEET, YOU ALSO OUGHT TO WASH ANOTHER'S FEET." –JOHN 13:13

Jesus said, "You call me Teacher and Lord, and you are right, for so I am. If I then, your Lord and Teacher, have washed your feet, you also ought to wash another's feet. For I have given you an example, that you also should do just as I have done to you. Truly, truly, I say to you, a servant is not greater than his master, nor is a messenger greater than the one who sent him. If you know these things, blessed are you if you do them" (John 13:13–17).

I don't want the president of the United States washing my feet. But I do want him to recognize that he ought to want to wash my feet, as well as the feet of all the constituents he serves.

NINE

CHRISTIANITY DOESN'T MEAN DEFENSELESSNESS: THE SECOND AMENDMENT SAVES

A well regulated Militia, being necessary to the security of a free State, the right of the people to keep and bear Arms, shall not be infringed.
—SECOND AMENDMENT, US CONSTITUTION

On July 20, 2012, a well-armed twenty-seven-year-old man named James Eagan Holmes entered a Century movie theater in Aurora, Colorado, tossed some smoke and gas canisters on the floor, and began shooting at the audience members. He ultimately killed twelve and injured another seventy.

A few days later, President Obama took to his national platform and called for stricter gun control.

"I, like most Americans, believe that the Second Amendment guarantees an individual the right to bear arms," he said during a conference of the National Urban League in New Orleans. "I think we recognized the traditions of gun ownership that passed on from generation to generation. That hunting and shooting are part of a cherished national heritage. But I also believe that a lot of gun owners would agree that AK-47s belong in the hands of soldiers, not in the hands of criminals. That they belong on the battlefield of war, not on the streets of our cities."[1]

On December 14, 2012, twenty-year-old Adam Lanza entered the halls of Sandy Hook Elementary School in Newtown, Connecticut, and began firing randomly at staff and students alike. Ultimately, twenty children and six adults were killed. Lanza, who had shot and killed his own mother before he left the house that morning, turned the gun on himself and committed suicide.

The nation mourned.

Two days later, Obama went on national television to announce his will to do something to end the violence—specifically, to use his White House office to press for more gun control.

His words came across as a scolding:

> This is our first task—caring for our children. It's our first job. If we don't get that right, we don't get anything right. That's how, as a society, we will be judged. And by that measure, can we truly say, as a nation, that we are meeting our obligations? Can we honestly say that we're doing enough to keep our children, all of them, safe from harm? . . . I've been reflecting on this the last few days and if we're honest with ourselves, the answer is no.[2]

He then vowed "in the coming weeks [to] use whatever power this office holds to engage my fellow citizens . . . in an effort aimed at preventing more tragedies like this."[3]

So he did.

By January 2013, Obama's White House had released fifteen pages of new gun control proposals, including federal background checks and bans on high-capacity magazines and on certain types of weapons deemed assault-style, while calling for more Justice Department oversight of states and state-compiled gun-related data.[4] The National Conference of State Legislatures described the document as "23 executive actions and three presidential memoranda, most of which will require congressional approval [and much] may have significant effect on the states."[5]

On September 16, 2013, lone gunman Aaron Alexis entered the Washington Navy Yard in southeast Washington, DC, and began nearly an hour's worth of firing inside the Naval Sea Systems Command building, leaving twelve dead and three injured. Police were able to shoot Alexis in the head and kill him at the scene.

Six days later, Obama gave remarks at the victims' eulogy and once again pressed the cause of gun control. "It may not happen tomorrow and it may not happen next week and it may not happen next month," he said. "But it will happen, because it's the change we need. Our tears are not enough. Our works and prayers are not enough. If Americans want to honor the 12 men and women who died at the Navy Yard, we're going to have to change. We're going to have to change."[6]

And on June 10, 2014, a fifteen-year-old boy named Jared Michael Padgett entered his Reynolds High School hallway in Troutdale, Oregon, and shot to death a fourteen-year-old freshman, Emilio Hoffman. A teacher was also wounded. Padgett then traded gunfire with police before fleeing to a bathroom and killing himself with his weapon.[7]

That same day, Obama vented about his inability to bring his gun control measures to fruition on the American people.

"We're the only developed country on earth where this happens," Obama griped in widely reported remarks. "Our levels of gun violence are off the charts. There's no advanced, developed country on earth that would put up with this."[8]

He also said of the Troutdale shooting, "My biggest frustration so far is the fact that this society has not been willing to take some basic steps to keep guns out of the hands of people who can do just unbelievable damage. . . . We should be ashamed of that. There's no place else like this."[9]

Notice the trend? Four shootings; four similar White House responses, each calling for more gun control. But it's not just Obama using emotionally charged situations to press a political agenda. Members of the faith community have joined in the gun control call, adopting a "can't we all get along" tone they suggest is rooted in biblical principles.

In late 2012, Rabbi David Saperstein of the Religious Action Center of Reform Judaism said at an interfaith gathering in Washington that participants had decided "sensible gun control" was necessary for the nation. "The indiscriminate distribution of guns is an offense against God and humanity," he continued. "Our gun-flooded, violence-prone society has turned weapons into idols. And the appropriate religious response to idolatry is sustained moral outrage."[10]

United Methodist bishop and United Methodist Council

of Bishops executive secretary Peter Weaver, speaking at this same interfaith event, agreed. "This must become a matter of moral conscience, not just politics," Weaver said. "It's not about Republicans or Democrats. It's about our children and what some have called a 'national epidemic' of gun violence."[11]

That's just a couple of the voices from the faith community calling for tighter gun laws. Faiths United to Prevent Gun Violence is a nonprofit that counts among its fifty or so supporters the Episcopal Church, the Evangelical Lutheran Church in America, the Islamic Society of North America, the Jewish Council for Public Affairs, the Presbyterian Church USA, the American Baptist Churches of the South, Catholics United, and the Unitarian Universalist Association.[12] Their mission? In part, to press Congress to require federal background checks on all gun buyers and to ban all so-called high-capacity assault weapons and cartridges. The group's website even touts a guide "to help faith leaders speak to congregants about gun violence prevention."[13]

Leftist politicians attempting to use high-profile gun-related acts of violence to sway voters into accepting clamps on the Second Amendment is one thing. It's come to be expected. But church and faith leaders coming together to pressure Congress to do the same, based on both explicit and implicit biblical interpretations, is an entirely new level of politicking—and one that's badly skewed. Yet their calls via direct petitions on Capitol Hill are growing louder. And freedom-loving America needs to get ahold of all the directions of attack, in order to launch an adequate defense.

The Bible doesn't speak to the use or ownership of guns, of course. But it does offer some practical guidance in this regard.

THE BIBLE DOESN'T SPEAK TO THE USE OR OWNERSHIP OF GUNS,

BUT IT DOES OFFER SOME PRACTICAL GUIDANCE IN THIS REGARD.

The gospels tell the story of Jesus, in the Garden of Gethsemane, praying and awaiting Judas, who would lead the Roman soldiers to arrest him—the pivotal moment toward His crucifixion. John tells how Jesus, surrounded by His disciples, did not try to disguise His identity when the soldiers arrived.

> Jesus therefore, knowing all things that should come upon him, went forth, and said unto them, Whom seek ye? They answered him, Jesus of Nazareth. Jesus saith unto them, I am he. . . . As soon then as he had said unto them, I am he, they went backward and fell to the ground. Then asked he them again, Whom seek ye? And they said, Jesus of Nazareth. Jesus answered, I have told you that I am he; if therefore ye seek me, let these go their way: that the saying might be fulfilled, which he spake, Of them which thou gavest me have I lost none. Then Simon Peter having a sword drew it, and smote the high priest's servant, and cut off his right ear. The servant's name was Malchus. Then said Jesus unto Peter, Put up thy sword into the sheath; the cup which my Father hath given me, shall I not drink it? (John 18:4–11 KJV)

Luke 22:49–51 fills in some more details from the scene: "When Jesus' followers saw what was going to happen, they said, 'Lord, should we strike with our swords?' And one of them struck the servant of the high priest, cutting off his right ear. But Jesus answered, 'No more of this!' And he touched the man's ear and healed him."

A quick reading might lead one to conclude that the main message of this passage is one of antiviolence—that Jesus obviously disdained Peter's use of his sword to defend him from the Roman soldiers and keep him from being arrested. In part, quite right. Jesus not only ordered Peter to put away his sword, but also healed the servant's ear. But the message of the passage is more of obedience—"the cup which my Father hath given men, shall I not drink it?"—than one expressly of antiviolence. Notice, too, that Peter and at least one other disciple carried swords—"should we strike with our swords?"—and they carried them openly, with the apparent blessing of Jesus.

Modern days have replaced the sword with the firearm. For those who think owning a firearm for defense and protection is in any way contrary to Christian beliefs, think again.

MODERN DAYS HAVE REPLACED THE SWORD WITH THE FIREARM.

FOR THOSE WHO THINK OWNING A FIREARM FOR DEFENSE AND

PROTECTION IS IN ANY WAY CONTRARY TO CHRISTIAN BELIEFS,

THINK AGAIN.

Matthew, the first of the four gospel accounts of Jesus' arrest, offers yet another perspective.

Jesus, in the garden, tells his betrayer, "'Do what you came to do.' Then [the soldiers] came up and laid hands on Jesus and seized him. And behold, one of those who were with Jesus stretched out his hand and drew his sword and struck the servant of the high priest and cut off his ear. Then Jesus said to him, 'Put your sword back into its place. For all who take the sword will perish by the sword'" (Matt. 26:50–52).

> THE SECOND AMENDMENT IN AMERICA IS ABOUT THE RIGHT OF INDIVIDUALS TO DEFEND THEMSELVES AND FAMILY. IT'S ABOUT THE POWER OF THE PEOPLE TO CONTROL THEIR GOVERNMENT WITH A TACIT BUT NOT-SO-SUBTLE MESSAGE: WE'RE ARMED.

The last phrase has been popularly cited as "Those who live by the sword will die by the sword," a sort of warning that violence begets violence. Well, that's true: those who choose a life of crime, violence, thuggery, thievery, murder, rape, and so forth are generally putting themselves into risky positions where the responses—from police, from victims, and from other criminal elements—could very well bring severe injury and death. But this rebuke from Jesus isn't about the soldier who must kill to save others, or the parents who shoot an intruder to save their children, or the victim who shoots her attacker to escape physical injury. Jesus knew full well where the soldiers were taking Him, and He had already accepted His fate.

Don't let anyone convince you gun ownership isn't compatible with biblical teachings and beliefs—or even with the principles of other spiritual groups. The Dalai Lama, a world-renowned symbol of pacifism in Tibetan Buddhist society, told a crowd of high school students at a 2001 "Educating the Heart Summit" in Portland, Oregon, "If someone has a gun and is trying to kill you, it would be reasonable to shoot back with your own gun," the *Seattle Times* reported.[14] He also clarified that the goal of the shooting should be to wound, not kill. But the message is, guns are logical objects of self-defense—the same idea the Founding Fathers had in mind while writing the Constitution.

The Second Amendment in America is about the right of individuals to defend themselves and family. It's about the power of the people to control their government with a tacit but not-so-subtle message: we're armed.

"What country can preserve its liberties if their rulers are not warned from time to time that their people preserve the spirit of resistance? Let them take arms," Thomas Jefferson wrote in a 1787 letter to William Stephens Smith.[15]

That spells it out pretty well. But so does history.

In 1933, Adolf Hitler used government firearms registration records to identify and disarm those he deemed political enemies, including the Jews.[16] Five years later, he signed the Nazi Weapon Law requiring citizens who wished to own firearms to obtain police permission. Shortly after, Hitler-led forces staged the "Night of Broken Glass," storming Jewish homes and synagogues and confiscating their weapons, arresting and imprisoning thousands. Two years later, after Germany took France, citizens there were subjected to the same harsh, antigun demands.[17]

Jews for the Preservation of Firearms Ownership elaborates, in this chart:[18]

GOVERNMENT	DATES	TARGETS
OTTOMAN TURKEY	1915-1917	ARMENIANS (MOSTLY CHRISTIANS)
SOVIET UNION	1929-1945	POLITICAL OPPONENTS; FARMING COMMUNITIES
NAZI GERMANY & OCCUPIED EUROPE	1933-1945	POLITICAL OPPONENTSJEWS; GYPSIES;CRITICS; "EXAMPLES"
CHINA, NATIONALIST	1927-1949	POLITICAL OPPONENTS; ARMY CONSCRIPTS; OTHERS
CHINA, RED	1949-1952, 1957-1960, 1966-1976	POLITICAL OPPONENTS; RURAL POPULATIONS, ENEMIES OF THE STATE
GUATEMALA	1960-1981	MAYANS & OTHER INDIANS; POLITICAL ENEMIES
UGANDA	1971-1979	CHRISTIANS POLITICAL ENEMIES
CAMBODIA (KHMER ROUGE)	1975-1979	EDUCATED PERSONS; POLITICAL ENEMIES
RWANDA	1994	TUTSI PEOPLE

Meanwhile, antigun activists and firearm control advocates continue to try and sell Americans on the need for tame-sounding registrations—with the government holding the key to the databases—or so-called commonsense curbs and bans on assault weapons that aren't seen as necessary for self-defense of home and family.

But the Second Amendment is sacrosanct. Without it, our other constitutional rights—not to mention our safety—are in

CIVILIANS KILLED	"GUN CONTROL" LAWS
1-1.5 MILLION	PERMITS REQUIRED • GOVERNMENT LIST OF OWNERS • BAN ON POSSESSION
20 MILLION	LICENSING OF OWNERS• BAN ON POSSESSION • SEVERE PENALTIES
20 MILLION	REGISTRATION & LICENSING • STRICTER HANDGUN LAWS • BAN ON POSSESSION
10 MILLION	GOVERNMENT PERMIT SYSTEM • BAN ON PRIVATE OWNERSHIP
20-35 MILLION	PRISON OR DEATH TO "COUNTER-REVOLUTIONARY CRIMINALS" AND ANYONE RESISTING ANY GOVERNMENT PROGRAM • DEATH PENALTY FOR SUPPLY GUNS TO SUCH "CRIMINALS"
100,000-200,000	REGISTER GUNS & OWNERS • LICENSING WITH HIGH FEES • PROHIBIT CARRYING GUNS • BANS ON GUNS, SHARP TOOLS • CONFISCATION POWERS
300,000	REGISTER ALL GUNS & OWNERS • LICENSES FOR TRANSACTIONS • WARRANTLESS SEARCHES • CONFISCATION POWERS
2 MILLION	LICENSES FOR GUNS, OWNERS, AMMUNITION & TRANSACTIONS • PHOTO ID WITH FINGERPRINTS • LICENSE INSPECTED QUARTERLY
800,000	REGISTER GUNS, OWNERS, AMMUNITION • OWNERS MUST JUSTIFY NEED • CONCEALABLE GUNS ILLEGAL • CONFISCATING POWERS

jeopardy. And nowhere in the Constitution does it give government the right to own weapons the average American isn't entitled to own, or to stipulate and restrict the types of acceptable firearms, size of acceptable magazine cartridges, caliber of acceptable bullets, and so forth that citizens are allowed to possess.

We can't let the government erode the Second Amendment with piecemeal regulations. Our safety and security are at stake.

In 2011, a fifty-three-year-old woman in Gwinnett County,

Georgia, emerged from a shower to find a man, armed with a knife, standing in her bathroom. She struggled with him, fell in her tub, and grabbed a shower rod to try to fight him off. He then ordered her into the bedroom, where she tricked him into believing she had money to offer him—and instead pulled out a .22 caliber handgun and shot him nine times. Police and neighbors credited her quick thinking, suggesting that had she been without weapon, the attack would have ended very differently.[19]

Thank goodness for the Second Amendment.

In 2012, a Phoenix, Arizona, fourteen-year-old boy, was home babysitting his younger siblings, ages eight, twelve, and twelve, when the doorbell rang. The teen didn't recognize the woman at the door, so he ignored her knock. Shortly after, he heard a loud banging and, in fear, ushered his siblings to an upstairs room while he grabbed a handgun from his parents' room. His instincts were correct; from the top of the stairs he watched an unknown man break through the front door, holding and pointing a gun. The teen fired at the intruder, seriously injuring him—but saving his siblings from harm. One responding police officer commended the boy for his actions, saying to the Associated Press that if he hadn't acted as he did, the community could have had "injured children on our hands."[20]

Again, hat tip to the Second Amendment.

In 2013, a Loganville, Georgia, mother and twin nine-year-old children tried hiding in the attic from a robber who chased them through their own home. But the criminal was persistent and, armed with a crowbar, opened the attic door. The terrified woman picked up her handgun and fired five times at the intruder, who then stumbled from the scene and into his car. Police apprehended him a short time later, crashed in his car and seriously injured. The woman, meanwhile, fled with her children to her neighbor's house for assistance.

"Thank God the homeowner had a .38," the neighbor later said to WGCL-TV Atlanta. "I'm not saying you should shoot people but you're going to defend your young children [and], for a woman, I think you should have a weapon."[21]

In 2014, parents of a seventeen-year-old girl watched in horror as two men confronted her in the driveway as she tried to get in her car. The attackers held a gun to the girl's head and used her as a human shield to gain entry into the home—where another child, age five, was also present. The mother and father grabbed their guns. As the suspects entered, the father fired off several shots at both men. The mother fired one shot, but missed. One suspect died at the scene; another scurried away, wounded. Police apprehended him a short time later, discovering he was the same man who was arrested for a 2010 murder that ended with dropped charges due to the failure of witnesses to cooperate. The mother, father, seventeen-year-old, and five-year-old were all saved from harm—once again, due largely to the Second Amendment.[22]

In 2015, a homeowner in Catawba County, North Carolina, was inside his residence with his wife when he heard the sound of breaking glass and went to retrieve his 12-gauge shotgun. The man called police but said the burglars—two men—charged him, so he shot. One suspect died at the scene, while the other fled. The sheriff on the scene, meanwhile, offered local WCNC this stoic response: "He was afraid that this subject was going to harm him or harm his wife, so he has a right to protect himself and he did."[23]

How many of those cases would have ended differently had

the victim or the victim's family been without a firearm?

It's that line of logic that should be paramount in making the case for Second Amendment rights to remain untouched by government control—the power of the gun to equalize the innocent with those of evil intent. As the Heritage Foundation reported, "Armed citizens are less likely to be injured by an attacker and the number of defensive gun uses may be as high as 2.1 million to 2.5 million times per year."[24]

Unfortunately, the debate over guns has taken on fever pitch, often by some of the very politicians who own guns, or, rather hypocritically, employ or otherwise use armed security officials for the protection of themselves and their families. But we can't afford to let emotionally charged and nonsensical reactions drive and shape this constitutional fight.

We also shouldn't lend any greater credence to those in the faith community who want to make some sort of biblical case for cracking down on the Second Amendment.

Jesus brought a crowd of armed Roman soldiers to the ground with the simple utterance "I am he." His very human disciples, however, carried swords—and it's a hard sell to say God would have preferred, say, the seventeen-year-old girl who was swiped as a human shield in her own driveway to suffer harm and perhaps death, over her mother and father pulling out their weapons and saving her. So what's the big takeaway?

Saving and maintaining the Second Amendment is a no-brainer.

Let's resist any federal and state call for new bans on weapons, ammunition, and cartridges. Let's fight any federal and state push to establish a gun registry and database of information on weapons' owners. Let's compel lawmakers to let those with rights of concealed carry to cross all borders within the United States, without fear of breaking another state's laws. Let's counter with fact any leftist, religiously based argument about the need to do away with guns because that's what Jesus would want. But mostly, let's put a stop to the notion that the government has our best interests—our safety and security—at heart by touting measures that water down or even abolish the Second Amendment. History and common sense prove otherwise.

TEN

TAKE ON THE LOCAL FIRST, THEN THE FEDERAL

Appoint judges and officials for each of your tribes in every town the Lord your God is giving you, and they shall judge the people fairly. Do not pervert justice or show partiality. Do not accept a bribe, for a bribe blinds the eyes of the wise and twists the words of the innocent. Follow justice and justice alone, so that you may live and possess the land the Lord your God is giving you. —DEUTERONOMY 16:18–20 (NIV)

On February 6, 1788, on the cusp of ratification of the newly created Constitution, the *New York Packet* published a brief essay popularly believed to have been penned by James Madison to the people of the state, describing the importance of structuring a government that allowed for checks and balances among the pertinent parties.[1] Federalist No. 51 laid out a concise and compelling case, based on a stark recognition of human nature, for the "members of each [department to] . . . have as little agency as possible in the appointment of the members of the others."[2]

He wrote:

But the great security against a gradual concentration of the several powers in the same department consists in giving to those who administer each department the necessary constitutional means and personal motives to resist encroachments of the others. The provision for defense must in this, as in all other cases, be made commensurate to the danger of attack. Ambition must be made to counteract ambition. The interest of the man must be connected with the constitutional rights of the place. It may be a reflection on human nature, that such devices should be necessary to control the abuses of government. But what is government itself, but the greatest of all reflections on human nature? If men were angels, no government would be necessary. If angels were to govern men, neither external nor internal controls on government would be necessary. In framing a government which is to be administered by men over men, the great difficulty lies in this: you must first enable the government to control the governed; and in the next place oblige it to control itself. A dependence on the people is, no doubt, the primary control on the government; but experience has taught mankind the necessity of auxiliary precautions.[3]

The eighty-five essays comprising the Federalist Papers were all published under the pseudonym "Publius" to avoid attacks on the authors—James Madison, Alexander Hamilton, and John Jay—so it's unclear if No. 51 was actually penned by Madison or Hamilton.[4] But what is clear is the message: the nature of humankind is such that the new government must include a way for the people to watchdog those in power.

> THE FOUNDERS CREATED THREE SEPARATE BRANCHES OF GOVERNMENT
>
> SO THAT A STRONGER ONE WOULDN'T EMERGE AND TRAMPLE THE
>
> RIGHTS AND POWERS OF THE WEAKER.

The recommendation was both simple and brilliant. Create three branches of government, "as little connected with each other" as possible, so that a stronger one wouldn't emerge and trample the rights and powers of the weaker.[5]

Just a few days earlier, Madison had published another essay in the *New York Packet* ensuring that the newly formed Constitution would not enable the federal government to run roughshod over the states—that the states, if so inclined, would always have the inherent ability to band together and resist national encroachments. He spoke directly to the sensibilities of a bottom-up, not top-down, approach to government, writing, "A local spirit will infallibly prevail much more in the members of the congress, than a national spirit will prevail in the legislatures of the particular states."[6]

His point? No need to guess. He also wrote, in that same Federalist No. 46, that "the ultimate authority, wherever the derivative may be found, resides in the people alone," and will not be subservient to whichever government entity—state or federal—rises in power.[7]

That's a terrific sentiment. But fast-forward a couple of centuries or so, and the sad realization is the Tenth Amendment, the constitutional provision giving states all powers not awarded to the federal bodies, is in tatters. Similarly, so is the Ninth

Amendment, reinforcing the Founders' views that the people, not the government, are the proper owners of rights not enumerated in the Constitution. The implicit warnings of Federalist No. 46, that politicians on the federal level would put their own interests above those who serve at the state levels, have borne as truth.

Yet all is not lost.

What we need to do is get hot on watchdogging the local and state levels of government, where those in power shop the same groceries, visit the same restaurants, and utilize the same schools as the rest of us. Politicians on Capitol Hill may be able to duck their constituents' wishes from the remoteness of Washington, DC. But it's hard for City Councilman Jane Q. Public to avoid speaking with an angry neighbor who bumps into her at the local deli and demands to know why she voted to hike fees for trash service, or close down hours of operation for the library.

As John Taylor, president of the Virginia Institute for Public Policy[8] and an experienced and successful fighter on the state and local public policy fronts said, these are the politicos who are "closer to the people, so they have to be more accountable to the people."[9]

And winning policy wars at these levels of government is much easier to accomplish than with the federal government. It's all in knowing how to play the game.

"TO BE SUCCESSFUL IN ANY KIND OF ACTIVIST ENDEAVOR, YOU NEED ...

GREAT GOBS OF MONEY OR GRASSROOTS SUPPORT." –JOHN TAYLOR

"To be successful in any kind of activist endeavor, you need one of two things," Taylor said. "You either need great gobs of money or grassroots support. A good grassroots game will always trump the money because in the end, you can only go in the voting booth and pull the lever once, no matter how much money you have. The disadvantage of going the grassroots route is that it is difficult to keep it mobilized over a long period of time unless you can show consistent victories that are making a difference."

Taylor, also the president of the nonprofit Tertium Quids, a 501(c)(4)-issue advocacy organization based in Virginia, for years held the monthly Tuesday Morning Group Coalition gathering of activists from around the state to discuss various political issues, plot certain policy strategies, and even more important, inspire and motivate action among the citizens.[10] He counts among his group's political wins the General Assembly passage of eminent domain legislation that corrected many of the wrongs from the US Supreme Court's decision in *Kelo v. City of New London* (Connecticut), which allowed private properties to be taken for economic development purposes. Virginia passed an eminent domain reform statute in 2007 and ultimately ratified a state constitutional amendment in 2012.

The group also helped pass into law an elimination of the state's death tax and pushed forward a measure that would have affixed expiration dates to all new tax provisions, winning approval in the House but not the Senate.[11]

"We did it by building a coalition of taxpayer associations, private property rights groups, and others," Taylor said. "If you organize these people, get them going in the same direction trying to achieve the same goal, you can bring enough pressure to bear to make lawmakers listen. They know there will be a price to be paid if they ignore you."[12]

Influencing policy at the local level is a different beast.

"Two of my children had the misfortune of attending a terrible school," Taylor told me. "The teachers knew it was a terrible school. The parents knew it was a terrible school. Taking my wife as a witness, I had a meeting with the principal and told her, 'This school is going to change. We can do that the easy way or we can do that the hard way.'"[13]

The principal opted for the hard way, so Taylor moved to step two in his campaign: he took out ads in local newspapers to announce a meeting for concerned parents of students attending the school.

When meeting day arrived, Taylor learned that all the parents who individually had gone to the school with complaints had been given the same rehearsed response by the administrators. "They were all told, 'You're the only parents we're having any problems with,'" Taylor said. "Turns out, once we got the parents in the same room, we realized there were many, many parents who had horror stories to tell, and who were willing to participate in fighting for change at the school."[14]

STANDING FIRM IN THE FACE OF AUTHORITY BRINGS RESULTS.

Armed with shared experiences, and motivated by a strength in numbers they hadn't before experienced, the parents quickly brought about change at the school. Taylor—who gave an example of a dean standing on a cafeteria table and screaming at the students to "shut up or you're all dead" as one example of egregious behaviors he wanted to eliminate—said it wasn't long before the poorly performing principal was gone.[15]

His learned message?

"Schools and local governments in particular are very sensitive to bad press," Taylor said. "As soon as the ad inviting parents to attend a community meeting hit the newspapers, the school was falling all over itself to fix the problem."[16]

He said he also learned standing firm in the face of authority brings results.

"First, they'll try to intimidate you, try to bluff you," he warned, recounting his initial experiences with school administrators. "But if you're not intimidated, they've got no Plan B. They've got nowhere to go from there."

Taylor suggested those seeking to make a policy difference on the local levels of government reach out to their local media outlets and make a case, not as a "wild-eyed radical" but rather as a concerned citizen, upset at injustice.

"At the local level, raise public awareness and shine the light of day on what is happening," he said. "The media reacts favorably when someone brings them a good story, if they are convinced it is not just some type of political vendetta. At the state level, you have to be able to bring pressure to bear, either money or the grassroots. If you have neither, you're just wasting your time."[17]

Good advice. He also said those hoping to change local and state policies ought to "be in it for the long term," because the wheels of change turn slowly.[18] The constitutional amendment for Virginia's eminent domain protections, for instance, took years to bring to fruition.

But that's still faster than at the federal level, where Big

Bureaucracy reigns.

For a comparative analysis—federal action versus state and local action—just look at the issue of police militarization.

On August 9, 2014, police officer Darren Wilson responded to a call for a burglary at a convenience store in Ferguson, Missouri, and shortly after, encountered eighteen-year-old Michael Brown in the street with a friend. Following a physical altercation and struggle, Wilson shot Brown, killing him.[19]

Subsequent investigation found Wilson acted within the boundaries of the law and fired his weapon at Brown in self-defense. Protesters, however, saw it differently and accused Wilson, who's white, of gunning down a defenseless Brown, who was black, in an act of violence fueled by racism. Hundreds took to the St. Louis–area streets to rage against the civil justice system, looting stores and tossing out Molotov cocktails in the process. Police responded with what critics called overkill—armored vehicles and military-type gear.

"Hands up, don't shoot" became the mantra of the moment, spreading across the nation as a coined phrase to describe the police shooting in Ferguson, despite forensic proof to the contrary—that Brown was not gunned down in cold blood with his hands in the air, à la surrender mode, as so-called witnesses, who were later debunked, had intoned.[20]

But to many, those facts didn't matter, and still don't. To them, the phrase "hands up, don't shoot" proved catchy—an easy, roll-off-the-tongue mantra to further their preconceived narratives.

Within months, the chaos of Ferguson, along with the videos of police response to the protesters, wrought a new national outrage: Have police become too militarized? Were they exhibiting ingrained racism toward members of the black community and using brutal tactics that were completely unnecessary?

"HANDS UP, DON'T SHOOT" BECAME THE MANTRA OF THE MOMENT, SPREADING ACROSS THE NATION AS A COINED PHRASE TO DESCRIBE THE POLICE SHOOTING IN FERGUSON, DESPITE FORENSIC PROOF TO THE CONTRARY.

Capitol Hill began to take notice. Sen. Claire McCaskill of Missouri questioned if police have "gotten carried away,"[21] Sen. Rand Paul of Kentucky and Rep. Hank Johnson of Georgia vowed legislation to rein in the Pentagon 1033 program gifting military gear to local police,[22] and both President Obama and his then attorney general, Eric Holder, promised to use the powers of the federal government to make sure law enforcement agents weren't acting in ways that violated the civil rights of innocent Americans.[23]

But more than a year later, and in the wake of a handful of other high-profile stories about alleged police abuses against suspects, the action on the federal stage proved largely stagnant—except in the case of Obama, who once again bypassed Congress and pulled out his pen to order his military heads to stop giving certain types of equipment to local police.[24]

Local and state governments, meanwhile, who were facing

the same questions and the same pressures from their constituents, did more than talk—and unlike Obama's, their action didn't involve the executive-level governors circumventing constitutional processes in some grandstanding show of power and authority. In March 2015, New Jersey governor Chris Christie signed into law a bill that blocked local government bodies from accepting equipment from the Pentagon's 1033 surplus and cast-off military gear program without first obtaining permission from the state.[25] In so doing, New Jersey became the first state in the nation to take such dramatic steps to rein in the controversial 1033 program. Bill supporters quickly cheered, pointing to the power of the states as a crucial aspect of America's constitutional system.

"New Jersey has taken the important first step towards ending this federal militarization and control of local police," said Michael Boldin with the Tenth Amendment Center. "As James Madison taught us, refusing to cooperate with federal programs in multiple states is the most effective way to bring them down."[26]

Several other states took similar action, or vowed similar action.

Tennessee state senator Brian Kelsey filed a bill in January 2015 to prohibit any state or local agency in the state from owning or operating certain types of military vehicles, aircraft, and weapons, and ordering any agency already in possession of this type of equipment to sell it or otherwise dispose of it.[27] New Hampshire legislators proposed similarly, right around the same time frame.[28]

Local governments, meanwhile, worked even faster to offset all the criticisms and concerns about police militarization that were raised by the Ferguson fiasco. In late August 2014, while Ferguson's streets were still filled with protesters, officials in two California cities, San Jose and Davis, drew up plans to get rid of their police departments' Mine Resistant Ambush Protected vehicles, MRAPs. At the same time, a New Jersey sheriff announced he would no longer seek to acquire an MRAP for his agency's use, while two police departments in North Carolina decided to hold community meetings to gauge the public's views of using military equipment.[29]

That's speedy.

THE FOUNDING FATHERS INTENDED THE NATION'S GOVERNMENT FOR A MORAL AND VIRTUOUS PEOPLE WHO WERE POSSESSED OF ENOUGH CONCERN ABOUT THE FATE AND FREEDOM OF THE NATION TO KEEP AN EDUCATED EYE ON LEADERS.

Also in late August 2014, during the midst of Ferguson, Missouri, street violence, the Pinal County Board of Supervisors in Arizona asked the county manager to kick off an audit of military equipment received by the local sheriff from the federal government. Locals had complained about police abuses with the equipment as far back as 2012. But in the wake of Ferguson and the national spotlight on police militarization, local government officials finally caved to pressure and requested a formal inquiry of the program.[30]

It's as Taylor said: "Local governing authorities don't like bad press, and they're only too accommodating when the right pressure's exerted."[31]

Remember: the Founding Fathers intended the nation's government for a moral and virtuous people who were possessed of enough concern about the fate and freedom of the nation to keep an educated eye on leaders. It's therefore incumbent upon us to bring forth leaders in this vein, and not only elect them, but make sure they remain virtuous and principled while in office. Where better to realize this standard than in state and local governments, where access to the political class is so much easier to obtain than on the federal front—and where so many of those who do serve on Capitol Hill get their political starts? Seems a good opportunity to train the career politicians in the fine art of public service, with an emphasis on service. Right?

Imagine—the zoning board member to whom you appeal for a reasonable resolution on a permit matter might actually sit near you in church. The supervisor you seek company with to discuss a property tax topic could show up at next week's graduation ceremony, or bake sale, or faith revival.

Adopt this tone: "First of all, then, I urge that supplications, prayers, intercessions, and thanksgivings be made for all people, for kings and all who are in high positions, that we may lead a peaceful and quiet life, godly and dignified in every way" (1 Tim. 2:1-2).

Then get involved in local government matters; stay abreast of state political goings-on. These are the bedrocks of our country's constitutional system, and if we can't contain the political powers that be on these levels, we certainly won't stand much of a chance at reining in the comparatively remote Big

Government in Washington, DC. Look at it this way: Going local, at the least, gives good practice for taking on the feds. For constituents, it can be both training ground and confidence builder in political activism, and truthfully, it's screaming for some commonsense, Christian, and conservative infusions.

ELEVEN

THE PRESS IS SECULAR— BE YOUR OWN WATCHDOG

"And you will know the truth, and the truth will set you free." —JESUS, IN JOHN 8:32

Acts 5 in the Holy Bible recounts a story of a man named Ananias and his wife, Sapphira, who sold some property with intent to give the proceeds to the apostles of Jesus, for charitable purposes. Ananias took some of the money he earned from the sale, however, and—with Sapphira's full knowledge—kept it for himself, giving Peter only a portion. Scripture indicates that he silently presented it as if he were giving the full amount from the sale. Peter, meanwhile, saw the deception and rebuked Ananias for acting as if he had given all when he'd given only some.

"Then Peter said, 'Ananias, how is it that Satan has so filled your heart that you have lied to the Holy Spirit and have kept for yourself some of the money you received for the land? Didn't it belong to you before it was sold? And after it was sold, wasn't the money at your disposal? What made you think of doing such a thing? You have not lied just to human beings but to God.' When Ananias heard this, he fell down and died" (vv. 3–5 NIV).

But the story goes on, picking up at a time about three hours later when Sapphira came into the presence of the apostles, unaware of her husband's fate.

"Peter asked her, 'Tell me, is this the price you and Ananias got for the land?' 'Yes,' she said, 'that is the price.' Peter said to her, 'How could you conspire to test the Spirit of the Lord? Listen! The feet of the men who buried your husband are at the door, and they will carry you out also.' At that moment she fell down at his feet and died" (vv. 8–10 NIV).

Their sin? At root, dishonesty.

Ananias and Sapphira wanted to present themselves as true followers of God—as selfless givers of their material blessings and gains—but for the wrong reasons: for the acclaim of fellow believers. They were more interested in the image than in the reality. The couple didn't have to give; they chose to. But they gave only a portion, while simultaneously trying to present that portion as if they had brought it all, and in so doing, they brought a false witness.

Here's a good synopsis of the situation the couple presented, from the website Bible.org:

> What was so wrong with their plan? They did not really lie to anybody, did they? They just gave the money and said nothing about what percentage of the total sale price it represented. They could not help what other people thought, could they? Evidently they could. Peter, with miraculous divine discernment, attributed

their scheme to Satan and called it lying to the Holy Spirit. He explained that they were under no obligation to sell their property. And even after they sold it, they were under no obligation to give all the money to the church. But they were obligated to be honest. The major sin of Ananias and Sapphira was dishonesty, deceit, hypocrisy, pretense, presenting a false image of themselves, implying a greater spirituality than they actually possessed, letting people think more highly of them than what they knew was warranted. They were more interested in appearances than in reality. Peter said, "You have not lied to men, but to God."[1]

Subtle lies—silent suggestions. The creation and furtherance of realities based on the omission of key facts and necessary contextual data. These are the deeds of much of today's media—are they not?

THE MEDIA, WHETHER BY OUTRIGHT LIE OR BY INTENTIONALLY CREATIVE STORYTELLING, OFTEN SKEW THE TRUTHS SO BADLY THAT THE NATION IS LEFT IN THE DARK, CONFUSED BETWEEN RIGHT AND WRONG, FACT VERSUS FICTION, FALSEHOOD OR REALITY.

The media, whether by outright lie or by intentionally creative storytelling, often skew the truths so badly that the nation is left in the dark, confused between right and wrong, fact versus fiction, falsehood or reality. And many in the news business do it with the nonchalance of an Ananias, as if they're not truly responsible for what others think—as if their hands are clean in the face of false conclusions derived from the messages they convey.

The particularly grievous aspect is that the media are supposed to be the truth-tellers on the government. How can the public be properly informed if the media aren't feeding truth?

More to the point: How can we have a nation of godly men and women, of principled leaders and moral and virtuous people, if we're constantly being fed, then swallowing, lies? It's going to be hard to retain God as our leader if we don't take the blinders off and live in truth.

Look at how Obamacare sailed through to fruition—on the wings of many lies, most of which went unchallenged by much of the media. In 2009, President Obama insisted to host George Stephanopoulos on ABC News that the individual mandate contained in the health care reform was not a tax.[2] Yet three years later, White House attorneys argued to the US Supreme Court that the mandate was indeed a tax, not a penalty, and that's how Obamacare finally passed constitutional muster—on that tax-based argument. Which version was the truth?

Doesn't matter. In the months between, the media went all out to wage a pro-universal health care campaign.

To ABC's Cokie Roberts, any resistance to Obamacare was simply due to a failure of the American public to understand its greatness. She said on *This Week* in December 2009, "A lot of people are going to like [Obamacare] a whole lot once they see what's in it. For the first time, it's got some long-term care in it, which everybody is desperate for as the population gets older. It's paid for, totally paid-for long-term care insurance. So

I think that there's a lot in the bill that people are going to like. It's just a question of understanding it."[3]

To fellow ABC News correspondent Sam Donaldson, any reluctance to embrace Obamacare was because of a concerted misinformation campaign launched solely by Republicans. He said in January 2010 on the same *This Week* program: "I'm on Medicare. People who've been in the military are on a government health program. And yet the Republicans were able to make the idea that being on a government health program is terrible. How absurd."[4]

And to Ed Schultz, host of *The Ed Show* on MSNBC, any lingering doubts over the benefits of Obamacare were due entirely to Republicans who would simply rather see Americans die than pay for their medical needs. He said, during a September 2009 broadcast, "The Republicans lie! They want to see you dead! They'd rather make money off your dead corpse. They kind of like it when that woman has cancer and they don't have anything for her."[5]

Where are the arbiters of truth in the media?

"THOSE OF US WHO WENT INTO JOURNALISM IN THE '50S OR '60S

[DID SO BECAUSE] IT WAS SORT OF A LIBERAL THING TO DO.

SAVE THE WORLD." —PETER JENNINGS

Peter Jennings, longtime ABC News anchor, admitted in a 2001 interview with the *Boston Globe* that "those of us who went into journalism in the '50s or '60s" did so because "it was sort of a liberal thing to do. Save the world." And since, he went on, "conservative voices in the US have not been as present as they might have been and should have been in the media."[6]

No kidding. A survey of 1,080 US journalists conducted in the fall of 2013 and published in 2014 found that 28 percent working in newsrooms across America identified as Democrat—down from 36 percent in 2002—compared to just over 7 percent as Republican. Another 50 percent or so claimed they were Independent, and the remainder didn't say.[7]

Other surveys and studies show an even greater schism between the number of self-declared Democratic and Republican journalists in America's newsrooms—a schism that's stretched for decades.

WHITE HOUSE CORRESPONDENTS DURING THE LATE '80S AND EARLY '90S VOTED FOR DEMOCRATS AT SEVEN TIMES THE RATE AT WHICH THEY VOTED FOR REPUBLICANS.

A FrontPageMag.com analysis, for example, found 94 percent of media professionals in 1964 voted for Democrat Lyndon Johnson over Republican Barry Goldwater; 86 percent in 1968 chose Democrat Hubert Humphrey over Republican Richard Nixon; 81 percent in 1972 went for Democrat George McGovern, not Nixon; 81 percent in 1976 picked Democrat Jimmy Carter over Republican Gerald Ford; and twice as many selected Carter in 1980 over Republican Ronald Reagan. Moreover, in 1984, the year Reagan won the largest landslide in presidential election history, 58 percent of media professionals nonetheless voted for his Democratic contender, Walter Mondale.[8]

The ensuing years brought more of the same.

"All told, White House correspondents during the late '80s and early '90s voted for Democrats at seven times the rate at which they voted for Republicans," FrontPageMag.com found. "In a 2004 nationwide poll of three hundred newspaper and television journalists, 52 percent supported Kerry, while 19 percent supported Bush."[9]

Other analysis found members of the news world were far more likely to donate their money to Democratic, not Republican, political candidates and causes.

It's not as if all these liberal-minded journalists and news members purposely set their minds on advancing a liberal or progressive policy or piece of legislation. Some did, and continue to do so, of course. But really, they don't even actually have to take purposeful steps for the bias to exist. Many journalists and editors advance a politically biased view naturally because their own circle of liberalism is so complete: their colleagues are liberal, their bosses are liberal, and the sources they tap and cite to explain and support their already liberal premises on their stories are generally liberal. A special report on media bias from the *Quarterly Journal of Economics* authored by Tim Groseclose and Jeffrey Milyo puts it well: "Only seldom do journalists make dishonest statements. . . . Instead, for every sin of commission . . . we believe that there are hundreds, and maybe thousands, of sins of omission—cases where a journalist chose facts or stories that only one side of the political spectrum is likely to mention."[10]

The sin of omission—kind of like Ananias, when he presented his offering and allowed others to believe he was giving the full amount of money he received for his land.

The bias in the media isn't to be taken lightly. The press wields great influence in our society, and it stands to reason that if the people who put out the day's news are liberal minded, and cite so-called scientific findings and research papers or studies that support their liberal-minded views and agendas, their news conclusions—whether explicitly stated or subtly suggested—are going to toe the liberal line. Oftentimes, news seems to have degenerated into little more than propaganda.

Just take a look at what many in the news profession believe, according to this same FrontPageMag.com analysis:

- More than 90 percent of them say they're pro-choice, with about 50 percent saying abortion should be legal for all circumstances, even in late-term cases.

- More than 80 percent say affirmative action is needed to balance the scales of unjust hiring practices in both academia and business worlds.

- Half say adultery is okay, depending on the circumstances.

- More than 65 percent say prayer in public schools is a big no-no.

- Fully 75 percent see government as the means of reducing income disparities between the rich and the poor.

- More than 50 percent believe the United States exploits the Third World nations for personal gain.

- Fewer than 8 percent attend church or other religious services with regularity.[11]

Do those findings seem representative of a nation that was founded on Judeo-Christian principles, and that counts among its greatest blessings a governing principle that rights come from God, not humankind?

It's the last bullet point—the fact that more than 90 percent of journalists don't attend religious services on a regular basis—that's particularly distressing. If it can be said that religion and belief in God are two of the biggest influences on a person's life, then a press that doesn't go to church certainly represents a great divide.

IF IT CAN BE SAID THAT RELIGION AND BELIEF IN GOD ARE

TWO OF THE BIGGEST INFLUENCES ON A PERSON'S LIFE, THEN

A PRESS THAT DOESN'T GO TO CHURCH CERTAINLY REPRESENTS

A GREAT DIVIDE.

Gallup reported in 2013 that 56 percent of Americans considered religion very important in their personal lives, and another 22 percent, fairly important. Twenty-two percent said religion wasn't very important at all. Another 59 percent claimed membership in a church or synagogue, down from 2000, when 70 percent touted affiliation. And when respondents were asked if they attended religious services in the last seven days, 39 percent in 2013 said yes, while 69 percent said no.[12]

In more of a breakdown, 27 percent of these same Gallup poll participants said they attended religious services once a week; 10 percent, almost every week; 13 percent about once a month; 25 percent seldom; and 22 percent, never.

A 1995 SURVEY OF JOURNALISTS FOUND PARTICULARLY SHARP DIFFERENCES BETWEEN JOURNALISTS AND THE PUBLIC WHEN IT CAME TO ATTITUDES TOWARD MORALITY AND HOMOSEXUALITY.

How's that fare with the journalism field?

Even adding together the percentages of the general public who said they "seldom" and "never" attend, a combined 47 percent, that figure is still vastly lower than the number of members in the media who don't attend with any regularity—more than 90 percent.[13]

No wonder religious views are often presented as radical, outdated, or outright discriminatory in the press. If you have a large percentage of the American public citing biblical reasons for resisting gay marriage, for example, and those views are being reported by an even larger percentage in the media who see such objections as rooted in bias—the Bible be hanged—then the subsequent stories aren't going to cast favorable lights on the religious objectors. Rather, the stories are going to trend toward outing those with biblical-based views as crazies.

Pew Research Center reported in 2004:

> The 1995 survey of journalists found particularly sharp differences between journalists and the public when it came to attitudes toward morality and homosexuality. A solid majority of Americans consistently have expressed the opinion that it is necessary to believe in God to be a moral person. Nearly six-in-ten (58 percent) expressed that view in a 2002 Pew Research Center survey, while 40 percent said that belief in God is not a prerequisite for morality. Journalists, regardless of their organization and position, take a decidedly different view. Fully 92 percent of those who work at national news organizations say it is not necessary to believe in God to be moral; 78 percent of local journalists agree.[14]

The same poll goes on to report that 88 percent of national journalists and 74 percent of local journalists believe homosexuality should be widely accepted in society.[15]

Society at large, meanwhile, isn't as accommodating. In this 2004 poll, only 51 percent of Americans agreed with the sentiment that homosexuality should be embraced as a norm.[16]

In another Pew poll conducted nearly a decade later—and notably, after a concerted gay rights movement swept the nation, weaving through all forms of media and into the courts, Congress, and state governments—only 37 percent of Americans found homosexuality morally unacceptable.[17] Twenty-three percent deemed it acceptable, and 35 percent claimed it wasn't a moral issue at all.[18]

But once again, that's still a stark difference between the press and the American public. And it certainly underscores what many already believe: that modern-day journalists are often on personal crusades to bring about their ideas of a perfect society.

"IN THE LATE 1950S AND EARLY 1960S . . . THE FOLKS IN THE NEWS MEDIA BEGAN TO PRESENT THEMSELVES AS UNBIASED PURSUERS OF 'THE TRUTH.' GONE WAS THE OUT-IN-FRONT BIAS AND INSTEAD THE MEDIA CLOAKED ITSELF IN A NEW AIR OF DETACHMENT, A NEW JUST-THE-FACTS MIEN." —WARNER TODD HUSTON

Western Journalism elaborates:

In the late 1950s and early 1960s . . . the folks in the news media began to present themselves as unbiased pursuers of "the truth." Gone was the out-in-front bias and instead the media cloaked itself in a new air of detachment, a new just-the-facts mien.

This new era in media conceit coincided with the advent of a liberal mindset that took on the weight of the world, a new era in which liberals felt that their ideals rose above God, tradition, and country. . . .

This new wave of "journalists" did not want to report what was going on in their local news as much as they wanted to "save the world."

It's an attitude that's popularly played among today's press. Some examples of egregious press behaviors:

- Edward Kennedy and Chappaquiddick and the failure of a young woman's drowning to keep a senator from serving so many years. When Kennedy died, the mainstream media spun long yarns about his reported work for the poor, the handicapped, the underserved of society—but nothing of Mary Jo Kopechne, the twenty-eight-year-old whose body Kennedy left in 1969 at the bottom of waters off Chappaquiddick Island, where the two partied and later, crashed their car. The married senator failed to call in the incident for fully ten hours, an omission of truth that later led to his one-year license suspension. But his senate career never seemed to suffer, and his death was trumpeted in the media as a near disaster for those of the less privileged classes.

- The coronation of Barack Obama to the presidency. Not only did the media during his campaign and early White House years go on an outright crusade to push Obama as the candidate of choice for a modern-day America. But members of the press practically dubbed the man the actual "Messiah," going above and beyond to portray him in photographs and videos with halos about his head, in posters in royal shades of gold and red as the true messenger of hope and peace, and on magazine covers, bathed in the soft glows of heavenly lights.[19] *Newsweek, Rolling Stone,* and wire services such as Reuters and the Associated

Press—they all lent their creative touches to putting Obama in the best, seemingly divinely inspired backdrops as possible.[20]

- ABC News host George Stephanopoulos, pretending to be an unbiased journalist during his critical questioning of *Clinton Cash* author Peter Schweizer during an April 2015 broadcast. Turns out, Stephanopoulos—who, as a former White House adviser to former president Bill Clinton, should have been regarded as a dubious newsman anyway—had given seventy-five thousand dollars over three years to the very same organization Schweizer highlighted in his book for possible scandal, the Clinton Foundation.[21]

SIX TYPES OF MEDIA BIAS: OMISSION, STORY SELECTION, SOURCE SELECTION, PLACEMENT, LABELING, AND SPIN.

Student News Daily warns of six types of media bias:[22] the first five are omission; story selection; source selection; physical placement of the report, or the order of reporting; and labeling, which includes the "tagging" of some sources as extreme as well as failing to identify others in their proper political or cultural contexts, for example, as liberal versus conservative. The sixth— called spin—is actually something Stephanopoulos spoke of doing during his White House stint in his 1999 memoir, *All Too Human: A Political Education*, and something that followed him in his after-years in television.[23] Even the liberally minded *New York Times* recognized his talent for skewed truth telling with a 2002 feature article of his career progressions, aptly titled, "From Spin Doctor to Reporter to Anchor."[24]

How are those with Christian views, or just those with full regard for the truth, supposed to deal with this?

Americans must take the majority of the media with a grain of salt. Seriously.

We can't any longer spend just a cursory few minutes glancing at headlines, tuning in to radio reports, catching nightly news broadcasts, and expect to be fully informed on the day's events. Instead, we must seek out several news sources, from numerous different news outlets, and on a daily basis. When possible, we must do our own due diligence and our own fact checking. The press can't be trusted to perform this service any longer, or in a way that presents all sides of the story in a fair, balanced measure.

IF JOE POLITICIAN SAYS ON CBS NEWS THAT HE'S VOTED FOR A TRADE TREATY THE PRESIDENT'S PUSHING, GO TO HTTP:// THOMAS.LOC.GOV, THE LIBRARY OF CONGRESS WEBSITE, AND CHECK ON HIS VOTE.

If Joe Politician says on CBS News that he's voted for a trade treaty the president's pushing, go to http://thomas.loc.gov, the Library of Congress website, and check on his vote.

If Jane Delegate is quoted by a state house news reporter

as voting against a funding measure for abortion clinics, go to Google or Bing and search on the pertinent General Assembly or state House and Senate, and click around for the current bill section. Check who sponsored, cosponsored, supported, and opposed it.

If City Councilman Bill Friendly is hailed by the local newspaper for funding a pet project that helps the elderly, check out the minutes of the meeting when the vote occurred, or listen to the audio of the clerk's recording of the meeting.

Watchdog the press. Because the press isn't acting as a watchdog for us any longer.

Think about it: how are Christians supposed to take a righteous stand for or against the people and issues of our day if those who are tasked with presenting the information are not only themselves secular, but also hostile to those who don't share their secular views?

As the story of Ananias and Sapphira indicates, God doesn't take truth lightly—and neither should we. If that means extra effort and time are needed to discern the truth, then those are things we should be prepared to expend. An apathetic, uneducated constituency is a slap in the face to the Founding Fathers and to those who fought and died to preserve our national freedoms. An apathetic, uneducated Christian is a slap in the face to the Founders, to the veterans—and to God.

WE MOCK GOD'S BLESSINGS BY FAILING TO STAY EDUCATED ON

THE ISSUES OF IMPORTANCE OF OUR TIME.

Psalm 119:160 says, "The sum of [God's] word is truth, and every one of [His] righteous rules endures forever." If media bias gets in the way of discerning this truth, then it's up to a righteous people to go out and dig it up, and set the nation back on that proper course.

TWELVE

STAND FAST IN THE FACE OF THE PROGRESSIVE, ATHEIST ONSLAUGHT

Blessed is the nation whose God is the Lord, the people He has chosen as His own inheritance. —PSALM 33:12 NKJV

Progressives and atheists are destroying America.

Their policies and campaigns as they play out in culture and politics are taking us not only farther down the path of socialism and total government control, but also toward a finish line of ungodly governance and utter devastation of our constitutional system. How? Look at their policies, their statements, their beliefs and mantras, and how they seek to gain influence in American society. The basic theme of all: No absolutes, no right versus wrong. The government, not God, is the wind beneath America's wings.

Here's an example of how they work, from a February 2015 op-ed by Jeff Schweitzer, a former White House senior policy analyst who identifies as a scientist with a "desire to introduce a stronger set of ethics into American efforts to improve the human condition worldwide."[1] (In other words, he's a do-gooder who wants the government to instill his personal vision of nirvana around the globe.) In a *Huffington Post* blog posting entitled "Founding Fathers: We Are Not a Christian Nation," he opened with a quote attributed to John Adams assuring readers that the newly formed United States government "is not, in any sense, founded on the Christian Religion." Schweitzer then wrote:

> As we witness yet again the brutal and bloody consequences of religious intolerance in the form of ISIS, we have a majority of Republicans pining for a Christian America. Proponents of converting the United States into a theocracy do not see the terrible parallel between religious excess in the Middle East and here at home, but they would not because blindness to reason is the inevitable consequence of religious zealotry. Conservatives who so proudly tout their fealty to the Constitution want to trash our founding document by violating the First Amendment in hopes of establishing Christianity as the nation's religion.[2]

This is wrong on so many levels; it's breathtaking.

The Far Left holds intolerant views that go so far as to compare Christianity to the bloodlust of ISIS terrorism, paint conservatives as religious zealots, and limit the First Amendment's guarantee for religious expression. Even Schweitzer's opening quote from the Treaty of Tripoli signed by Adams and then ratified by the US Senate in 1797 is clever spin.[3]

While it's true the treaty Adams signed did contain the claim that "the government of the United States of America is not, in any sense, founded on the Christian Religion," the context of that sentence packs a slightly different punch. The United States, no longer under the protection of the British navy, faced frequent pirate attack from the Muslim-dominated regions of the Barbary Coast. Pirates from Morocco, Tunis, Algiers, and Tripoli had grown so aggressive that they were not just taking US ships, but also capturing US sailors and selling them into slavery. And of crucial note: "The Barbary Powers often declared that they were 'at war with all Christian nations' unless and until a treaty was signed," said Ian W. Toll, author of the book *Six Frigates*, in an interview with PolitiFact.[4]

So the United States worked a deal with the Muslim powers in order to make the Mediterranean safe for commercial travel, underscoring the point of America's non-Christian government because of the Muslims' declaration of war against Christians.

"THE GENERAL PRINCIPLES ON WHICH THE FATHERS ACHIEVED INDEPENDENCE, WERE THE ONLY PRINCIPLES IN WHICH THAT BEAUTIFUL ASSEMBLY OF YOUNG MEN COULD UNITE. . . . AND WHAT WERE THESE GENERAL PRINCIPLES? I ANSWER, THE GENERAL PRINCIPLES OF CHRISTIANITY." –JOHN ADAMS

It's clear the Barbary Powers regarded America as a nation founded on Christianity; why else would the United States have to insert language ensuring the secular nature of the deal?

In another interesting aside: Adams may have signed this treaty, but he nonetheless recognized the United States as a country rooted in Christian principles. In a letter to Thomas Jefferson dated June 28, 1813, Adams said: "The general principles on which the fathers achieved independence, were the only principles in which that beautiful assembly of young men could unite. . . . And what were these general principles? I answer, the general principles of Christianity."[5]

Adams also issued a proclamation while president declaring April 25 a national "day of solemn humiliation, fasting, and prayer; that the citizens on that day abstain as far as may be from their secular occupations, devote the time to the sacred duties of religion in public and in private; that they call to mind our numerous offenses against the Most High God, confess them before Him with the sincerest penitence, implore His pardoning mercy . . . and that he would extend the blessings of knowledge, of true liberty, and of pure and undefiled religion throughout the world."[6]

Does that sound like the talk of an atheist, a secularist—a man who wanted government devoid of religion or God?

But Schweitzer went on in his op-ed: "We were born a secular nation and must remain one to sustain our future, unless we want to go the way of ISIS. Our founding fathers understood well the extraordinary danger of mixing religion and politics; we forget that lesson at our great peril. If we forget, just glance over to the Middle East. . . . In mixing religion and politics, the religious right subverts both. And the world suffers."[7]

It's incomprehensible to draw a moral equivalency between Christians and murderous Islamist thugs who see beheadings as justifiable acts of faith—and yet, this is what both progressives and atheists commonly do. In their world, one religion is the same as another, and mixing religion with politics automatically brings theocracy and harsh government rule. Their line of argument is that any expression of faith by a governing official, any display of religious belief, must be swept from public view. But that's not only counter to our nation's founding; it's outright aligned with the mind-sets of the North Korean and former USSR regimes.

ORTHODOX CHRISTIANITY HAD A VERY SIGNIFICANT INFLUENCE ON AMERICA'S FOUNDERS.

"My contention," said Mark David Hall in his Heritage Foundation lecture on the influence of Christianity on America's founding, "is merely that orthodox Christianity had a very significant influence on America's founders."[8] This was part of Hall's excellent analysis of the long-running dispute about the religious beliefs of the Founding Fathers. Some were deists, some were Christians of varying denominations and intensities, some were very private in their beliefs and likely tussled with the same religious challenges and questions that those of modern day faith do—but none were Muslims. None were Buddhists, Hindus, Taoists, Rastafarians, or one of a score of other religions, or even nonreligions, for that matter. Even those with a more subdued passion for the faith could hardly be called atheists— and definitely not radicalized atheists, the type and tone of today who want to rid all mention of God from the public sector.

They may have held differing views on how much religion should influence day-to-day life, including politics, as well as how much God intervened on Earth and for individuals. But the fact is, they hailed from Christian backgrounds, settled the lands with wives of predominantly Christian beliefs, and forged a government based on the thought processes, mind-sets, and beliefs that stemmed from often-intimate knowledge of the Bible.

AMERICA'S COLONIAL ORIGINS WERE ROOTED IN MASSACHUSETTS GOVERNOR JOHN WINTHROP'S HOPE FOR HIS FELLOW PURITANS TO CREATE THE SHINING CITY UPON A HILL REFERENCED IN MATTHEW 5:14.

Among Hall's research: America's colonial origins were rooted in Massachusetts governor John Winthrop's hope for his fellow Puritans to create the shining city upon a hill referenced in Matthew 5:14. Some of our nation's earliest governing documents—the Mayflower Compact and other rules of governance for Massachusetts and Connecticut—contained entire sections of text either quoting or referring to the Bible. For instance, the 1681 Charter of Liberties and Frame of Government of the Province of Pennsylvania quoted Romans 13 to make clear that government was ordained by God, and included a list of "offenses against God" that were punishable by law. Some of those offenses? "Swearing, cursing, lying, profane talking, drunkenness, drinking of healths (toasts), obscene words, incest, sodomy . . . stage-plays, cards, dice, May-games, gamesters, masques, revels, bull-baiting, cock-fighting, bear-baiting, and the like, which excite the people to rudeness, cruelty, looseness and irreligion."[9]

No wonder atheists and those on the Far Left hate the idea of religion mixing with politics. They're afraid of being told what to do, how to act—what's right versus what's wrong.

Yet a society that wants to function and not devolve into chaos must have some sort of moral code that reins in the more radical and criminal of elements. Christians find that code in the Bible; atheists and progressives seek it in the individual. In an essay entitled "Ethics Without Gods," Frank Zindler, former president of American Atheists, makes clear that morals and values have "nothing to do with the presence or absence of religious belief." Rather, he says, they stem from an evolutionary process that has given human beings "nervous systems biased in favor of social, rather than antisocial, behaviors." The essay is long and complex, but several twists and turns later, Zindler's logic seems to be this: Humans derive their moral codes from nature because, like the animals, "it is in our natures to desire love, to seek beauty, and to thrill at the act of creation."[10] And we know we won't get love unless we treat others with love—so we do.

So terrorists who want to chop off heads, are they simply expressing the love they desire? That's ridiculous. Take God as the arbiter of ethics and morals out of the picture, and what the human mind can devise to self-direct is oftentimes anything but moral or ethical.

Progressives, meanwhile, aren't necessarily atheists. But they do tout their own special brand of biblical interpretation.

Roger Wolsey, writing for *The Holy Kiss,* a self-described progressive Christian blog, said, "We don't think that God wrote the Bible. We think it was written by fallible human beings who were inspired by (not dictated to by) the Holy Spirit. Hence, we don't consider it to be infallible or inerrant." He also wrote that progressive Christians believe there is "no 'objective, one, right way' to interpret a passage," that the true meaning of biblical passages cannot be discerned except through the application of an individual's "own personal experiences, education, upbringing [and] socio-political context," and that readers of the Bible are free to junk those excerpts that don't fit their views.[11]

"We follow Jesus' example," Wolsey added, "in being willing to reject certain passages & theologies in the Bible and to affirm other ones. (He did it a lot)."[12]

Not taking away from the progressive Christian's professed love for God and the Bible, but all that's just a long-winded way of saying "we don't believe in absolutes."

THE ATHEIST AND PROGRESSIVE WORLDVIEWS PERMEATE OUR CULTURE AND PRODUCE ABORTION ON DEMAND, GAY MARRIAGE, AND A HIGHLY SEXUALIZED CULTURE THAT ENCOURAGES YOUTH TO PUSH SEXUAL BOUNDARIES.

The atheist and progressive worldviews permeate our culture and produce abortion on demand, gay marriage, and a highly sexualized culture that encourages youth to push sexual boundaries.

A clamor for transgender rights has led public venues, including schools and colleges, to do away with gender-specific restrooms and showering areas. Fairfax County Public Schools, for instance, in May 2015 voted to add "gender identity" to its nondiscrimination policy, a move that angry parents said would eventually allow boys who claim to be girls—biological evidence to the contrary—to use the female changing and showering areas, and vice versa. School board chair Tamara Derenak Kaufax said the measure would promote equality, protect "our students and staff from discrimination," and bring local policy in line with the US Department of Education's Office of Civil Rights, thus ensuring the continuance of federal funding.[13]

On the other side of the country, a West Hollywood law mandating that all single-stall bathrooms in businesses and other public locations be gender-neutral took effect in January 2015. West Hollywood Transgender Advisory Board member Drian Juarez praised the city council for the passage of the ordinance, and thanked members for "giving that protection to transgender people," the *Los Angeles Times* reported.[14]

Needless to say, transgender rights are typically seen by progressives and atheists as a social justice and civil rights cause to embrace. Dave Muscato, public relations director for American Atheists, announced in 2014 that he would slowly transition into a woman. He even picked the name—Danielle—and said he "fully support[ed] intersectionality and working together with LBGTQ activists on mutual goals," though atheism came first.[15] And transgender activist Kayley Whalen—who was born a male and raised a Catholic, but who now self-labels as a "proud, queer, atheist woman"—said in an interview posted on Religious News Service, "We must stand together in celebrating this diversity as healthy to our society, and stand against anyone who dismissed LGBTQ identities as unnatural or immoral."[16] Well, the biological and psychological unnaturalness of morphing from the gender of birth to a gender of choice would seem obvious.

But as for the morals—desiring to keep girls' showers in schools for girls only is hardly an immoral stance. It's what most would call a norm. Not to understate, but it just doesn't seem right to uproot and overhaul long-accepted societal standards and practices that separate bathroom and shower areas based on gender for a segment of society that one study found only totaled about 0.3 percent of the US population.[17]

It's not a matter of relegating transgender people to second-class status: no human has the right to treat another as inferior, especially those who claim belief in Christianity.

It's not a matter, either, of condemning homosexuals, those who support abortion—or even those who've had abortions.

AMERICA HAS BECOME A SOCIETY THAT MOCKS GOD BY TURNING THE RIGHT UPSIDE DOWN AND MAKING THE WRONG THE ACCEPTABLE NORM.

What is the matter is that America has become a society that mocks God by turning the right upside down and making the wrong the acceptable norm.

We can't expect God to continue to bless our nation if we don't obey His Word.

We can't continue to walk a path of moral decay and expect God just to nod and smile and continue to bless us. It won't be long before He will take action against our idolatrous behaviors.

Jeremiah 22 explains: "And many nations will pass by this city, and every man will say to his neighbor, 'Why has the Lord dealt thus with this great city?' And they will answer, 'Because they have forsaken the covenant of the Lord their God and worshiped other gods and served them'" (vv. 8–9).

IF AMERICA WAS INDEED FOUNDED BY THE GRACE OF GOD AND SET AS A SHINING CITY ON A HILL FOR AN EXAMPLE TO OTHER NATIONS, THEN WE NEED TO PAY ATTENTION TO JEREMIAH'S PROPHECIES.

If America was indeed founded by the grace of God and set as a shining city on a hill for an example to other nations, then we need to pay attention to Jeremiah's prophecies.

Progressives and atheists may have the right to live in America and enjoy the freedoms guaranteed by our Constitution. They also have the right to completely dismiss the notions of Jeremiah, or similar warnings based on God and the Bible. But progressives and atheists don't have the right to completely uproot our Constitution or disdain the very greatness of our nation—the core belief that our rights come from God, not government—by pushing legislation and campaigns directly opposed to our founding principles and governing documents. And they don't have the right to expect moral America to stand idly by and allow our country to degrade into a cultural cesspool, all in the name of gender equality, or individual rights, or some sense of skewed entitlement reasoning.

Our Founding Fathers did not fight for the First Amendment so that pop star Miley Cyrus could swing naked from a wrecking ball in a music video. That's not what freedom of speech is about.

The battle for America was much more inspired than that.

If polls bear true, though, we've got a long and uphill climb to overcome the anti-American, anti-Christian forces that are degrading the country. A Pew Research Center poll in May 2015 found that "fully 36 percent of the youngest members of the Millennial generation—those between the ages of 18 and 24 when the survey was conducted in 2014—eschew an affiliation with a formal religion."[18]

The gist of the survey is that the number of Americans self-identifying as "nones," or those with no particular religious affiliation or belief, is on the upswing.

> For years, surveys have indicated that members of the youngest generation of adults in the U.S. are far less likely than older Americans to identify with a religious group. But . . . [Pew] finds that, as time goes on, the already-large share of religiously unaffiliated Millennial adults is increasing significantly.
>
> A high percentage of younger members of the Millennial generation—those who have entered adulthood in just the last

several years—are religious "nones" (saying they are atheists or agnostics, or that their religion is "nothing in particular"). At the same time, an increasing share of older Millennials also identify as "nones," with more members of that group rejecting religious labels in recent years.[19]

THIRTY-FIVE PERCENT OF ADULT MILLENNIALS CLAIM NO RELIGIOUS AFFILIATION; 21 PERCENT IDENTIFIED AS EVANGELICAL PROTESTANT, 16 PERCENT AS CATHOLIC, AND 11 PERCENT AS MAINLINE PROTESTANT.

Pew found that 35 percent of those born between 1981 and 1996, the adult Millennials, claimed no religious affiliation. By comparison, 21 percent of this same age group identified as evangelical Protestant; 16 percent as Catholic; and 11 percent as mainline Protestant.[20]

What that means to some is America is getting less religious, and the upcoming generations—so far, at least—don't seem the least bit bothered by this loss of religious identification.

Good news for the progressives and atheists; not so good for those who believe in the need for God to guide our government, our society, and our homes. So what to do?

Perhaps this story shines light on some solutions.

In 2013, a couple of Carroll County, Maryland, residents kicked off a lawsuit to halt their board of commissioners from opening meetings with prayers that invoked the name of Jesus Christ. The plaintiffs won an injunction in March 2014 to stop the prayers until the US District Court could weigh in and issue its own ruling. Shortly after, board member Robin Bartlett Frazier made national headlines with her response to the injunction, telling her colleagues and the community that there was no way she was going to cease and desist speaking the name of Jesus. Her statement, as reported by CBN News: "Thinking of what Jesus did for me on the cross, I would not say his name because I might go to jail? I just couldn't do that."[21]

And one day after the injunction was handed down, Frazier made this statement at the board of commissioners' meeting:

> I think that is an infringement on my freedom of speech and freedom of religion, and I think it's a wrong ruling. And just as I wouldn't give up my guns or I wouldn't allow my children to be palm-scanned or I wouldn't give up my property rights . . . I'm not going to give up those rights. But out of respect for my colleagues— I'm not sure how strongly they feel about it—I'm willing to go to jail over it. I believe this is a fundamental of America. And if we cease to believe that our rights come from God, we cease to be America. We've been told to be careful, but we're going to be careful all the way to communism if we don't start standing up and saying, "no." So, I say no to this ruling.[22]

And then?

Frazier led the board and the community in a prayer that she said George Washington once delivered—a prayer that invoked the name of Jesus Christ.[23]

Bravo. That, ladies and gentlemen, is how you do it. It's

how John Hancock did it when he swirled his name on the Declaration of Independence in extra-large script—so the story goes, the better for the king to see his signature. It's how Christians of bold and determined faith should do it—draw a line in the sand beyond which atheists and progressives can't pass, and then stand tall and strong, ready to defend.

To counter the messages and purposes of atheists and progressives and those who would seek to bring permanent policy and cultural harm to America, one need only take a page out of Frazier's book and refuse to cave—refuse to be silent—even if the possible price is pain, discomfort, personal inconvenience or, in her case, jail time.

"Be on your guard," 1 Corinthians 16:13 tells us. "Stand firm in the faith; be courageous, be strong" (NIV).

We only have to do our part, and then trust in the fact that God will do His.

THIRTEEN

GET IN THE BATTLE OF PRINCIPALITIES

An unjust man is an abomination to the righteous, but one whose way is straight is an abomination to the wicked. —PROVERBS 29:27

Is it too late to save our nation?

The Bible recounts the story of Daniel standing at the Tigris River, in mourning for his people, who were living in rebellion to God and facing drastic punishment, when a heavenly body—some say Jesus; others, an angel, most likely Gabriel—appeared and spoke.

> Then he said to me, "Fear not, Daniel, for from the first day that you set your heart to understand and humbled yourself before your God, your words have been heard, and I have come because of your words. The prince of the kingdom of Persia withstood me twenty-one days, but Michael, one of the chief princes, came to help me, for I was left there with the kings of Persia, and came to make you understand what is to happen to your people in the latter days. For the vision is for days yet to come." (Dan. 10:12–14)

There are several lessons to be learned from this brief passage. First: faith. Prayers are heard; they don't fall on deaf ears. Second: patience. Prayers, even after being heard, may take time to address.

And third: not only does God work in the day-to-day matters of nations, but also the fate of the world rests in discerning and doing God's will.

IF WE WANT A NATION THAT'S BLESSED BY GOD, LED BY GOD, AND PROTECTED BY GOD, WE NEED TO RECOGNIZE AND RESPECT WHO'S TRULY IN CHARGE.

As the passage recounts, for three weeks a battle was playing in the background as the rulers of Persia wrestled with a governing decision that couldn't be seen by human eyes—a battle that pitted the "prince of the kingdom of Persia," or Satan, versus the heavenly being who appeared to Daniel. The fight, which probably played out to the ruling entities as whispers in the ear or sudden thoughts and visions to the head, ultimately required the assistance of Michael, the Bible's powerful archangel, to win. So what's that got to do with America's future?

Quite a bit, actually. For believers, this is a story that we should keep front and center, not only while going about daily business but also while considering the political and cultural status of America. The real fight America's facing isn't over partisan politics, or electing a candidate with an R next to his or her name versus a D. As this biblical story indicates, what happens in the day-to-day, as well as in government and politics, is all centered on one great premise: the battle against the principalities.

The book of Ephesians tells us that "we wrestle not against flesh and blood, but against principalities, against powers, against the rulers of the darkness of this world, against spiritual wickedness in high places. Wherefore take unto you the whole armour of *God*" (6:12 KJV, emphasis added).

If we want a nation that's blessed by God, led by God, and protected by God, we need to recognize and respect who's truly in charge versus who's actually mounting the rebellion, so we can better plot the paths of the future, both individually and as a nation, accordingly.

That's a freeing notion because it means the ultimate fate of America doesn't depend on the outcome of something as earthly as a political election, a mostly uncontrollable entity. But it's also a sobering principle because it means if we as a nation don't become more penitent and humble, obedient to God's Word, then it really doesn't matter whom we elect to lead our government—our country will crumble regardless.

America's annual National Day of Prayer recognizes this basic idea.

The most recent May 7, 2015, event drew what organizers said was one of the largest crowds ever to Capitol Hill, all for the common 1 Kings 8:28 theme, "Lord, Hear Our Cry," and to entice the nation to "repentance and prayer," as National Day of Prayer Task Force leader Shirley Dobson put it.[1]

And it's an inspiring get-together that brings together some of the most noted Christians—and those of other faiths—in American politics, culture, and the pulpit to take bended knee in the middle of one of the most powerful sites in the world and humbly pray for divine intervention for the country. As Jack Graham, pastor of the Prestonwood Baptist Church in North Texas and the honorary chairman of the 2015 gathering, put it during his prayerful remarks: "More than anything, in this desperate hour, may our hearts cry out to God for the healing of our nation's spiritual brokenness. May Jesus be exalted and may God's people be awakened to a new obedience to fulfill the Great Commission."[2]

What is this Great Commission to which Graham referred?

Basically, it's about spreading the Word of God to as many people in as many areas of the world as possible.[3] It's based on a command from Jesus to His disciples:

> Then the eleven disciples went to Galilee, to the mountain where Jesus had told them to go. When they saw him, they worshiped him; but some doubted. Then Jesus came to them and said, "All authority in heaven and on earth has been given to me. Therefore go and make disciples of all nations, baptizing them in the name of the Father and of the Son and of the Holy Spirit, and teaching them to obey everything I have commanded you. And surely I am with you always, to the very end of the age." (Matt. 28:16–50 NIV)

Atheists, of course, think this principle, or those put forth by the National Day of Prayer, have no business in America's government. They even hold their own counter to the National Day of Prayer, called America's National Day of Reason, in hopes of gathering some of the greatest agnostics, skeptics, humanists, and atheists together to show solidarity among the secularists of society.[4]

But it's the atheists who are wrong.

THE FOUNDING FATHERS MAY HAVE HELD DIFFERENT VIEWS ABOUT
CHRISTIANITY, BUT EVEN THE MOST IRRELIGIOUS WERE STILL
RELIGIOUS BY TODAY'S STANDARDS.

In America, it's prayer—not atheism—that hearkens back
to our nation's roots. The Founding Fathers may have held different views about Christianity, but even the most irreligious
were still religious by today's standards. They would have
been puzzled by the concerted modern-day campaigns surging
through America to rid the public sector of all mentions of God.

At its first meeting in 1774, Congress reached out to the
Reverend Jacob Duché of Christ Church in Philadelphia for an
opening prayer. Among his words:

> O Lord our Heavenly Father, high and mighty King of kings, and
> Lord of lords, who dost from thy throne behold all the dwellers on
> earth and reignest with power supreme and uncontrolled over all
> the Kingdoms, Empires and Governments; look down in mercy,
> we beseech Thee, on these our American States, who have fled
> to Thee from the rod of the oppressor and thrown themselves
> on Thy gracious protection, desiring to be henceforth dependent
> only on Thee. To Thee have they appealed for the righteousness
> of their cause; to Thee do they now look up for that countenance
> and support, which Thou alone canst give. Take them, therefore,

Heavenly Father, under Thy nurturing care; give them wisdom in Council and valor in the field; defeat the malicious designs of our cruel adversaries; convince them of the unrighteousness of their Cause . . . All this we ask in the name and through the merits of Jesus Christ, Thy Son and our Savior.[5]

Note the recognition of God as the sovereign over nations and governments—and the appeal through Jesus Christ at the end. This really is the stuff of our nation, as history clearly shows. A few more examples:

- Congress named John Adams, Thomas Jefferson, and Benjamin Franklin in July 1776 to come up with a suitable image for the seal of the United States of America. Franklin suggested a biblical adaptation of the parting of the Red Sea; Jefferson, one that showed the "Children of Israel in the Wilderness, led by a Cloud by Day and a Pillar of Fire by night." After seeing Franklin's idea, Jefferson backed it, rewrote it, and then the two presented it to Congress via a committee a month later. Neither was accepted, but the drafts clearly indicate that when it came to selecting something as important as the national seal, both these Founders turned to the one source they thought most inspiring for the task at hand: the Bible.[6]

- In May 1776, Congress declared a "day of Humiliation, Fasting and Prayer," urging colonists to "confess and bewail our manifold sins and transgressions, and by a sincere repentance and amendment of life, appease [God's] righteous displeasure, and through the merits and mediation of Jesus Christ, obtain his pardon and forgiveness."[7] Congress proclaimed many more such days of fasting and prayer throughout the Revolutionary War.

- Congress declared December 18, 1777, a day of thanksgiving for all Americans to "express the grateful feelings of their hearts and consecrate themselves to the service of their divine benefactor . . . [and] join the penitent confession of their manifold sins . . . that it may please God, through the merits of Jesus Christ, mercifully to forgive and blot them out of remembrance." That same day, Congress also suggested Americans ask God "to prosper the means of religion for the promotion and enlargement of that kingdom which consisteth in righteousness, peace and joy in the Holy Ghost"—just the sort of Great Commission principle elevated at the 2015 National Day of Prayer.[8]

- Congress, concerned about morality in the military, added clauses in the Articles of War in 1775 that pressed army and navy members to attend church, going so far in Article 2 as to "earnestly recommend to all officers and soldiers to attend divine services." Meanwhile, the Rules and Regulations of the Navy adopted in 1775 ordered commanders "to be very vigilant . . . to discountenance and suppress all dissolute, immoral and disorderly practices" and to "take care, that divine services be performed twice a day on board, and a sermon preached on Sundays." (Today's Michael "Mikey" Weinstein, founder and president of the Military Religious Freedom Foundation—whose group regularly fights against public shows of religion in the armed forces, particularly in the US Air Force he once served— would certainly oppose.[9])

- While debating the settling of the newly acquired western territories, from the Alleghenies to the Mississippi River, Congress suggested in 1785 the middle of each declared township be set aside for schools and the area "immediately adjoining the same to the northward, for the support of religions." That plan was voted down but just a couple of years later Congress passed the Northwest Ordinance, containing the language: "Religion, Morality and knowledge being necessary to good government and the happiness of mankind, Schools and the means of education shall be forever encouraged."[10]

It's odd that a nation supposedly not built on Judeo-Christian principles, and forged by Founders who purportedly insisted on the separation of all things religious from the public sector, would contain so many religious references in its early documents and politics, isn't it? Or, could it be that modern-day America is being sold a constant stream of lies by those who want a totally secular society?

I think so.

THE MYTH OF OUR NATION'S POLITICS AND GOVERNMENT BEING SEPARATED AT BIRTH FROM RELIGION IS JUST THAT – A MYTH.

It's the Big Lie of modern times—the myth of our nation's politics and government being separated at birth from religion. It's just not true. And if we lose sight of that—if we ignore and dismiss the God-blessed roots of our country's creation—we lose sight of the bigger battle, the one that crosses petty partisan lines and involves an oft-unseen enemy who works, much of the time, in stealth.

We lose sight of the one whom Daniel patiently waited out while unseen forces fought.

This is what happens to a nation that cedes the battlefield to forces antithetical to God:

> Your rich men are full of violence; your inhabitants speak lies, and their tongue is deceitful in their mouth. Therefore I have begun to smite you, making you desolate because of your sins. You shall eat, but not be satisfied, and there shall be hunger in your inward parts; you shall put away, but not save, and what you save I will give to the sword. You shall sow, but not reap; you shall tread olives, but not anoint yourselves with oil; you shall tread grapes, but not drink wine . . . I may make you a desolation, and your inhabitants a hissing; so you shall bear the scorn of the peoples. (Mic. 8:12–16 RSV)

That's according to God's Word in Micah, anyway, and it's hardly a trifling alert. In fact, many in America presently feel its sting—the ever-increasing lust for possessions; the never-satisfied quest for more; the economic downturns that have led to longer and longer work hours for little gain and little savings; the falling respect for our country in the eyes of other nations.

The reverse course, way back starts with a recognition of where we are as a nation, on the path toward the demise that Micah describes. It then calls for action, beginning with prayer.

Come on, Christians. The nation needs your fight.

Get in the battle of principalities—start with confession and repentance; then move on to prayer for our nation and its leaders; our families and social circles; our local churches, communities, and organizations; our neighbors; and our friends— and just as important, our enemies. Confess. Repent. Pray. It's the trifecta of spiritual warfare, and what's more—recall the congressional call for "Humiliation, Fasting and Prayer" in 1776—it's in our national DNA.

GET IN THE BATTLE OF PRINCIPALITIES: CONFESS AND REPENT

OF YOUR OWN SINS; THEN PRAY FOR THE NATION AND ITS

LEADERS, YOUR FAMILY, YOUR CHURCH, AND YOUR COMMUNITY.

AND JUST AS IMPORTANT, PRAY FOR YOUR ENEMIES.

We've done it before, with stellar results.

The Constitutional Conventional of 1787 hit a brick wall a few weeks into discussions, and the delegates were already packing up and heading home to their respective states. That's when Benjamin Franklin, generally regarded as one of the more secular of the Founders, whom history paints as a deist who didn't believe in the daily interventions of a kind and loving God, spoke up:[11] "In this situation of this Assembly," he began, "groping as it were in the dark to find political truth, and scarce able to distinguish it when presented to us, how has it happened . . . that we have not hitherto once thought of humbly applying to the Father of Lights to illuminate our understanding?"

He then reminded the delegates that on previous contests of will with Britain, those present for the Constitutional Convention held daily prayer services that usually brought positive results:

Our prayers, Sir, were heard, and they were graciously answered. . . . And have we now forgotten that powerful Friend [Providence]? Or do we imagine we no longer need His assistance? I have lived, sir, a long time, and the longer I live, the more convincing proofs I see of this truth—that God governs in the affairs of men. And if a sparrow cannot fall to the ground without His notice, is it probable that an empire can rise without His aid? We have been assured, sir, in the Sacred Writings, that "except the Lord build the House, they labor in vain that build it." I firmly believe this, and I also believe that without His concurring aid we shall succeed in this political building no better than the builders of Babel.

He finished with a call for all Convention participants to engage in "prayers imploring the assistance of Heaven, and its blessings on our deliberations," each and every morning, at the outset of business.

"THE LONGER I LIVE, THE MORE CONVINCING PROOFS I SEE OF THIS TRUTH—THAT GOD GOVERNS IN THE AFFAIRS OF MEN."

—BENJAMIN FRANKLIN

Accounts differ as to what happened after Franklin made this call for prayer; some sources say the Convention members adjourned without taking a vote.[12]

Regardless, the participants did later attend a church service conducted by Rev. William Rogers, who called for God to favor the group and their discussions with His wisdom and strength and to bless the Convention members "from day to day, with thy immediate presence; be thou their wisdom and their strength. Enable them to devise such measures as may prove happily instrumental for healing all divisions and promoting the good of the great whole."[13]

Weeks later, the Constitutional Convention brought forth one of the greatest political governing documents of all time.

Was it the hand of God or the common sense of mankind that brought the Convention to a state of success? Some dispute the validity of histories that retell of Franklin's call to prayer, saying few of his colleagues actually agreed to take part, or saw the need to call on God for help with the proceedings.[14] But different writings from others in attendance underscore the belief that God was indeed a guiding hand, and without Him the Constitutional Convention would have gone down in flames.

Remarking on the difficulty of achieving consensus at the Convention, James Madison wrote in his 1788 Federalist No. 37: "It is impossible for any man of candor to reflect on this circumstance without partaking of the astonishment. It is impossible for the man of pious reflection not to perceive in it a finger of that Almighty hand which has been so frequently and signally extended to our relief in the critical stages of the revolution."[15]

Alexander Hamilton said similarly, shortly after the Convention wrapped up: "For my own part, I sincerely esteem it a system [of government] which without the finger of God, never could have been suggested and agreed upon by such a diversity of interest."[16]

These entreaties to God, and recognition of God's guiding

hand, from America's political class have some modern-day equivalents. Just look at the Congressional Prayer Caucus and its advocacy spinoff, the Congressional Prayer Caucus Foundation.

Each week before the legislation session starts, congressional members meet in room 219 of the US Capitol and, no matter the political party, pray for each other, for their government, and for the country. And it's not just on Capitol Hill anymore. Congressional Prayer Caucus efforts are fanning out across the nation, and individuals in different states are forming their own 219 Prayer Groups to take nonpartisan, faith-based action for the benefit of America as a whole.[17]

Meanwhile, the foundation's Pray USA initiative, where members of government at federal, state, and local levels make public calls for "prayer and repentance" in order to see "God's hand of healing and restoration for America," is gaining steam. By June 2015, just a few weeks after its launch, the campaign had already grabbed the support of more than 650 government leaders.[18]

They take their motivation from 2 Chronicles 7:14, one of the most quoted biblical passages to show the power of national repentance: "If my people, who are called by my name, will humble themselves and pray and seek my face and turn from their wicked ways, then I will hear from heaven, and I will forgive their sin and will heal their land" (NIV).

We ought to do similarly.

The Congressional Prayer Caucus Foundation even offers a quick and easy way for all Americans, both civilian and government, to affirm "In God We Trust" as our national motto, just as Congress did once again in 2011. Called the "In God

We Trust. Put It Up!" initiative, the campaign seeks to have the motto displayed in as many places as possible around the nation, from homes and schools to businesses and government buildings.[19]

Those are but a few suitable counters to the secular forces that are currently sweeping the nation, ones the average citizen can easily get behind and support with both public affirmations and financial donations. More important, however, is to realize that electing new faces to Congress won't solve all our nation's problems. Rather, doing as our Founders did—doing as the Bible commands—and turning to God for help with the spiritual battles we all face, both individually and as a country, will do wonders.

"THE KINGS OF THE EARTH SET THEMSELVES, AND THE RULERS TAKE COUNSEL TOGETHER, AGAINST THE LORD, AND AGAINST HIS ANOINTED, SAYING, LET US BREAK THEIR BANDS ASUNDER, AND CAST AWAY THEIR CORDS FROM US. HE THAT SITTETH IN THE HEAVENS SHALL LAUGH: THE LORD SHALL HAVE THEM IN DERISION." –PSALM 2:2-4 KJV

Remember, God rules the rulers. The Psalmist wrote, "The kings of the earth set themselves, and the rulers take counsel together, against the Lord, and against his anointed, saying, Let us break their bands asunder, and cast away their cords from us.

He that sitteth in the heavens shall laugh: the Lord shall have them in derision" (Psalm 2:2–4 KJV).

So let's get in the game—the spiritual one—and stop exhausting ourselves with the skirmishes of political bickering and instead jump into the main battle of principalities. Maybe by focusing there, and starting from there, we can win back the America that the Founders envisioned and that God wants to bless.

FOURTEEN

LOOKING FOR A FEW GOOD JONAHS

Righteousness exalts a nation, but sin is a reproach to any people.
—PROVERBS 14:34

In 1922, the traveling English writer, philosopher, poet, journalist, and orator Gilbert Keith "G. K." Chesterton published his book *What I Saw in America*, based on his visit of the previous year. Among his findings: America is like no other nation.

"America is the only nation in the world that is founded on a creed ... It clearly names the Creator as the ultimate authority from whom ... equal rights are derived," Chesterton wrote. The power of his words still resonates.[1]

That's an amazing observation, and a humbling one. Chesterton's unique insights as a British citizen who nonetheless immersed himself in American culture were not only spot-on, fully in accord with Founding Father intents—but they also indicated that 135 years after the signing of the Constitution, the moral compass of the country was still headed in the right direction.

Now, more than 225 years since the signing of the Constitution, can we still claim the same?

Are we still a nation that regards the Creator as our ultimate authority?

> "AMERICA IS THE ONLY NATION IN THE WORLD THAT IS FOUNDED ON A CREED ... IT CLEARLY NAMES THE CREATOR AS THE ULTIMATE AUTHORITY FROM WHOM ... EQUAL RIGHTS ARE DERIVED."
>
> —G. K. CHESTERTON

Former US ambassador to the United Nations Ken Blackwell touched on that very issue during a June 2015 radio interview with Joe Miller. He then spoke of the overregulation of government, the porous borders and dramatic influx of illegal immigrants, the Obama administration's reluctance to view America through the lens of exceptionalism, the failure of the same White House to address the outright terrorist-fueled slaughter of Christians around the world—and he summed these degradations up in a single, simple, powerful statement: "Our reputation as a shining city on a hill . . . as a defender of freedom, has waned," Blackwell said.[2]

Many would agree.

"WE'RE ALL INVESTED WITH CERTAIN HUMAN RIGHTS, NOT BY
GOVERNMENT BUT BY GOD ... BUT OBAMA'S TURNED IT ON ITS
HEAD. HE WANTS US TO BELIEVE IT'S GOVERNMENT WHO GAVE
RIGHTS ... [SO] INSTEAD OF A GOD-CENTERED CULTURE, WE
HAVE A GOVERNMENT-CENTERED CULTURE." —KEN BLACKWELL,
FORMER UN AMBASSADOR

Blackwell, who also headed up family empowerment issues
for the Family Research Council, went on to say, "We're all
invested with certain human rights, not by government but
by God . . . but Obama's turned it on its head. He wants us
to believe it's government who gave rights . . . [so] instead of a
God-centered culture, we have a government-centered culture."[3]

When that happens, you can be sure an internal crumbling
is right around the corner.

Suddenly, rights become a commodity of government to
dole out and trade and barter, often going to the party with the
loudest voice, or the deepest pockets. Think gay marriage. As
Blackwell pointed out, marriage has for thousands of years been
defined as a God-designed union of one man to one woman.
But a couple of decades of concerted pressure from the homosexual lobbies, combined with a somewhat disturbing quieting
of Christians in the political arena, and the creative minds of five
Supreme Court justices, and what's left is a complete upheaval

of this definition—a wholesale crumbling of that cultural and moral boundary.

Compliments of the Supreme Court's 2015 decision in *Obergefell v. Hodges*, what's left is an order for all fifty states to recognize the rights of gays to marry.[4] What a thud to the Bible most Christians hold dear.

"Tear down the family, silence the church, you change the nature of who we are as a people," Blackwell warned.[5]

Richard Land, president of Southern Evangelical Seminary, said the *Obergefell v. Hodges* decision completely trashed God's intentions for marriage.[6] Pastor Mark Biltz, author of the prophetic *Blood Moons: Decoding the Imminent Heavenly Signs*, compared the gay marriage ruling to the biblical days of Lot, saying the "very fabric of what makes up a moral society is being ripped apart,"[7] Sam Rohrer, president of the American Pastors Network and the Pennsylvania Pastors Network, said "the fact that this issue even made it to the Supreme Court of the United States was an indictment against American Christians and against American churches."[8] And pastor Carl Gallups, a best-selling author whose most recent work is titled *Be Thou Prepared: Equipping the Church for Persecution and Times of Trouble*, said the ruling was the "most monumental" in the history of the world and "could prove the death-nail of divine judgment upon our once great nation."[9]

"TEAR DOWN THE FAMILY, SILENCE THE CHURCH, YOU CHANGE THE NATURE OF WHO WE ARE AS A PEOPLE." –KEN BLACKWELL

For believers, such reaction and narratives are hardly overdramatic.

Still, the high court's *Obergefell v. Hodges* decision was only the latest in a long line of offenses against God that have been committed in recent years by an increasingly callous nation. It's not a decision that came out of left field; rather, it was an outcome of years of rebellion against biblical principles. But now, we should be a bit worried at what could befall.

Isaiah 1:5 reads, "Why should ye be stricken any more? Ye will revolt more and more: the whole head is sick, and the whole heart faint" (KJV). And that, in a nutshell, is where Dr. Chuck Harding, missionary evangelist and founder of the nonprofit Awake America, sees the nation now standing.[10] Harding, who conducts Christian heritage and constitutional awareness conferences in both pastoral and political settings around the country, had this to say about the condition of modern-day society: "America is suffering from what I call an America's Alzheimer's disease. A large portion of our country has forgotten God."[11]

"AMERICA IS SUFFERING FROM WHAT I CALL AN AMERICA'S ALZHEIMER'S DISEASE. A LARGE PORTION OF OUR COUNTRY HAS FORGOTTEN GOD." –DR. CHUCK HARDING

Like Israel, who turned from God's Word and began to forsake His laws and commandments, so goes our nation today—we are starting to "follow false gods," Harding continued. "That is what we see in America and it is reflected in our politics, our culture, and our morality. Bottom line: our national problem is a spiritual problem in that we have forgotten God."[12]

Too true. But what's especially pitiful about that summation is the fact that most Americans—"more than six in ten," according to the Public Religion Research Institute (PRRI)—still believe God selected this country to fulfill "a special role in human history."[13]

> "MORE THAN SIX IN TEN AMERICANS BELIEVE THAT GOD HAS GRANTED AMERICA A SPECIAL ROLE IN HUMAN HISTORY." –PUBLIC RELIGION RESEARCH INSTITUTE

Conservatives, of course, are more apt to see the country in this light. According to PRRI, fully 80 percent of conservatives believe God chose America for a special role (only 45 percent of liberals think similarly).[14]

Both Democrats and Republicans agree America sets a moral standard on the world stage. Unfortunately, says PRRI, fully 54 percent of Republicans and 47 percent of Democrats admitted the country wasn't setting a good moral example for other nations.[15]

"AMERICA IS IN AN ASTONISHING MORAL DECLINE. WE ARE IN

A STATE OF SPIRITUAL DISTRESS. I AM FREQUENTLY ASKED

IF GOD'S JUDGMENT IS REALLY GETTING READY TO FALL UPON

AMERICA. MY ANSWER IS THAT IT, MOST LIKELY, HAS ALREADY

BEGUN." –PASTOR CARL GALLUPS

"There can be little doubt," Gallups told me in a June 2015 interview, "that America is in an astonishing moral decline. We are in a state of spiritual distress. I am frequently asked if God's judgment is really getting ready to fall upon America. My answer is that it, most likely, has already begun."

The proof, he said, is everywhere.

"Approximately one-third of the entire population of the United States currently has a sexually transmitted disease," he reported. "America now has the highest STD rate in the entire industrialized world. America produces an astounding 89 percent of all the world's pornography. American has the highest divorce rate, by a wide margin, in the world."[16]

That doesn't even touch on the abortion rate. The Guttmacher Institute recently reported that half of all pregnancies in America are unintended, and four in ten of those end in abortion.[17]

"AT LEAST HALF OF AMERICAN WOMEN WILL EXPERIENCE AN UNINTENDED PREGNANCY BY AGE 45 ... ONE IN 10 WOMEN WILL HAVE AN ABORTION BY AGE 20, ONE IN FOUR BY AGE 30 AND THREE IN 10 BY AGE 45." —GUTTMACHER INSTITUTE

"At least half of American women will experience an unintended pregnancy by age 45 . . . [O]ne in 10 women will have an abortion by age 20, one in four by age 30 and three in 10 by age 45," the report continued.[18]

A quick look at past trends is even more shocking. In 2011 alone, 1.06 million babies were aborted. From 1973 through 2011, almost 53 million abortions took place in this nation.[19]

One doesn't have to pick a side, pro-life versus pro-choice, to agree this is a sorry state of affairs for the country—a pitiful commentary on the moral compass that's now guiding us. That both men and women regard abortion as a form of birth control is apparent; the fact that our culture accepts this with such widespread embrace is abhorrent—and not just in earthly eyes. As Gallups remarked on these statistics: "There is already a monumental moral collapse taking place in America."

Just step back, observe, and try to discern the situation through God's eyes.

"The definition of marriage, the bedrock of any society's foundation, is specifically being targeted," Gallups told me. "Along with the attacks upon that pillar of human existence—a pillar that dates back to the garden of Eden—comes the frontal assaults upon home, family, human sexuality, womanhood, manhood, childhood, [and] the sanctity of life, [as well as] the direct exploitation of America's children. Once a culture goes far enough down these paths, that society will eventually grow to hate the Word of God and the people of God who hold to that sacred foundation. Make no mistake: if we continue to collectively spit in God's face, the full judgment of God will come to our shores."[20]

So you don't think that STD and abortion rates have anything to do with a heavenly judgment? Well, think again. The Bible is quite clear about what happens to a people who rebel: "If at any time I declare concerning a nation . . . that I will build and plant it, and if it does evil in my sight, not listening to my voice, then I will relent of [any] good that I had intended to do to it" (Jer. 18:9–10).

"BUT MY PEOPLE WOULD NOT LISTEN TO ME; ISRAEL WOULD NOT SUBMIT TO ME. SO I GAVE THEM OVER TO THEIR STUBBORN HEARTS TO FOLLOW THEIR OWN DEVICES." –PSALM 81:11-12 (NIV)

That the people don't heed God's commands plays out in modern days like this: Go ahead and treat sex as if it's a recreational activity, an adulterous excursion, a fun pastime to be enjoyed with multiple partners—of either gender. Ignore or dismiss God's words on these points; be stubborn. But here are the consequences: abortion, STDs, unwanted and unprepared-for pregnancies, single motherhood, wayward and undisciplined children, economic struggle, and outright poverty, to name a few.

Forget God, and He'll eventually leave you alone. The apostle Paul underscored that hard fact:

> And since they did not see fit to acknowledge God, God gave them up to a debased mind to do what ought not to be done. They were filled with all manner of unrighteousness, evil, covetousness, malice. They are full of envy, murder, strife, deceit, maliciousness. They are gossips, slanderers, haters of God, insolent, haughty, boastful, inventors of evil, disobedient to parents, foolish, faithless, heartless, ruthless. Though they know God's righteous decrees that those who practice such things deserve to die, they not only do them but give approval to those who practice them. (Rom. 1:28–32)

Sound like any country you know?

Here in America, the righteous cry out against politicians on Capitol Hill, wondering why their elected leaders ignore the Constitution, ignore their constituents, ignore and condemn those who speak truth, and instead align and partner with deceivers—think of the attacks on principled conservatives like Sen. Ted Cruz from members of his own party, when he refused to toe the GOP line.

The insolent, haughty judiciary rubber-stamps what ought to be tossed, and creatively circumvents established laws to bring about malicious ends—think of the Obamacare decisions and gay marriage.

The arrogant executive boasts, as President Obama did, of "fundamentally transforming the United States of America,"[21] something that's been pressed in a ruthless manner in recent years—think of Obama's many bypasses of Congress on immigration, the environment, and gun control.

Meanwhile, on the moral front, marijuana is making inroads as a legal recreational substance in several states, teen sex is commonplace—and the unwed mother birthrate completely unacceptable—and the national debt has soared to the point that America actually lost its AAA credit rating.[22] Our televisions blare filth; and our public school educators promote *Fifty Shades of Grey* to middle schoolers.[23]

As Gallups said, the "spiritual law of 'reaping what you sow'" is alive and well.[24]

IF WE AS A NATION TURN OUR BACK ON GOD, IT'S ONLY THAT

"REAP WHAT YOU SOW" REALITY THAT'S ON DISPLAY WHEN ALL

THESE NEGATIVE REPERCUSSIONS BEFALL.

Harding put it this way: if we break our founding vows to God, He won't be so available for help when the tough times come calling.

"Do we, as a nation, have a covenant with God? In the early years of our founding, we made a compact with God," Harding said. "One could term it a covenant but I prefer to use the term compact. We told God that we would establish a nation that would be the base for the evangelism of the gospel of Jesus Christ. . . . The further we walk away from it, the more judgment will ensue. God brought Israel into bondage and then delivered them back to their land on many occasions. If America turns completely from our binding compact with God, He won't simply chastise us. He will bring our country to its demise—as Psalm 9:17 says, 'the wicked shall be turned into hell, and all the nations that forget God [KJV].'"[25]

IT'S HARD TO IMAGINE OUR COUNTRY CRUMBLING, BUT THE

ANCIENT ROMANS PROBABLY COULDN'T IMAGINE THEIR COUNTRY

CRUMBLING EITHER.

Dire times for America? It's hard to imagine our country crumbling to such a degree—but then again, the ancient Romans probably couldn't imagine their country crumbling either. What's needed, to avoid their same fate, are some strong church voices to fight a fearless battle, and to get outside the pulpit and into the streets.

In January 2015, a trio of religious leaders—bishops Harry Jackson and T. D. Jakes and pastor James Robison—hosted a summit called "The Reconciled Church: Healing the Racial Divide."[26] Nearly one hundred church leaders gathered to try to find solutions to the race-tinged upheaval and civil unrest that were coursing through the country, sparked in part by the violent Ferguson, Missouri, protests that surged after a white police officer shot and killed a black eighteen-year-old man in self-defense. More than six thousand people attended this church-sponsored event, which was held at the Potter's House in Dallas, Texas.

A common theme that day was complacency, as summit speakers collectively bemoaned a passive church community that has stood idly by, watching the nation fall into a state of degradation. Had God's people hoped that government would intervene? If so, unfortunately, as these clergymen obviously recognized, government is not the solution for what ails the heart. "The church should lead the way," said Bishop Jakes. "We can't complain about Congress and community if we don't communicate with one another. . . . Our silence is costing lives. I'm praying that we [the church] would care enough to do better with the resources and influence that we have. . . . We can do better regarding civic engagement in our churches."

Bishop Jackson agreed. "Church leaders need to go up into the gap and be courageous and catalytic to make a difference. . . . The church is divided black and white and not as connected as we should be. The first thing we can do is come together united as the church. A group like this can shake the foundations of the nation—for God and for good."

There's no room for spectators in this battle. "Today's complacency is tomorrow's complicity," said Dr. Samuel Rodriguez, president of the National Hispanic Christian Leadership Conference/Conela. "There is no such thing as a silent Christianity."

And Jack Graham, senior pastor of Prestonwood Baptist Church in Plano, Texas, remarked, "There are a lot of good people in our churches who are sinfully silent. It is our responsibility to engage them on what matters most."

Others have said similarly, at various venues around the

nation. Ronnie Lloyd, a pastor of nearly forty years who currently serves at the Cross Church's Springdale campus in Arkansas, wrote the following for the National Day of Prayer's 2015 event:

> Much of the church in America sleeps. Spiritual lukewarmness is plaguing the church, resulting in the infrequency of church attendance, declining churches, lagging evangelism, sagging giving, and generational disconnectedness. Complacency and conflict categorize the church more than contrition and compassion. Among the people of God, announcements and promotions within the church gain a higher priority in planning and follow through than prayer.[27]

Ouch.

David Lane, founder of the American Renewal Project, a nonprofit aimed at bringing ministers into political offices, offered a similarly blunt assessment, saying the time for Christians to get off the sidelines is now—God requires it.

"NO ONE I KNOW IS UNDER THE ILLUSION THAT POLITICIANS ARE GOING TO SAVE AMERICA. SPIRITUAL MEN AND WOMEN ARE TRANSMISSION AGENTS CALLED TO BRING WISDOM AND RIGHTEOUSNESS TO EVERY AREA OF SOCIETY. VIRTUE IS A KEY COMPONENT OF FREEDOM." -DAVID LANE

"No one I know is under the illusion that politicians are going to save America," Lane said. "Spiritual men and women are transmission agents called to bring wisdom and righteousness to every area of society. Virtue is a key component of freedom."[28]

Indeed—isn't it well past the hour for Christians to step forward and demand a return to the nation's founding roots, to the Judeo-Christian principles that require a government of moral individuals? One doesn't even have to agree with the politics of all those speaking at the Potter's House summit to join forces with them on this simple view: the church community most certainly needs to get in the game.

Jerry Falwell Jr., chancellor and president of the Christian-based Liberty University in Lynchburg, Virginia, told conservative news talker Glenn Beck back in 2010 that even those of different faiths could and should set aside their theological judgments to band together for issues of national importance. "If we don't hang together, we'll hang separately," Falwell said. "I mean, that's what my father believed when he formed Moral Majority . . . an organization of Mormons, Catholics, Protestants, Jews, people of no faith. And there are bigger issues now. We can argue about theology after we save the country. And I really think that we really do need to stand together; it's a critical time in our nation's history."[29]

That seems like some sound advice for churches to adopt and adapt to help navigate these dangerous days we face in America. As individuals, we need to carry that tone outside the congregation, too.

"MY CALL TO ACTION? AS WE'RE TOLD IN THE SCRIPTURES, BE UNAFRAID. TAKE A STAND. SHOW UP. PUNCH HOLES IN THE DARKNESS BY MAKING SURE YOU HOLD YOUR SPECIAL LIGHT HIGH AND STRONG." —KEN BLACKWELL

"My call to action?" said Ken Blackwell. "As we're told in the scriptures, be unafraid. Take a stand. Show up. Punch holes in the darkness by making sure you hold your special light high and strong."[30]

Just because America's government has fallen into a free fall of dishonesty, and the culture into a pit of moral decay, that doesn't absolve the individual believer of responsibility to fight for what's right. Amen? Besides, hope springs eternal.

Just think of Jonah, Harding told me, likening the stresses of twenty-first-century America to the biblical man chosen by God to deliver an important message, but whose disobedience landed him for a time in the belly of a giant fish. "The wicked nation of Nineveh was under a forty-day judgment call from God. Jonah the unwilling preacher, after being redirected by God, showed up and preached an eight-word message: 'Yet forty days, and Nineveh shall be overthrown,'" Harding said, citing Jonah 3:4. "The people repented and God postponed His judgment to over a century later."[31]

The larger message?

Hey, if it happened in Nineveh, it could happen in America.

If repentance turned away God's wrath from the very wicked Nineveh, then repentance could turn God's wrath from America too.

Americans just need to listen—and more Jonahs (Christians) need to speak up.

"Proverbs 28:2 states, 'For the transgression of a land many are the princes thereof; but by a man of understanding the state thereof shall be prolonged' [KJV]. Herein lies our hope, for God is the same yesterday, today, and forever," Harding said. "We need to be praying for God to have mercy upon us for the sins of our nation and postpone his judgment."[32]

That's a message that's not likely to go over well with individuals used to doing their own thing, acting according to their own will. But it's really the only way this country is going to realize the full extent of God's glory and recapture America's essence as a shining city on a hill. The status quo—which brought us socialized health care, gay marriage, and score upon score of disappointments from both the political and the cultural worlds—isn't working. It's time to usher in something new—which is really something old.

"Prayer, repentance, turning back to God, and moral renewal are the only solutions Americans can pursue to cure the deep rot that has settled within [their] culture," Gallups said. And yet, he continued, "a large number of Americans mistakenly believe we can correct our problems solely through the political process."

We've tried, but we can't. Isn't it time to lay down that burden and put the fate of the nation on the shoulders of Him who holds it anyway?

"Our problems go far deeper than that political makeup of Washington, DC," Gallups concluded. "It is the heart of

America that needs cleansing first—the rest will follow. America does not need more patriotism at this point in our history—it needs more repentance. We need to turn back to a national reverence for God and His Word."

Yes, indeed. And in so doing, maybe then we can win back our internationally recognized label as a nation that regards God as our ultimate provider, savior, and authority.

FIFTEEN

CHRISTIANS, WAKE UP! THE CULTURE WAR IS RAGING

Do not be deceived: God is not mocked, for whatever one sows, that will he also reap. —GALATIANS 6:7

On June 26, 2015, the US Supreme Court in a 5-4 decision struck down states' constitutional abilities to ban gay marriage. For many, especially those of Christian faith, it was as Sen. Ted Cruz opined, on his presidential campaign trail: "Today is some of the darkest 24 hours in our nation's history."[1]

Cruz was referring to the double whammy to conservatives on Obamacare and gay marriage, when in the course of just a few short hours, justices released one ruling upholding the government's fight to keep Obamacare intact and another striking down the legal authority of states to bar the issuance of marriage certificates to same-sex couples.

But look at the gay marriage ruling by itself, and Cruz was

still spot-on. That's because the fight over gay marriage was never about equality, as its principal players often claimed. Had it been, the battle would have waged against the IRS and the medical industry, and the arguments would have been along the lines of demanding tax filing changes and legal access to loved ones' health care records. And on those causes, the battle would likely have been waged in a manner that didn't generate much controversy, even from the Christian or religious crowd.

THE SO-CALLED GAY RIGHTS BATTLE HAS ALWAYS BEEN ABOUT TEARING DOWN THE TRADITIONS OF RELIGION AND CULTURE—OF REDEFINING WHAT GOD HIMSELF ORDAINED.

Instead, the so-called gay rights battle has always been about tearing down the traditions of religion and culture—of redefining what God Himself ordained.

Genesis 2:22–24 states, "And the rib, which the Lord God had taken from man, made he a woman, and brought her unto the man. And Adam said, This is now bone of my bones and flesh of my flesh; she shall be called Woman, because she was taken out of Man. Therefore shall a man leave his father and his mother, and shall cleave unto his wife: and they shall be one flesh" (KJV).

The Supreme Court mocked that standard—mocked God's Word—and America will face repercussions.

"In *Obergefell v. Hodges*, the Supreme Court didn't just

confect a new right to same-sex civil marriage," the Catholic World Report stated. "In some ways, it inaugurated a new phase in American law, culture and religion."[2]

That it did.

THE *OBERGEFELL V. HODGES* RULING WAS THE RESULT OF A DRAMATIC CULTURAL AND MORAL SHIFT IN AMERICA THAT HAS TAKEN ROOT AND SPREAD FOR YEARS, DUE IN LARGE PART TO THE QUIETING OF THE VOICES ON THE CHRISTIAN FRONT.

But we didn't get here overnight. The *Obergefell v. Hodges* ruling didn't exactly come out of the blue—more to truth, it was the result of a dramatic cultural and moral shift in America that has taken root and spread for years, due in large part to the quieting of the voices on the Christian front. On this, the Supreme Court justices were only holding a mirror to the American people. Look at this Bible passage as both a record of the past and a warning of what's to come:

> Therefore God gave them over in the sinful desires of their hearts to sexual impurity for the degrading of their bodies with one another. They exchanged the truth about God for a lie, and worshiped and served created things rather than the Creator—who is forever praised. Amen. Because of this, God gave them over to shameful lusts. Even their women exchanged natural sexual relations for

unnatural ones. In the same way the men also abandoned natural relations with women and were inflamed with lust for one another. Men committed shameful acts with other men, and received in themselves the due penalty for their error. (Rom. 1:24–27 NIV)

Have those of faith become too fearful of violating Romans 13, the biblical directive to "be subject to the governing authorities" or else "incur judgment" from God? Is that part of the reason the whole gay rights movement, leading to gay marriage, was allowed to capture such widespread attention in recent years, planting itself in both the media and minds of the youth as a norm, not an aberration? Perhaps.

WE HAVE TO LOOK INWARD AND NOT JUST CAST BLAME FOR OUR COUNTRY'S CULTURAL DEMISE ON THOSE WHO CREATE THE LEGISLATION, OR PEN THE ORDERS, OR ISSUE THE RULINGS.

We have to look inward, too, and not just cast blame for our country's cultural demise on those who create the legislation, or pen the orders, or issue the rulings.

Or perhaps it's that those in Christian camps have decided they don't want to rock the boat or cause trouble—that life is pretty good, the 401(k) is in decent shape, the kids are headed off to college, and retirement to Florida is right around the corner. Yes? Sound familiar?

Or, maybe it's the opposite. Maybe it's the thought that the country's in such turmoil and shambles and it's so difficult to make economic ends meet at home—there's no time or energy left to fight the cultural battle with any sort of effectiveness after paying the bills, getting the kids to school, taking care of the ailing in-law, juggling two jobs. And now, it's all despair. Besides, what can one Christian do to change a nation?

Whatever the reason, it's not good enough any longer to justify inaction. America's in deep trouble, facing deep danger. It's time to pick up another cross and help save the nation.

First off, our country is a republic, founded on the idea of an informed citizenry keeping watch on government officials— and government branches keeping watch on other government branches—and holding them accountable. So sitting on the sidelines and calling it "God's will" doesn't really apply in America. The second justification is selfish; the third, leading to despair and shoulder shrugging, is faithless.

CHRISTIANS CAN'T AFFORD TO STRADDLE THE LINES OF POLITICS AND RELIGION ANY LONGER, LETTING THE CULTURE CONTINUE TO ROT WHILE CLAIMING ADHERENCE TO A HIGHER PURPOSE AND BIBLICAL CALLING.

Christians can't afford to straddle the lines of politics and religion any longer, letting the culture continue to rot while claiming adherence to a higher purpose and biblical calling.

Obergefell v. Hodges, if nothing else, ought to serve as a blunt wake-up. Christians, it's time to take action. Put on the breastplate of righteousness; buckle that belt of truth, and take up that sword of the Spirit. Dress in the full armor of God. And get into the battle.

The nation now stands on a precipice that threatens to crash the First Amendment's religious freedoms—the premise that founded our nation—smack into the politically driven will of government entities who are demanding that such rights become subservient to the interests of the state.

Christians and those who value our country's religious freedoms may soon have to choose sides—stay quiet and stand silent, or rise up and speak out against the persecution, even if it brings fines, jail time, and government-backed punishments.

Consider the case of Aaron and Melissa Klein, the Christian owners of the Gresham, Oregon, bakery Sweet Cakes by Melissa, who, in January 2013, refused to make a wedding cake for a lesbian couple. Their reason? The Kleins had religious objections, based on biblical views of homosexuals.

The lesbians, Laurel Bowman-Cryer and Rachel Bowman-Cryer, didn't like that answer, however, and sought redress through the government.

More than two years later, after fighting a determined gay rights lobby, a widespread media smear that harped about perceived discrimination and some heavy-handed state civil rights authorities, the Kleins were finally ordered by Brad Avakian, the commissioner of the Oregon Bureau of Labor and Industries (OBLI), to pay the gay couple a total of $135,000 for damages and suffering. That wasn't the only bruising the Kleins took. Over the span of two years, the couple had to deal with death threats, harassment of their five children, and ultimately, the shuttering of cake-making operations at their shop and the relocation of baking operations.[3]

Yet in the government's eyes, it was the lesbian couple, not the Christian bakers, who were aggrieved.

The OBLI wrote in its order: "This case is not about a wedding cake or marriage. It is about a business's refusal to serve someone because of their sexual orientation. Under Oregon law, that is illegal." Their final determination also pointed to the great emotional anguish the lesbians had suffered because of the bakery's denial to make them a wedding cake, to the point where one "felt depressed and questioned whether there was something inherently wrong with the sexual orientation she was born with," and the other professed "extreme anger, outrage, embarrassment," and other draining emotions.[4]

Coincidentally enough, the Oregon labor group released its findings just a few days after the Supreme Court issued its gay marriage findings in *Obergefell v. Hodges*. Fox News's Todd Starnes, who covers religious-themed issues for the cable outlet and who authored *God Less America: Real Stories From the Front Lines of the Attack on Traditional Values*, summed up the dangers of the Kleins' case: "The Klein case has demonstrated once again that gay rights trump religious liberty. Other Christian business owners should pay close attention. The Kleins had a choice. They could obey the government or they could obey God. They chose God—and now they must pay the price."[5]

How godless does America have to become before those of faith say enough is enough, and open their mouths to fight?

> IT'S ONE THING TO ABIDE BY THE BIBLICAL COMMAND TO SUBJECT ONESELF TO THE AUTHORITIES THAT GOD APPOINTS AND ALLOWS. IT'S ANOTHER THING ENTIRELY TO STAND QUIET WHILE WICKEDNESS SPREADS.

It's one thing to abide by the biblical command to subject oneself to the authorities that God appoints and allows. It's another thing entirely to stand quiet while wickedness spreads.

Herb Titus, a constitutional attorney, scholar, and Bible teacher, warned that the Supreme Court decision is evidence of a nation adrift from its Founding Father governing principles, and from biblical teachings. He also lamented the silence of believers. "[Christians have] abandoned civil society to the heathen and to the enemy," and could soon find themselves facing concerted and intense attacks, he said during a July 2015 interview with former Alaska senate candidate and Tea Party favorite Joe Miller.[6]

Titus makes a valid point. If those of faith won't speak up and fight for the religious freedoms of the persecuted, who will?

Franklin Graham, president of Samaritan's Purse and the world-renowned Billy Graham Evangelistic Association, addressed just this matter in a June 5, 2015, post on his Facebook page:

Have you ever asked yourself—how can we fight the tide of moral decay that is being crammed down our throats by big business, the media, and the gay & lesbian community? Every day it is something else! Tiffany's started advertising wedding rings for gay couples. Wells Fargo bank is using a same-sex couple in their advertising. And there are more. But it has dawned on me that we don't have to do business with them. At the Billy Graham Evangelistic Association, we are moving our accounts from Wells Fargo to another bank. And guess what—we don't have to shop at Tiffany & Co, there are plenty of other jewelry stores. This is one way we as Christians can speak out—we have the power of choice. Let's just stop doing business with those who promote sin and stand against Almighty God's laws and His standards. Maybe if enough of us do this, it will get their attention.[7]

How easy is that? Christians could do that with about any business, if so inclined.

The Shepherd's Guide offers a simple, online search tool for individuals to find Christian-owned businesses—"Your Christian Connection," its website states.[8]

The Christian Business Marketplace is another online source that offers similarly, and even boasts a stringent vetting process to separate the sheep from the wolves. "All members have been checked against the BBB database at their time of application and have agreed to our Christian Statement of Faith and Christian Business Code of Ethics," the site claims on its Frequently Asked Questions page.[9]

Of course, just because a business identifies as Christian, or professes observance of some sort of values-based mission statement, this doesn't guarantee alliance with biblical principles.

But Graham's call for followers of the faith to fight back against the homosexual lobby with a boycott hit to the pocketbook is a valid, albeit nuclear, option and call to arms.

THE GAY RIGHTS CROWD ISN'T PLAYING AROUND. WHY SHOULD CHRISTIANS, ESPECIALLY ON MATTERS OF SUCH CRUCIAL CONCERN TO OUR NATION'S FUTURE?

The Kleins' case hit at more than freedom of religion rights. When OBLI issued the ruling, Avarkian also ordered the Kleins to "cease and desist from publishing, circulating, issuing or displaying, or causing to be published, circulated, issued or displayed, any communication, notice, advertisement or sign of any kind to the effect that any of the accommodations, advantages, facilities, services or privileges of a place of public accommodation will be refused, withheld from or denied to, or that any discrimination will be made against, any person on account of sexual orientation."[10]

In other words, the state put a gag order on the Kleins.

Melissa Klein took to Facebook to express outrage: "This effectively strips us of all our First Amendment rights. According to the state of Oregon, we neither have freedom of religion or freedom of speech."[11] That's a government action that should outrage and anger all Americans, regardless of religion, political party, race, sexual preference, or any other cultural divide and demographic.

The justification for the OBLI's determination against the Kleins was the Oregon Equality Act of 2007,[12] which bars private business owners from denying service to any protected class, which includes sexual orientation, as well as race, gender, disability, age, and religion. But in practice, what occurred with the Kleins is their US constitutional rights to exercise their religious beliefs were trumped by the state's insistence to uphold gay rights—and then their US constitutional rights to freedom of speech were trumped by the state's granting of special protections to gays.

Is this really where we want our country to head?

> TO BELIEVE GAY MARRIAGE IS EQUAL TO HETEROSEXUAL MARRIAGE ASKS THOSE OF FAITH TO DECLARE GOD MADE A MISTAKE—THAT HE EITHER ERRONEOUSLY CREATED HOMOSEXUALS, OR THAT HE ERRONEOUSLY LABELED HOMOSEXUALITY AS A SINFUL ABOMINATION.

To believe gay marriage is equal to heterosexual marriage asks those of faith to declare God made a mistake—that He either erroneously created homosexuals, or that He erroneously labeled homosexuality as a sinful abomination.

This redefinition of marriage the US Supreme Court nailed to America's coffin truly opens the door to a societal collapse. People like Melissa and Aaron Klein, who are just trying to abide by their Christian precepts, will be painted as discriminatory outcasts, the segment of society to despise. People like Laurel and Rachel Bowman-Cryer—the lesbians who could just as easily have gone elsewhere for a wedding cake, and done so without drawing the attention they claimed in their complaint caused them such embarrassment and distress—will be accorded automatic victimhood status. Move over, religious freedoms. Move over, rule of law. Move over, history, tradition, and biblically based values and commands.

AMERICA'S POLITICAL AND COURT SYSTEMS WILL BE BASED ON THE EVER-CHANGING FANCIES AND DEMANDS OF SOCIAL JUSTICE CRUSADERS WHOSE TRUE INTENT IS THE BREAKDOWN OF MORAL CODES AND RESTRAINTS. GAY MARRIAGE WAS JUST THEIR WEAPON OF CHOICE TO ACCOMPLISH THIS GREATER GOAL.

America's political and court systems will instead be based on the ever-changing fancies and demands of social justice crusaders who mask their true intent—the breakdown of moral codes and restraints—as necessary reforms for equality. Gay marriage was just their weapon of choice to accomplish this greater goal.

One lesson learned? What the government giveth, the government can taketh away. But as Rand Paul, Kentucky senator and 2016 presidential hopeful, suggested, marriage was never really a matter that belonged in the hands of the government in the first place.

"The government should not prevent people from making contracts, but that does not mean that the government must confer a special imprimatur upon a new definition of marriage," Paul wrote, in the days after the Supreme Court issued its gay marriage ruling. "Perhaps the time has come to examine whether or not governmental recognition of marriage is a good idea, for either party."[13]

The idea is not as startling as it sounds.

Government hasn't always had its nose in marriages. To many, in God's eyes, a marriage is made as soon as a man and a woman share intimacies. Up until the Civil War, in man's eyes, a marriage was made when couples lived together for at least seven years. Called "common-law marriages," the unions were fully recognized as legal by local courts and governing officials.[14] In that era, only the wealthiest or those of more formal upbringing were officially joined in matrimony in public settings attended by family and friends, and blessed by priests, pastors, or other religious leaders. But even in those cases, the government didn't rubber-stamp them.

Shortly after the Civil War, however, state governments began to take an interest in marriages, first with the issuance of licenses—when racially mixed couples, for instance, couldn't get local religious officials to perform the service—and then with increasing frequency and abandon, justifying the intrusions as a means of collecting child support or maintaining the integrity of the food stamp program.[15] States also began to watchdog for polygamy, for pensions—to determine who were the rightful recipients—and for moral depravities.[16]

"States started regulating marriage in order to affirm racial and gender hierarchies," wrote the *Wall Street Journal* in January 2010. "You also couldn't marry 'drunkards,' or TB patients. States really pulled back on the whole notion of common-law marriages."[17]

The federal government, meanwhile, became an active, regular player in the marriage game in the 1920s, in part because of a Supreme Court case over contested miscegenation laws that subsequently opened the door for government to make money off inheritance taxes.[18]

But many see modern-day government's role in marriage as an unconstitutional intrusion, and the *Obergefell v. Hodges* ruling a sort of par for the course for a morally collapsed republic.

> "IT'S A VERY SMALL MINORITY OF PEOPLE WHO HAVE ANY SENSE WHATSOEVER OF THE LAW OF NATURE AND OF NATURE'S GOD."
>
> —HERB TITUS

"It's a very small minority of people [nowadays] who have any sense whatsoever of the law of Nature and of Nature's God—that is, the law as revealed by God in Nature and in the Holy Scriptures," said attorney Herb Titus.[19] That's a harsh assessment for a nation supposedly founded by individuals who regularly prayed to their heavenly Creator for daily intervention and direction. But it's true, as well as what logically follows: the state of marriage in America is only symptomatic of the demise of the country's culture, Constitution, and collective virtues.

Constitutional and administrative attorney, author, and columnist Jonathan Emord,[20] whose long list of career accomplishments began as a lawyer with the Federal Communications Commission under President Ronald Reagan and included, in later years, enough court wins against the oft-tyrannical US Food and Drug Administration to earn him the nickname "FDA Dragon Slayer,"[21] offered an interesting take on the state of marriages in modern-day America:

> The licensing of marriage presupposes that the state must grant authority for two people to be married. Marriage is, however, an individual right and an exercise of religious liberty. Licensing of marriage presupposes that marriage is not a right but a privilege granted by the state. If marriage is a privilege, and not a right, then it can be made subject to restrictions, such as a demand that those who wish to marry first obtain a blood test and prove their "eligibility." . . . Our nation was founded on the proposition that rights to life, liberty and property are unalienable, meaning that they are a birth right, preceding citizenship [and] . . . freedom of religion means little if the sacred covenant of marriage is made subservient to the dictates of the state. While people of faith accept God as a party to a marriage through the church, the state may not substitute itself for God in that compact nor constrict or define the marital relationship without usurping the liberty to define it according to one's own religious preference.

Emord then offered a conclusion about *Obergefell v. Hodges:* it should have been tossed from court because logically and legally speaking, the system of government-run marriage licensing cannot coexist with freedom of religion, as it's guaranteed in the First Amendment. "Because it is an unalienable liberty right," he said, "the state may not condition marriage on satisfaction of any requirement."[22]

That, in essence, mirrors Rand Paul's view: the government doesn't belong in marriage.

What a concept.

As David Harsanyi, author and senior editor at the *Federalist*, wrote, "Imagine if government had no interest in the definition of marriage. Individuals could commit to each other, head to the local priest or rabbi or shaman—or no one at all—and enter into contractual agreements, call their blissful union whatever they felt it should be called and go about the business of their lives."[23]

How simple that all sounds—and how biblical.

REMOVE GOVERNMENT FROM MARRIAGE AND WHAT'S LEFT? JUST

THE COUPLE, ENTERING A COVENANT WITH GOD.

After all, remove government from marriage and what's left? Just the couple, entering a covenant with God.

Robert Scott Bell and his wife did just that.[24] Bell, a talk radio host and homeopath who lives in Florida, said he and his wife joined in holy matrimony more than two decades ago, not by government permit or license, but rather via a "covenant of celestial marriage," effected by the filing of declaratory paperwork in the courthouse of the county they lived in at the time. The benefit of this type of union, Bell told me during a July

2015 phone interview, is that it puts God, not government, at the helm of the marriage.

"This [was] a big concern for me about getting a marriage license. When people ask permission of government, you don't realize how much you're inviting government in," Bell said. "It's the difference between rights versus privileges."

He described marriage as a "spiritual commitment" involving God, "completely devoid of government interference. . . . Why would I want the government to be a party to this contract? I don't. The government pretty much screws things up."

His advice to others?

"Stop asking permission where none is required, and when it comes to marriage, none is required," Bell said.

> "STOP ASKING PERMISSION WHERE NONE IS REQUIRED AND WHEN IT COMES TO MARRIAGE, NONE IS REQUIRED." –ROBERT SCOTT BELL

The website Boundaries for Effective Ministry repeats a similar mantra. In an article titled, "Marriage Without License Prevents 'Strange Gods' from Controlling Families," the writer goes on to say:

A Christian marriage without license from the State is necessary for the couple seeking to wed so they may honor the First Commandment. God cannot bless a union that violates the Commandments. The First Commandment requires that neither Christians nor their ministers enslave themselves by allegiance to the law of strange gods that replaces their allegiance to God who freed them from slavery. You cannot serve God and mammon . . . it is either one or the other but not both.[25]

THAT THE IDEA OF BYPASSING THE GOVERNMENT TO MARRY SEEMS STRANGE AND PERHAPS RADICAL ONLY SHOWS HOW CONDITIONED AMERICA HAS BECOME TO THE PUBLIC SERVICE SECTOR'S DABBLING IN PERSONAL AND PRIVATE AFFAIRS.

If the idea of bypassing the now-normal government system to marry—absent county clerk, absent notarized license, absent mandated blood tests—seems strange and perhaps radical, that only shows how conditioned America has become to the public service sector's dabbling in personal and private affairs.

It's not even been that long ago that the book of record for most households was the family Bible, where the names of newborns and couples who'd exchanged vows were written among the pages, and those pages then served as the official certificates of birth or marriage. Nowadays, that system's been supplanted by government agencies, from the Social Security Administration to the Internal Revenue Service.

This new normal doesn't necessarily mean better. As Bell suggested, sometimes taking "the road less traveled" leads to a freer existence, one where a godless government can't tread.[26] For Christians confounded by the moral implications of the

Supreme Court's marriage decisions, and the cultural changes that are sure to come, the opt-out of government-stamped marriage may prove an appropriate choice.

But the bigger takeaway is this: Christians and others of faith have at their disposal plenty of means to strike back at a government that fails to recognize and respect the First Amendment's freedom of religion clause. Don't like where government's taking marriage? Don't let government control marriage. Don't like how government's persecuting Christian beliefs and trampling religious freedoms? Don't stand silent and let the government claim more battleground.

Take inspiration from the Kleins. They didn't quit their fight, even after they were handed the $135,000 fine.

As Aaron Klein said in July 2015 on *Washington Watch*, a broadcast of the Family Research Council, about the Oregon ruling signed by Avarkian: "I don't believe that a man who sits in an office like that has the authority to do that. The Constitution has given me freedom of speech and I'm going to stand behind what the Constitution has to say. I think that every American should be very afraid when a public official seems to think that they have the right to strip them of any of their constitutional freedoms. We need to be very outspoken about that."[27]

Amen—with a caveat. Truly, think God-given, even more than Constitution-given.

And to those of faith who fear speaking out, or who are otherwise timid and reluctant to challenge the wicked forces that seek to root all things Christian and all things biblical from our society, remember this biblical prescription: "Take no part in the unfruitful works of darkness, but instead expose them" (Eph. 5:11).

It's imperative that we put that ideal to work. Our country needs a strong Christian voice to keep politicians in check, to serve as the gate guard of moral principles, and to keep the cultural decay at bay. Take up the armor—you know the deal—and work boldly to not only expose but also rid the country of the influences of those who seek to destroy.

SIXTEEN

CHURCHES TO THE RESCUE—HOPEFULLY

For we do not wrestle against flesh and blood, but against principalities, against powers, against the rulers of the darkness of this
age, against spiritual hosts of wickedness in the heavenly places.
—EPHESIANS 6:12 NKJV

America is still an amazingly faith-filled nation.

Even now, with all the problems—degradations to our
Constitution, political corruptions, cultural demises, judicial
activisms, and outright evil permeations we see on a daily
basis—even now, an undercurrent of Christ-loving outreach
courses across the country.

On July 11, 2015, amid the doom and gloom of the
Supreme Court's rulings on Obamacare and on gay marriage,
Christians from a multitude of denominations rallied together in
the heart of what some see as the very cesspool of sin for America,
downtown New York City, for one of the largest outdoor prayer
and preaching events in US history.

Called CityFest, the event was choreographed by famed evangelist Luis Palau, an octogenarian who has preached to more than 30 million people in seventy-five countries. The event took roughly three years to plan.[1]

The seed for CityFest was planted when Palau helped create NY CityServe, a group that partnered the local government with roughly seventeen hundred different churches of various denominations—Presbyterians, Assemblies of God, Southern Baptists, Methodists, and more—to help the poor.[2] Over the years, NY CityServe participants raised the idea several times of holding a massive gospel event in New York City, and after concerted planning, collaboration, and hard work, CityFest was born, in a section of one of the best-known venues the Big Apple has to offer, Central Park.

"Since I was a pretty young guy, I felt the Lord called me to the big cities. New York has always been on the radar but it always seemed so daunting and large and complicated," Palau said in an interview with Religion News Service just days before the big event. "But we got an invitation. It came from a group of youth pastors. It started with the Hispanics but it spread to the major ethnic groups, or language groups, and churches."[3]

CityFest was free, but participants needed tickets because by law, the number attending couldn't exceed sixty thousand. And inspiringly enough, in the days before the event, there were no extra tickets to be found.

"Sixty thousand is the maximum they will allow inside this section of the park, or any section," Palau said. "That is what we have to live with. I think if it had been open and we could have gone anywhere in the park, we would have had a quarter of a million or a half a million."[4]

What an encouragement. In the heart of desolation, despair, worry—God is still knocking.

"ASK AND IT WILL BE GIVEN TO YOU; SEEK AND YOU WILL FIND; KNOCK AND THE DOOR WILL BE OPENED FOR YOU. FOR EVERYONE WHO ASKS RECEIVES, AND THE ONE WHO SEEKS FINDS, AND TO THE ONE WHO KNOCKS, THE DOOR WILL BE OPENED." —MATTHEW 7:7-8 NET

It's as the Bible teaches: "Ask and it will be given to you; seek and you will find; knock and the door will be opened for you. For everyone who asks receives, and the one who seeks finds, and to the one who knocks, the door will be opened" (Matt. 7:7–8 NET).

What's more inspiring is that people are still asking and seeking and knocking, and the door is still being opened.

In July 2015, world-renowned evangelist Franklin Graham put out a plea for prayer and participation, first referencing the Supreme Court's ruling on gay marriage and the "defining moment for our nation" that case brought, and then saying:

> There is no hope for this nation from any political party: Republican, Democrat, tea party, independent, or any other. The only hope for America is God, and that's why I'm going to be holding Crusades in Oklahoma City and Birmingham in the next few weeks, to preach the truth of the Gospel that can bring real change in hearts and

lives, not just now but for all eternity. And that's why I'll be going to all 50 states in 2016—to declare the Gospel of Jesus Christ, to call on the church to take a stand, to urge Christians to vote and to run for public office at every level, and to call the people of our nation to prayer and repentance.[5]

Graham called it the Decision America Tour, a means for citizens to come together and plead for God's mercy and grace, to avoid the types of harsh judgment and punishments He inflicted on a disobedient Israel.

"As a nation, we have arrogantly turned our back on God, and I believe God's judgment will come against our country," Graham said. "I don't know any country on earth that has been more blessed than America, but it seems as though immorality not only reigns but is now celebrated."[6]

Can't argue with that.

"AS A NATION, WE HAVE ARROGANTLY TURNED OUR BACK ON GOD,

AND I BELIEVE GOD'S JUDGMENT WILL COME AGAINST OUR COUNTRY.

I DON'T KNOW ANY COUNTRY ON EARTH THAT HAS BEEN MORE

BLESSED THAN AMERICA, BUT IT SEEMS AS THOUGH IMMORALITY

NOT ONLY REIGNS BUT IS NOW CELEBRATED." -FRANKLIN GRAHAM

Just head south during spring break season and walk some of the beaches to check out the hedonism that passes for normal behaviors among the college-age crowd nowadays. Try and put a stop to it and you're a killjoy, not the voice of sanity.

But the moral deprivation of our nation is not confined to just a season, or a geographical spot. The country's inundated with what used to shock but now passes as acceptable, on television, at the movie theater, in the lyrics and stage antics of musicians, and on magazine covers in plain view of youngsters. As Graham said, immorality nowadays is "celebrated," not shamed.

Our nation's soul is sick.

In mid-2014, Sam Sorbo—described on Talk Radio Network's website as a writer, philosopher, international fashion model, real estate developer, actress, wife, and mother of three[7]—was kind enough to have me on her radio show to discuss my first book, *Police State USA: How Orwell's Nightmare Is Becoming Our Reality*. During the course of our chat, she aptly summarized what she saw as the solution to America's ills—as the healing salve for a massively overreaching government and slow collapse of our constitutional system: people needed to get back to church.[8]

Exactly. That's hitting the nail on the head.

If God's not leading, who is? An America adrift from God's guiding hand and moral compass is an America that's opened the door for government to lead. And once government has that open door, it's not long before freedom's crowded out of the room. If patriotic and freedom-loving Americans want to know the root of Big Government, they need only look to the empty church pews on Sunday morning.

It's only common sense that the key to reversing America's

downward trend is for churches to ratchet up their influence—a mantra Sam's Hollywood husband, Kevin Sorbo, star of the '90s TV series *Hercules* and, more recently, the Christian film *God's Not Dead*, picked up and repeated in mid-2015—albeit, with a bit of a sharper tone.

"Seventy-five percent of Christians . . . didn't even vote in the last two elections," he said, during a podcast of the *Church Boys* that soon after went viral. "Well, you know what? You get the government you deserve. You've got to get out there. Pastors have got to wake their congregations up. You can't sit there and say that religion and politics shouldn't be mixed—of course they're mixed."

And his big finish? "This country was founded on Christianity, for crying out loud."[9]

THE SPIRITUAL AWAKENING IN THIS NATION IS ALIVE, GROWING, AND COURSING STRONG EVEN IN THOSE GEOGRAPHICAL PLACES IN AMERICA KNOWN MORE FOR SIN THAN CHRISTIANITY.

Look at what's taking place. From New York City to Hollywood, California, to all fifty states in 2016, the spiritual awakening in this nation is alive, growing, and—as CityFest and the Sorbos show—coursing strong even in those geographical placces in America known more for sin than Christianity.

But now the churches need to step up their game.

In the book of Revelation, the apostle John wrote letters to seven churches in the Roman province of Asia, based on visions God gave him, pointing out their various problems, pitfalls, and, in some cases, failings. A summary of John's letters:

- The church at Ephesus was warned to jealously guard their love for God's truth and His people.

- The church at Smyrna was warned to keep the faith, regardless of what trials and tribulations arose, including abject poverty.

- The church at Pergamos was warned to fight against Satan, no matter how furious that fight became.

- The church at Thyatira was warned to boot false teaching from both pews and pulpit.

- The church at Sardis was warned to walk a line of purity, and to keep up their zealous preaching.

- The church at Philadelphia was warned to stand strong in the faith and walk on the paths God directs.

- The church at Laodicea was warned to guard against a cooling faith—to keep the passion when it came to abiding in God's will.[10]

Different times, different countries. But America can still look at these letters and learn. If nothing else, these letters point to what's important to Christ. And what's important to Christ ought to be important to all Christian churches, no matter the year, no matter the location.

Can we say with assurance these same or similar ills and diseases haven't taken root in modern-day churches in America? Or has there been a cooling of the faith, a watering down of the message, a straying from the biblical truths in too many of today's places of worship?

If the answer lies in looking at the fruit—the couples who think nothing of divorcing, the politicians who think nothing of lying, the youth who think nothing of premarital sex, the crime rates, drug abuse rates, out-of-wedlock childbirth rates, abortion rates, and so forth—then the obvious conclusion is that we've gone off track.

Sadly, it seems too many of today's churches have been corrupted with pursuits that have less to do with saving souls and more with filling pews or offering plates—pursuits that drive out life-changing and biblical preaching on sin and repentance in favor of less offensive spiritual messages, family barbeques, and feel-good get-togethers.

Here's an opinion from Chelsen Vicari, author of *Distortion: How the Christian Left Is Twisting the Gospel and Damaging the Faith*, about the degradations that have come to America's churches:

> The goal of the Christian Left is to undermine the authority of the Bible by painting inconsistencies in Scripture, which they hope will breed confusion and, at times, doubt. Once the lines of truth are blurred, young evangelicals begin reconciling their faith with liberal political platforms like same-sex marriage, taxpayer funded abortions and contraception, feminism, pacifism, and big government.

The danger is that this distorted, liberal theology breaks down the moral values outlined in Scripture. It also encourages young evangelicals to deny the Judeo-Christian principles our Founding Fathers used to establish a just, prosperous nation.[11]

That's just a brilliant assessment of the current goings-on in church, in politics, and in how they intermingle and relate. It's why the main message being touted by Graham, by the Sorbos, by Palau—that Christians need to rise up and speak up and blast back the political and cultural wickedness confronting our nation—seems so sane and sensible to some, yet so radical and off base to others. The real division in America isn't between Republicans and Democrats. It's between the powers of good and the powers of evil—the battle Satan is waging against God. And Satan, the father of lies, does some of his most far-reaching and long-lasting work when he's at his most subtle—when he works through the minds of the easily influenced to flip-flop what's wrong and turn it into right.

IF CHURCHES WON'T PREACH THE TRUTHS OF THE BIBLE, WE CAN'T EXPECT THOSE WHO ATTEND TO DON THE ARMOR OF GOD AND FIGHT THE GOOD FIGHT ON THE CULTURAL AND POLITICAL FRONTS.

If churches won't preach the truths of the Bible, we can't expect those who attend those biblically skewed churches to don the armor of God and fight the good fight on the cultural and political fronts. At the same time, if those who do attend churches that boldly preach biblical truths fail to speak out against what ails the nation, or to publicly support those who do, then as Kevin Sorbo said, we'll get the government we deserve.[12]

Unfortunately, the one we have now has sent many churches into defense mode.

In 1954, the Johnson Amendment, named for its sponsor, former president Lyndon B. Johnson, went into effect, amending Section 501(c)(3) of the Internal Revenue Code so that non-profit tax-exempt entities couldn't "participate in, or intervene in (including the publishing or distributing of statements), any political campaign on behalf of or in opposition to any candidate for public office."[13] The code has generally been interpreted to mean churches cannot appear to support one political candidate over another, and preachers cannot appear to favor one political candidate over another, or else risk losing their tax exemptions.

In 2008, the Alliance Defending Freedom launched Pulpit Free Sunday, a sort of rebellion against government control of the pulpits that encouraged preachers, pastors, and other heads of churches to speak freely before their congregations, at least for one day, on campaigns, candidates, and policies. The drive included the participation of 33 pastors, a number that rose to 84 at the next year's event, and then to 100 the year after that.[14] By 2011, fully 539 pastors from forty-seven states and Puerto Rico participated.[15] Participation soared again in the next couple of years, and by 2013, almost 1,100 pastors in all fifty states had taken part.[16]

Inspiring, right? Not so fast. It didn't take long for the atheists to send out the battle cry. In 2009, the Freedom from Religion

Foundation (FFRF) sued the IRS over the agency's failure to control these supposed wayward churches, and again in 2012, when the first suit didn't bring the desired clampdown on political speech.[17] In July 2014, the FFRF reached a settlement with the IRS, but the terms were unclear, and the Alliance Defending Freedom demanded to know how exactly the federal agency was planning to enforce the Johnson Amendment going forward.[18]

> "CHURCHES, NOT THE IRS, SHOULD BE ALLOWED TO DECIDE WHAT THEY WANT TO TALK ABOUT FROM THE PULPIT." –ERIK STANLEY

"Churches, not the IRS, should be allowed to decide what they want to talk about from the pulpit," said Erik Stanley, senior legal counsel for the ADF and director of its "Pulpit Free Sunday" campaign, months after the settlement. "The IRS should not have vague tax laws that can arbitrarily be enforced against churches to revoke their tax-exempt status. Churches and other religious congregations deserve clearer tax guidelines so they can enjoy their constitutionally protected freedoms without fear of government retaliation."[19]

The ADF was quite right to worry.

To say the FFRF has been on an aggressive search-and-destroy mission against politics in the pulpit would be an understatement. The nonprofit's filed more than fifty complaints to the IRS since 2006—twenty-eight in 2012 alone—aimed at enforcing the Johnson Amendment.[20]

Yet some of the FFRF's complaints have gone far beyond the law's basic justification to keep taxpayer dollars from supporting specific political candidates.

In a 2012 letter to the IRS, the FFRF accused Madison, Wisconsin, bishop Robert Morlino of violating tax laws by emphasizing the Catholic Church's opposition to abortion and gay marriage in a letter published in the *Catholic Herald*, the news arm of his diocese, a few days before an election. These are the so-called egregious statements Morlino made, according to the FFRF's complaint:

- "No Catholic may, in good conscience, vote for 'pro-choice' candidates."

- "No Catholic may, in good conscience, vote for laws or candidates who would promote laws that would infringe upon our religious liberties and freedom of conscience."

- "No Catholic may, in good conscience, vote for candidates who promote 'same-sex marriage.'"[21]

For that, Morlino was accused by the FFRF of "inappropriately" intervening in a political campaign and of violating IRS laws against electioneering. Some would say Morlino was simply reminding his diocese of biblical principles—thou shalt not kill, for example, or homosexuality is an abomination to God.

But the FFRF found even more cause to call for IRS action against Morlino. The group's letter continued:

The issues identified by [his letter] are generally what distinguish Republican and Democratic social platforms. In Wisconsin, these issues differentiate candidates for federal and state offices, i.e., one candidate for US Senate is anti-abortion and anti-gay marriage, and the other candidate is a lesbian who supports marriage equality and abortion rights. Bishop Morlino's article, published and distributed just five days before Election Day, is clearly urging people not to vote for candidates that embrace these positions. Likewise, the paragraph about "religious freedom and freedom of conscience" is a clear reference to the current [Health and Human Services] mandate of the current incumbent for president, Barack Obama. Though he does not explicitly state, "Vote for Romney" or any other political candidate, it is clear to the reader that Morlino is urging members of his diocese to vote against President Obama and other Democratic candidates in today's elections.[22]

The FFRF finished by requesting that the IRS "commence an immediate investigation" of Morlino and his diocese, and take appropriate enforcement action.

This is hardly the spirit in which our nation was founded. But attempts to scale back or abolish the Johnson Amendment have gone down in flames. In a report issued in two parts in December 2012 and August 2013, the Commission on Accountability and Policy for Religious Organizations came up with a commonsense way for tax-exempt religious organizations to maintain their freedom of speech rights without abusing taxpayer dollars for political causes. One of the Commission's recommendations?

Members of the clergy should be able to say whatever they want in the context of their religious services or their other regular religious activities without fear of IRS reprisal—even when these communications include content related to political candidates. Such communications would be permissible provided that the organization does not expend incremental funds in making them. In other words, as long as the organization's costs would be the same with or without a political communication, the communication would be permissible.[23]

The Commission then gave an example to illustrate its point: Say a minister who, during the course of delivering a regularly scheduled sermon, mentions the benefits of a particular political candidate and urges those in the congregation to vote for that particular candidate. Now say that same minister's statements are captured on the church's audio and video devices, and are then made freely available for public access and distribution, post-sermon. Should that minister face IRS scrutiny and punishment?

Under current laws, yes. But the Commission said that should change.

The minister in that example should be allowed to pick a candidate, announce the name of the preferred candidate, and even allow the distribution of the recording and video of the sermon in which the particular candidate was shown favor, the Commission concluded.

"No additional or incremental costs are incurred by [the church] in connection with the minister's statements during the worship service or in the dissemination of the content of the minister's sermon containing those statements," the Commission wrote. "The minister's communications related to the candidate would be considered no-cost political communications, and would not constitute prohibited participation or intervention in a political campaign."[24]

What's wrong with that? It's not as if those in the congregation or anyone hearing the preacher's political recommendations have to vote for the church-chosen candidate. After all, we're all alone when we cast our ballots.

> TRULY, THE ONLY REASON THE JOHNSON AMENDMENT HANGS AROUND IS TO MAKE A POLITICAL POWER PLAY: IT GIVES THE IRS AND LEFTIST-PROGRESSIVE GROUPS—NOT TO MENTION ATHEISTS—AN INROAD TO ATTACK AND SILENCE CONSERVATIVE SPEECH.

Truly, the only reason the Johnson Amendment hangs around is to make a political power play: it gives the IRS and leftist-progressive groups—not to mention atheists—an inroad to attack and silence conservative speech. Recall the IRS scandal in which leading agency officials applied extra scrutiny to patriotic or Tea Party–type groups seeking nonprofit status, effectively delaying their permit applications for months and in some cases, years. Lois Lerner, the then IRS official who oversaw the nonprofit organization division, actually apologized during a May 2013 conference hosted by the American Bar Association for the agency's targeting of applications that contained the words *tea party* or *patriot* in their names. But then she blunted that mea culpa by claiming the targeting wasn't partisan—it was aimed, she said, at ratcheting up office efficiency to handle a flood of nonprofit applications sent to the agency between 2010 and 2012.[25]

Predictably perhaps, the scandal didn't fade, despite a rather shocking attempt by President Obama to deny during a July 2015 appearance on *The Daily Show* with Jon Stewart that the IRS ever targeted conservatives. Then, he told Stewart, "turns out," the targeting story wasn't true—it was actually Congress that "passed a crummy law" that didn't give the IRS good advice, and agency workers in turn interpreted and implemented that law "poorly and stupidly."[26] Even Stewart had to chuckle at that lame spin of truth.

"Boy, you really do have only a year left," he said to the president, in apparent reference to Obama's lame-duck status and devil-may-care attitude.[27]

Regardless, in April 2015, a federal judge ordered the IRS to turn over a list of 298 Tea Party groups it had admittedly peppered with over-the-top and intrusive questions during their nonprofit application stage.[28] Whether America ever gets the full truth, and those guilty ever get held accountable, is something to await and see. But the lesson from the fiasco is something that should give us all chills.

This is exactly the type of free speech–crushing atmosphere churches face from the IRS in modern-day America.

As the *National Review* posited in a mid-2014 examination of the FFRF's seemingly cozy relationship with the IRS: "Is the Internal Revenue Service a threat to religious liberty? . . . Indeed, if the IRS actually enforced FFRF's suggested standards, it would be downright frightening. It would mean . . . not only that pastors could be forbidden from candidate endorsements, but also that they could not even inform their congregants about the real-world tenets of their faith."[29]

THE GOAL OF THE PROGRESSIVE, ATHEISTIC FRONT IS TO BLOT OUT THE LAST VESTIGES OF BIBLICAL PRINCIPLES THAT HAVE SHAPED AND MAINTAINED OUR POLITICAL AND CULTURAL CIRCLES SINCE THE DAWN OF THE UNITED STATES.

And that is the whole goal of the progressive, atheistic front—abolish all things religious from the public sector. Wipe out the standards of morality from American society. Blot out the last vestiges of biblical principles that have shaped and maintained our political and cultural circles since the dawn of the United States, and instill instead something that relies on a human, secular view and will—government, not God.

It wasn't always this way. America's churches used to be fierce defenders of the faith and active fighters for freedom.

During the American Revolution, the churches of the thirteen colonies were filled with fiery pleas from the ministers to fight for the cause of freedom—to get in the mix of battle with the British and win independence for the side of righteousness. These Protestant pastors spoke at length about the rights of those guided by God versus kings, paving the way—first with rhetoric and then by taking up their own arms—for the dawn of the Minutemen, the famed fighters of the British at Bunker Hill.[30] One story recounts how John Peter Gabriel Muhlenberg, ordained as a priest in April 1772 by the bishop of London, ultimately served as pastor of the Lutheran congregation in Woodstock, Virginia. "In January 1776, he preached his farewell sermon on Ecclesiastes 3, which mentions 'a time for war, and a time for peace.' At the end of the service, he removed his clerical gown, revealing under it his military uniform," the Episcopal Church recounted.[31]

Other accounts explain how the men in the congregation were immediately moved to join his battle cry, and that he actually served nearly eight years in the Continental Army, first as colonel, and upon retirement, as a brevetted major general. Moreover, Muhlenberg achieved so much military success that history records him, by nickname, as the "fighting parson."

Another story recounts how Presbyterian preacher Abraham Keteltas told his colonial congregants in no uncertain terms the Revolutionary War against the British was approved by God. In one sermon, he characterized the fight of the Americans as "the cause of truth, against error and falsehood . . . the cause of pure and undefiled religion, against, bigotry, superstition, and human invention . . . In short, it is the cause of heaven against hell—of the kind Parent of the Universe against the prince of darkness, and the destroyer of the human race."[32]

And yet in one other story, Congregationalist minister Jonathan Mayhew famously told his West Church faithful in Boston that resistance to tyranny was a good Christian's duty.

We may very safety assert these two things in general, without
undermining government: One is, That no civil rulers are to be
obeyed when they enjoin things that are inconsistent with the commands of God: All such disobedience is lawful and glorious; . . .
Another thing that may be asserted with equal truth and safety,
is, That no government is to be submitted to, at the expense of
that which is the sole end of all government,—the common good
and safety of society. . . . The only reason of the institution of
civil government; and the only rational ground of submission to
it, is the common safety and utility. If therefore, in any case, the
common safety and utility would not be promoted by submission
to government, but the contrary, there is no ground or motive for
obedience and submission, but, for the contrary.[33]

The phrase "for the contrary" means Christians are called
to fight when laws go against God.

So, what are we waiting for?

PASTORS, IT'S TIME TO PICK UP POLITICAL STEAM, POINT OUT

THE BIBLICAL PRINCIPLES AS THEY PERTAIN TO MODERN-DAY

AMERICA, AND FIRE UP CONGREGANTS TO ACT.

This is a call for all who stand in the pulpits of America's
churches: It's time to pick up political steam, point out the
biblical principles , pointing out the wickedness that's perme-
ated our modern-day culture and politics. It's time to fire up

congregants to act. The churches are the last wall of defense for a rapidly approaching secular, socialistic society. If not you, who? If not the Bible, what?

As Jesus told His disciples during the Last Supper: "If you love me, you will keep my commandments." (John 15:15 RSV).

Do this, churches, in remembrance and honor of the truth the cross represents—and in duty and regard for the Constitution that keeps us free. The nation is starving for leadership.

SEVENTEEN

A CRASH COURSE IN LETTING GOD LEAD

"For I know the plans I have for you, declares the Lord, plans for welfare and not for evil, to give you a future and a hope. Then you will call upon me and come and pray to me, and I will hear you. You will seek me and find me, when you seek me with all your heart. I will be found by you, declares the Lord, and I will restore your fortunes and gather you from all the nations and all the places where I have driven you, declares the Lord, and I will bring you back to the place from which I sent you into exile." —JEREMIAH 29:11–14

It seems the people of our country are standing at a crossroads.

To the left is the status quo, the path of political bickering, economic instability, national security danger, constitutional degradations, cultural and moral depravity.

To the right—a return to godly principles, biblical beliefs, and a disciplined, restrained, and respectful government.

It's not as if America has historically walked a continuous line on one path or the other. The nation, to varying degrees, has always suffered spots and spells of financial trouble; always wrestled with security issues; always dabbled in morally questionable activities. But the intensity and frequency of our national troubles seem sharper nowadays.

The feeling in the air seems darker, more unsettled.

The needle on our moral compass seems to have done a one-eighty.

The messages coming out of our schools, out of the mouths of our youth, seem more at odds with the notions upon which our nation was founded than in previous generations.

The sieve we call the border keeps filtering through some of the worst of the worst—the repeat criminals, the murderers, rapists, and drunkards—who do mischief on US soil and then dodge justice, either by their own fleeing devices or at the complicit hands of our amnesty-driven government.

The country's collective values haven't just degraded— they've flipped. What was once considered despicable is now cheered; what used to be seen as shameful is flaunted and embraced; the dignity and respect of the past is mocked and derided today.

IT'S AS IF WE'RE CRUMBLING FROM WITHIN—AMERICA IS FALLING WITHOUT A SHOT FIRED, WITHOUT A MISSILE LAUNCHED.

It's as if we're crumbling from within—America is falling without a shot fired, without a missile launched.

But remember this? From the mouth of a great leader: "You

can call it mysticism if you want to, but I have always believed that there was some divine plan that placed this great continent between two oceans to be sought out by those who were possessed of an abiding love of freedom and a special kind of courage."[1]

That was former president Ronald Reagan, speaking of his beloved America during a speech he gave in 1974. But does his assessment still hold true—can the characterization of a God-blessed and freedom-seeking America still be ascribed to our country?

Many say yes.

The real question, though, is this: do enough Americans believe it to be true nowadays, or do they think that description is an antiquated notion, the quaint ramblings of a now-deceased president whose views of America are no longer valid?

Truthfully, the pendulum seems to be swinging in the latter direction, and that's a very sad reality.

UNFORTUNATELY, TOO MANY CHRISTIANS HAVE SAT ON THE SIDELINES FOR TOO LONG, AND NOW THE FIGHT FOR AMERICA'S SOUL HAS TURNED FEROCIOUS.

Unfortunately, too many Christians have sat on the sidelines for too long, and now the fight for America's soul has turned ferocious.

Progressives, atheists, secularists, and outright evil forces have been allowed to spring up, root in, and dig deep in recent years. It'll take quite an effort to rip their influences away and replant the seeds the Founders sowed.

But the dream's still alive. And the pursuit's still worthy.

Really, our last hope rests with our first hope. As God promised: "If at any time I announce that a nation or kingdom is to be uprooted, torn down and destroyed, and if that nation I warned repents of its evil, then I will relent and not inflict on it the disaster I had planned. And if at another time, I announce that a nation or kingdom is to be built up and planted, and if it does evil in my sight and does not obey me, then I will reconsider the good I had intended to do for it" (Jer. 18:7–10 NIV).

America, God has not left the building. It's actually we who have turned from Him. How many more years of His patience do we have, you think?

It's probably prudent not to wait much longer to take action—to show God we are humbled and repentant and willing to let Him lead.

LET'S NOT BE LIKE THE PEOPLE OF NOAH'S TIME WHO MOCKED AND

RIDICULED THE BUILDING OF THE ARK—UNTIL THE RAIN BEGAN.

Let's not be like the people of Noah's time who mocked and ridiculed the building of the ark—until the rain began, that is. By then, it was too late; all but the faithful few of Noah's family died during the forty-day flood. So the plan of action?

First and foremost, we need to confess our sins, individually and as a nation, and then turn from them and pray for the strength, commitment, faith, and humility to abide by God's will. Without this—without confession, repentance, and prayer—all of our other attempts to reform the country will likely fail.

Second, we need to realize that, yes, one person—just one—really can make a difference.

Exodus 32 (KJV) recounts how Moses went up Mount Sinai to meet with God, leaving his brother, Aaron, in charge of the Israelites. It wasn't long before the Israelites became impatient and said to Aaron, "Make us gods" (v. 1). Aaron was only too obliging, and told the people, "Break off the golden earrings, which are in the ears of your wives, of your sons, and of your daughters, and bring them unto me" (v. 2). The people did and Aaron took them and made a molten calf.

"These be thy gods, O Israel, which brought thee up out of the land of Egypt," the Israelites said (v. 4).

Then Aaron built an altar before the calf and declared a feast "to the Lord" for the following day (v. 5). The Israelites rose the next day and offered burnt offerings at the altar, provided peace offerings, and ate, drank, and partied. Soon, an angry God alerted Moses.

"And the Lord said unto Moses, Go, get thee down; for thy people, which thou broughtest out of the land of Egypt, have corrupted themselves," the passage reads. "They have turned aside quickly out of the way which I commanded them: they have made them a molten calf, and have worshipped it, and have sacrificed thereunto, and said, These be thy gods, O Israel, which have brought thee up out of the land of Egypt. . . . Now therefore let me alone, that my wrath may wax hot against them, and that I may consume them: and I will make of thee a great nation" (vv. 7–10 KJV).

All looked lost for the disobedient Israelites—the same group who had just experienced God's miracles, including the parting of the Red Sea, while fleeing Egypt, and who really should have known better than to trifle with their Creator. But Moses intervened. And his petition to God should prove a valuable lesson for those in America suffering under the current moral collapse of society and hoping for a return to saner times. The passage continues:

> And Moses besought the Lord his God, and said, Lord, why doth thy wrath wax hot against thy people, which thou hast brought forth out of the land of Egypt with great power, and with a mighty hand? Wherefore should the Egyptians speak, and say, For mischief did he bring them out, to slay them in the mountains, and to consume them from the face of the earth? Turn from thy fierce wrath, and repent of this evil against thy people. Remember Abraham, Isaac, and Israel, thy servants, to whom thou swarest by thine own self, and saidst unto them, I will multiply your seed as the stars of heaven, and all this land that I have spoken of will I give unto your seed, and they shall inherit it for ever. And the Lord repented of the evil which he thought to do unto his people. (vv. 11–14 KJV)

Moses was a righteous man, chosen by God for His own purposes—but that fact shouldn't let an important message of this chapter go down the tubes: one person, with and through God, can save a people.

Let's get busy. God's waiting for us to take the first steps. Here's a quick summary, from previous chapters, of recommended actions:

- Confess, repent, and pray. All else stems from this. Without confession, without repentance, without prayer, our hopes as a nation and dreams for the country will stall and stumble. We need to humble ourselves before God so He will listen.

- Quit relying on political parties to bail out the country. Neither the Republican nor the Democratic party holds the constituents' interests first and foremost. Stop funding them—stop donating to the party coffers and, in most cases, specific candidates' coffers. Better to give money to the nonprofits and lobby groups that do the real fighting on the political and cultural fronts for the average Joes and Janes in America.

- Give both time and money to charity and charitable endeavors. If you want to reel in government and make it irrelevant, or at least downsized, then the best pursuit is to make costly tax-paid entitlement programs unnecessary. Charity helps keep us free.

- Bring the Bible back to school systems in America. Support the efforts already under way to that end. We're not talking Bible-thumping, but rather, historical teachings with an undercurrent of moral consciousness. After all, if we can allow puzzles with sexually graphic terms to be distributed to our students, why not the Bible?

- Do not cede the border fight, under any circumstances, to those who claim that letting in illegals is a civil justice matter, or worse, God's will. This is a skewing of truth that will lead to a speedy downfall of our constitutional system of governance.

- Pay off debt, individually, as a family, and then, as a country. Get rid of the credit cards; live within your paycheck means; consider the tithe to church. Quit borrowing money for dumb things. Press for a return to the gold standard and the halt to all quantitative easing. And teach your children the fine art of saving and spending only what one earns.

- Be discerning when choosing at the ballot box. Look for politicians who possess track records and personalities of true public service—where they display their understanding that the taxpayer is the boss. In the meantime, be bold about insisting that those already in the public sector remember who pays their salaries. Remind them, over and over, if necessary. Better yet, run for office yourself and become the Christian light at the political table.

- Go back to our roots and read the Constitution. Teach it to your children—because the schools sure won't. Learn and pass along the history of our nation's founding, too. Right now, public schools and government bodies are busy teaching the next generation that George Washington was racist and Tea Party types are extremists, and that America's founding had nothing to do with religious liberty.

- Executive orders are antithetical to the Constitution and to the biblical ideals of a humble servant-leader. Fight to do away with this horrible executive privilege, for presidents of all political parties.

- The Second Amendment saves, and the government has no business or right watering down this provision. Fight all attempts to do so, especially the ones that come disguised as commonsense restrictions that will help save lives. They don't—and they won't. And yes, Christians have the God-given right to defend themselves and their families.

- Watchdog the local and state governments. Go to the local board meetings; sign up for your three minutes to speak to the council. Attending these will prove eye-opening as you witness the number of constitutional dings that are inflicted. It's a good place to hone some political activism skills, inject some Christian-based views into the procedures at hand, and ultimately, enact change. Remember: that local zoning or school board member could be the person you run into at the grocery. Translation: they're easy access and easier to influence than their federal counterparts.

- The press is unreliable and often biased to the point of purposeful dishonesty. You're going to have to do some digging to get the real truth on any given topic, and it's incumbent that you do so. Check out different television news broadcasts, online news sites, talk radio shows, and print outlets. Catch the headlines every day, at the least. This is your duty as an American, as a Christian, as a patriot, as a lover of freedom.

- Fight aggressively the onslaught of atheist and progressive influence that's sweeping the nation. Atheists and progressives are destroying our nation. If you don't actively battle these forces, you're only helping them and enabling their spread. There is no sideline in this fight.

- Recognize the root of what's tearing up America—the spiritual wickedness, the forces of evil, the powers of darkness, the "principalities" referred to in Ephesians 6:12 (KJV) —and get your prayer on to combat them. Recall the 1776 call for "Humiliation, Fasting and Prayer"? (See chapter 13.) This is the trifecta of spiritual warfare, and it's in our national DNA. After all, God rules the rulers, right?

- Today's America touts gay marriage as a good thing and those who oppose it on religious grounds as discriminatory and hateful. Where are the churches—where are the churchgoers? It's imperative that Christians get louder, bolder, on this issue and others that impact the family, the foundation and building block of God's plans for humanity. We're losing the country quickly to moral depravity of all kinds.

America's lamp must not be allowed to go dark. Will you get in the fight?

Let's not cede the battle just yet. Our country may be only of earthly substance, rather than heavenly, and we may all be here just biding our time until the Second Coming. But until then, we need something to do, and why not make it something for the greater good—for the glory of God? It seems only proper for those who see the evil to fight it, and for those who discern the wicked to teach others to be aware and act. At least then, if Christ asks, "When the Son of man cometh, shall he find faith on the earth?" [2]—we might be able to answer, resoundingly and with glad hearts, "Yes!"

NOTES

FOREWORD

1. Fox News Insider, "Huckabee on Indiana Law: 'This Is a Manufactured Crisis by the Left," The Official Blog of Fox News Channel as seen on *The Kelly File*, April 1, 2015, http://insider.foxnews.com/2015/04/01/huckabee-indiana-law-manufactured-crisis-left.

CHAPTER 1: PARTISAN POLITICS WON'T WIN THE NATION

1. Andrew Krietz, "Dave Brat: Eric Cantor's Fall From Political Grace Comes at Hands of Hope College Grad," MLive.com, June 11, 2014, http://www.mlive.com/news/grand-rapids/index.ssf/2014/06/hope_college_graduate_dave_bra.html.
2. Zach Noble, "Eric Cantor's Wall Street Buddy Just Gave Him a Job. Guess How Many Millions of Dollars He's Getting Paid," *The Blaze*, September 2, 2014, http://www.theblaze.com/stories/2014/09/02/eric-cantors-wall-street-buddy-just-gave-him-a-job-guess-how-how-many-millions-of-dollars-hes-getting-paid/.
3. Rasmussen Reports, "Voters Think Congress Cheats to Get Reelected," September 3, 2014, http://www.rasmussenreports.com/public_content/archive/mood_of_america_archive/congressional_performance/voters_think_congress_cheats_to_get_reelected; "Congressional Performance: Is Congress for Sale?," July 9, 2015, http://www.rasmus-senreports.com/public_content/politics/top_stories/congressional_performance.
4. Rasmussen Reports, "Congressional Performance: Is Congress for Sale?"
5. Rasmussen Reports, "Voters Think Congress Cheats to Get Reelected."
6. Ibid.

7. USHistory.org, "19c. Two Parties Emerge," http://www.ushistory.org/us/19c.asp, accessed September 3, 2014.

8. Robert Alexander, "Washington (George) Got It Right," CNN, October 16, 2013, http://www.cnn.com/2013/10/16/opinion/alexander-washington-george/.

9. John Adams, "John Adams to Thomas Jefferson, 9 July 1813," Founders Online, http://founders.archives.gov/documents/Jefferson/03-06-02-0230, accessed September 3, 2014.

10. Jeffrey M. Jones, "In U.S., Perceived Need for Third Party Reaches New High," Gallup, http://www.gallup.com/poll/165392/perceived-need-third-party-reaches-new-high.aspx, Oct. 11, 2013.

11. George Washington, Washington's Farewell Address 1796, Yale Law School Lillian Goldman Law Library, the Avalon Project, http://avalon.law.yale.edu/18th_century/washing.asp, accessed September 3, 2014.

12. USHistory.org, "5a. Political Parties," http://www.ushistory.org/gov/5a.asp, accessed September 3, 2014.

13. Center for Responsive Politics, "Top Organization Contributors," 2002-2014, OpenSecrets.org, accessed October 17, 2015, https://www.opensecrets.org/orgs/list.php. (See also the "Top All-Time Donors" list at https://www.opensecrets.org/orgs/.)

14. Ibid.

15. Ibid.

16. Ibid., "Top Organization Contributors," based on SEC data current to March 2015, accessed October 17, 2015.

17. Bill Scher, "Boehner Caves. Again," Campaign for America's Future, October 10, 2013, http://ourfuture.org/20131010/boehner-caves-again.

18. The Right Scoop, "Sarah Palin Calls Out Marco Rubio for Flip-Flopping on Amnesty," June 23, 2013, http://therightscoop.com/sarah-palin-calls-out-marco-rubio-for-flip-flopping-on-amnesty/.

19. Susan Milligan, "A Towering Record, Painstakingly Built," Boston.com, February 20, 2009, http://www.boston.com/news/nation/articles/2009/02/20/a_towering_record_painstakingly_built/.

20. GovTrack.us, "S.811, (108th): American Dream Downpayment Act," signed into law December 16, 2003, https://www.govtrack.us/congress/bills/108/s811#summary/libraryofcongress.

21. CNN, "Miers Withdraws Supreme Court Nomination," CNN.com, October 28, 2005, http://www.cnn.com/2005/POLITICS/10/27/miers.nominations/.

22. "Majority and Minority Leaders and Party Whips," the website of the United States Senate, accessed September 3, 2014, http://www.senate.gov/artandhistory/history/common/briefing/Majority_Minority_Leaders.htm; and United States House of Representatives, "Speakers of the House, 1789 to Present," History, Art & Archives website, accessed September 3, 2014, http://history.house.gov/People/Office/Speakers/.

23. Isaiah Thompson, "Philly DA Sued Over $5.8 Million Civil Forfeiture Machine," Philadelphia *CityPaper*, August 12, 2014, http://citypaper.net/article.php?Philly-DA-sued-over-5.8-million-civil-forfeiture-machine.-20953.

24. Nick Sibilla, "Philadelphia Earns Millions by Seizing Cash and Homes from People Never Charged with a Crime," *Forbes*, August 26, 2014, http://www.forbes.com/sites/instituteforjustice/2014/08/26/philadelphia-civil-forfeiture-class-action-lawsuit/.

25. Radley Balko, "Rand Paul Introduces Bill to Reform Civil Asset Forfeiture," *Washington Post*, July 25, 2014, http://www.washingtonpost.com/news/the-watch/wp/2014/07/25/rand-paul-introduces-bill-to-reform-civil-asset-forfeiture/.

26. Congress.Gov, "S. 2644, FAIR Act," https://beta.congress.gov/bill/113th-congress/senate-bill/2644/text?q={%22search%22%3A[%22s.+2644%22]}, accessed September 3, 2014.

27. Ibid.

28. Nick Sibilla, "Cops in Texas Seize Millions by 'Policing for Profit,'" *Forbes*, June 5, 2014, http://www.forbes.com/sites/instituteforjustice/2014/06/05/cops-in-texas-seize-millions-by-policing-for-profit/.

29. Press Room, "Benghazi Documents Point to White House on Misleading Talking Points," *Judicial Watch*, April 29, 2014, http://www.judicialwatch.org/press-room/press-releases/judicial-watch-benghazi-documents-point-white-house-misleading-talking-points/.

30. Matthew Clark, "President Obama Says, 'We Don't Have a Strategy on ISIS,' Except He Does," American Center for Law and Justice, September 2, 2014, http://aclj.org/radical-islam/president-obama-says-we-dont-have-a-strategy-on-isis-except-he-does.

31. Aaron Blake, "Why Obama's 'We Don't Have a Strategy' Gaffe Stings," *The Fix* (blog), August 29, 2014, http://www.washingtonpost.com/blogs/the-fix/wp/2014/08/29/why-obamas-we-dont-have-a-strategy-gaffe-stings/.

32. Jennifer Van Laar, "CNN's Jake Tapper Calls Out Obama & White House on Labeling ISIS the 'JV' Terror Team," *IJReview*, August 2014, http://www.ijreview.com/2014/08/166093-isis-jv-team-jake-tapper/.

33. American Civil Liberties Union, "War Comes Home: The Excessive Militarization of American Policing," ACLU website, accessed September 3, 2014, https://www.aclu.org/report/war-comes-home-excessive-militarization-american-police.

34. Center for Responsive Politics, "Political Nonprofits (Dark Money)," OpenSecrets.org, accessed July 27, 2015, https://www.opensecrets.org/outsidespending/nonprof_summ. php?cycle=All&type=viewpt.

CHAPTER TWO: CHARITY KEEPS US FREE

1. Edward Sylvester Ellis, *The Life of Colonel David Crockett: comprising his adventures as backwoodsman and hunter* (Philadelphia: Porter & Coates, 1884), 138.
2. Ibid., 139.
3. Ibid., 140.
4. Ibid., 143–45.
5. Ibid., 146–47.
6. USA.gov, "Administration on Aging," https://www.usa.gov/federal-agencies/administration-on-aging, accessed August 17, 2015.
7. USA.gov, "African Development Foundation," https://www.usa.gov/federal-agencies/african-development-foundation, accessed August 17, 2015.
8. USA.gov, "Fair Housing and Equal Opportunity (FHEO)," https://www.usa.gov/federal-agencies/fair-housing-and-equal-opportunity, accessed August 17, 2015.
9. USA.gov, James Madison Memorial Fellowship Foundation, https://www.usa.gov/federal-agencies/james-madison-memorial-fellowship-foundation, accessed August 17, 2015.
10. Meals on Wheels America, http://www.mealsonwheelsamerica.org/, accessed April 18, 2015.
11. Independent Transportation Network of America, "Dignified Transportation for Seniors," http://www.itnamerica.org/, accessed April 18, 2015.
12. The Pets for the Elderly Foundation, "Joining Friends Together for Life," http://www. petsfortheelderly.org/, accessed April 18, 2015.
13. AARP Foundation, http://www.aarp.org/aarp-foundation/, accessed April 18, 2015.
14. Habitat for Humanity, https://www.habitat.org/cd/giving/one/donate. aspx?link=271&source_code=DHQOW1407W1GGP&iq_id=86202156-VQ6-42874363281-VQ16-c, accessed April 18, 2015.
15. Mercy Housing, "Vision, Mission, Values," https://www.mercyhousing.org/vision-mission-values, accessed April 18, 2015.
16. National Housing Law Project, https://www.nhlp.org/, accessed April 18, 2015.
17. The Leadership Conference on Civil and Human Rights, http://www.civilrights.org/about/, accessed April 18, 2015.
18. HAND, http://www.handhousing.org/, accessed April 18, 2015.
19. Shelter Partnership Inc., http://www.shelterpartnership.org/, accessed April 18, 2015.

20. Save the Children, "Where We Work," http://www.savethechildren.org/site/
c.8rKLIXMGIpI4E/b.6146359/k.9C15/Where_We_Work.htm, accessed April 18,
2015.

21. Charity International, "Our Mission," http://www.charityinternational.com/our-
mission.cfm, accessed April 18, 2015.

22. Africare, "Mission & Vision," https://www.africare.org/who-we-are/mission-vision/,
accessed April 18, 2015.

23. James Madison Memorial Fellowship Foundation, "About the Foundation," http://
www.jamesmadison.gov/about.php, accessed April 13, 2015.

24. Ibid., "Fellows List," http://www.jamesmadison.gov/fellows_list.php, accessed April
13, 2015.

25. Ibid., "About the Foundation."

26. Melinda Lemke, "The Progressive Movement (1890–1919) and WWI (1914-1920),
Suffrage During the Progressive Movement and WWI," lesson plan on the website of
the James Madison Memorial Fellowship Foundation, http://www.jamesmadison.gov/
lessons/progressive_movement.pdf, accessed April 13, 2015.

27. Robert Drapner, "Fisher Ames: Proto-Freshman," *Constitution Daily* (blog), May 14,
2012, http://blog.constitutioncenter.org/2012/05/fisher-ames-proto-freshman/.

28. Barbara Bradley Hagerty, "Debating America's Christian Character," May 5, 2005,
NPR, http://www.npr.org/templates/story/story.php?storyId=4631001, accessed April
13, 2015.

29. Hillsdale College, "Understand the Constitution like never before—for FREE,"
http://lp.hillsdale.edu/constitution-101-signup-tv/?utm_source=general&utm_
medium=drtv&utm_content=website&utm_campaign=con101, accessed April 17,
2015.

30. The Heritage Foundation, "The Heritage Guide to the Constitution," http://www.
heritage.org/constitution, accessed April 17, 2015.

31. The Cato Institute, Cato University Home Study Course, http://www.cato.org/cato-
university/home-study-course, accessed April 17, 2015.

32. Government Accountability Office, Opportunities to Reduce Potential Duplication
in Government Programs, Save Tax Dollars and Enhance Revenue (GAO-11-318SP),
March 2011, http://www.gao.gov/new.items/d11318sp.pdf.

33. Gus Lubin, "500 Government Programs and Agencies That Should Be Closed Right
Now," *Business Insider*, March 1, 2011, http://www.businessinsider.com/gao-govern-
ment-waste-2011-3, accessed April 13, 2015.

34. Wynton Hall, "14 Million More on Food Stamps under Obama," *Breitbart*, July 6,
2014, http://www.breitbart.com/big-government/2014/07/06/14-million-more-on-
food-stamps-under-obama/.

35. USDA.gov, "Supplemental Nutrition Assistance Program Participation and Costs," data as of April 10, 2015, http://www.fns.usda.gov/sites/default/files/pd/SNAPsummary.pdf, accessed April 13, 2015.

36. House of Representatives Committee on the Budget, "The War on Poverty: 50 Years Later," March 3, 2014, http://budget.house.gov/waronpoverty/, accessed April 13, 2015.

37. U.S. Senate Committee on the Budget, "Budget Background" on total welfare spending, December 7, 2012, http://www.budget.senate.gov/republican/public/index.cfm/2012/12/total-welfare-spending-equates-to-168-per-day-for-every-household-in-poverty.

38. Michael Tanner, "The American Welfare State: How We Spend Nearly $1 Trillion Per Year Fighting Poverty—and Fail," Policy Analysis, April 11, 2012, p. 1, http://www.cato.org/sites/cato.org/files/pubs/pdf/PA694.pdf, accessed April 13, 2015.

39. Ibid.

40. USGovernmentSpending.com, "U.S. Government Welfare Spending from 1900," http://www.usgovernmentspending.com/welfare_spending, accessed April 14, 2015.

41. Benjamin Franklin, "On the Price of Corn and Management of the Poor, 1766," Founding.com, http://www.founding.com/founders_library/pageID.2146/default.asp, accessed April 17, 2014.

42. White House Office of the Press Secretary, "Remarks by the President in State of the Union Address, January 20, 2015," WhiteHouse.gov, January 20, 2015, https://www.whitehouse.gov/the-press-office/2015/01/20/remarks-president-state-union-address-january-20-2015.

CHAPTER THREE: PUTTING THE BIBLE BACK IN SCHOOLS

1. Janet Y. Thomas and Kevin P. Brady, "Chapter 3: The Elementary and Secondary Education Act at 40," Review of Research in Education 29 (2005), 51–53, http://isites.harvard.edu/fs/docs/icb.topic460284.files/ESEA%20at%2040.pdf.

2. New America Foundation, "No Child Left Behind," http://febp.newamerica.net/background-analysis/no-child-left-behind-overview, upd. July 7, 2015.

3. Andrew Rudalevige, "The Politics of No Child Left Behind," Education Next 3, no. 4 (Fall 2003), http://educationnext.org/the-politics-of-no-child-left-behind/.

4. New American Foundation, "No Child Left Behind."

5. Fred Bauer, "Revising No Child Left Behind," National Review, February 3, 2015, http://www.nationalreview.com/article/397799/revising-no-child-left-behind-fred-bauer.

6. Share My Lesson, "History of the Common Core Standards," http://www.sharemyles-son.com/article.aspx?storycode=50000149, accessed February 25, 2015.
7. Truth in American Education, "Race to the Top," http://truthinamericaneducation. com/race-to-the-top/, accessed Feb. 25, 2015.
8. Share My Lesson, "History of the Common Core Standards."
9. Fawn Johnson, "Did Obama Screw Up Common Core?" National Journal, December 8, 2014.
10. Ibid.
11. Lyndsey Layton, "Louisiana Gov. Bobby Jindal Sues Obama over Common Core State Standards," *Washington Post*, August 27, 2014, http://www.washingtonpost. com/local/education/louisiana-gov-bobby-jindal-sues-obama-over-common-core-state-standards/2014/08/27/34d98102-2dfb-11e4-bb9b-997ae96fad33_story.html.
12. David Jackson, "CPAC Highlights, From the Speeches to the Swag: Strong Words from Jindal," *USA Today*, February 26, 2015, http://www.usatoday.com/story/news/ politics/elections/2015/02/26/cpac-highlights-christie-carson-cruz-walker/24049167/.
13. C. N. Trueman, "Adolf Hitler and Education," History Learning Site, August 2012, http://www.historylearningsite.co.uk/adolf_hitler_education.htm.
14. Yad Vashem, "How did the Nazis control education?," The Holocaust Explained, http://www.theholocaustexplained.org/ks3/life-in-nazi-occupied-europe/controlling-everyday-life/controlling-education/#.VPCiAS6ATLU, accessed February 27, 2015.
15. "Proposals Relating to the Youth of Education in Pennsylvania [October 1749]," Founders Online, National Archives, http://founders.archives.gov/documents/Frank-lin/01-03-02-0166, upd. June 29, 2015, from *The Papers of Benjamin Franklin*, vol. 3, January 1, 1745, through June 30, 1750, ed. Leonard W. Labaree (New Haven: Yale University Press, 1961), 397–421.
16. Ibid.
17. Ibid.
18. Stephanie Lulay, "Fifth Grade Sex Ed Plan Horrifies Chicago Parents Who Say It's Obscene," DNAInfo, November 14, 2014, http://www.dnainfo.com/chi-cago/20141114/university-village/fifth-grade-sex-ed-plan-horrifies-chicago-parents-who-say-its-obscene.
19. The Associated Press, "Pennsylvania Middle Schoolers Given 'Fifty Shades of Grey' Word Search Puzzle," *New York Daily News*, February 11, 2015, http://www. nydailynews.com/news/national/pa-middle-schoolers-fifty-shades-grey-puzzle-arti-cle-1.2111683.
20. Todd Starnes, "Teacher Tells Student He Can't Read the Bible in Classroom," Fox News, May 5, 2014, http://www.foxnews.com/opinion/2014/05/05/teacher-tells-student-cant-read-bible-in-my-classroom/.

21. Cato Institute, "Policy Recommendation for the 108th Congress: Department of Education," CATO Handbook for Congress (Washington, DC: CATO Institute, n.d.), 295–96, http://object.cato.org/sites/cato.org/files/serials/files/cato-handbook-policymakers/2003/9/hb108-28.pdf.

22. Monica Davey and Steven Greenhouse, "Angry Demonstrations in Wisconsin as Cuts Loom," *The New York Times*, February 16, 2011, http://www.nytimes.com/2011/02/17/us/17wisconsin.html.

23. Rush Limbaugh, "Union Thugs Turn Wisconsin into Greece as Freeloaders Protest," February 17, 2011, *The Rush Limbaugh Show* (transcript), http://www.rushlimbaugh.com/daily/2011/02/17/union_thugs_turn_wisconsin_into_greece_as_the_freeloaders_protest.

24. Dwight D. Eisenhower, "Remarks Recorded for the 'Back to God' Program of the American Legion," February 20, 1955, from the website of the Dwight D. Eisenhower Presidential Library, Museum and Boyhood Home, Quotes: Religion, http://www.eisenhower.archives.gov/all_about_ike/quotes.html, accessed February 25, 2015.

25. Robert Simonds, "Teaching the Bible in Public Schools?" Institute for Creation Research, http://www.icr.org/article/teaching-bible-public-schools/, accessed April 18, 2015.

26. U.S. Supreme Court, *Stone v. Graham*, 449 U.S. 39 (1980), no. 80-321, Justia, https://supreme.justia.com/cases/federal/us/449/39/case.html, p. 449 U.S. 42, accessed April 18, 2015.

27. American Bible Society and the Barna Group, The State of the Bible 2014, http://www.americanbible.org/uploads/content/state-of-the-bible-data-analysis-american-bible-society-2014.pdf, 24.

28. Ibid. 7.

29. Nicola Menzie, "Most Americans Want the Bible in Public Schools," *Christian Post*, August 28, 2013, http://www.christianpost.com/news/most-americans-want-the-bible-in-public-schools-103216/.

30. Emily Hardman, "High School Student in New Jersey Defends Pledge of Allegiance from Atheist Group's Attack," The Becket Fund for Religious Liberty, September 23, 2014, http://www.becketfund.org/high-school-student-new-jersey-defends-pledge-allegiance-atheist-groups-attack/.

31. FoxNews.com, "New Jersey Student Wins Court Case to Keep 'Under God' in Pledge of Allegiance," Fox News, February 6, 2015, http://www.foxnews.com/us/2015/02/06/new-jersey-student-wins-court-case-to-keep-under-god-in-pledge-allegiance/.

32. Secular Coalition for America, "Michael Newdow, MD" (bio), Secular Coalition website, https://www.secular.org/bios/Michael_Newdow.html, accessed February 27, 2015.

33. United States Supreme Court, *Elk Grove Unified School District et al v. Newdow et al*, no. 02-1624, argued March 24, 2004: Decided June 14, 2004, Find Law, accessed February 27, 2015, http://caselaw.lp.findlaw.com/scripts/getcase.pl?court=US&vol=0 00&invol=02-1624.

34. Elizabeth Ridenour, "It's coming back . . . and it's our constitutional right!," National Council on Bible Curriculum in Public Schools, http://bibleinschools.net/, accessed February 27, 2015.

35. Noah Webster, ed., *History of the United States* (New Haven: Durrie & Peck, 1832), 339.

CHAPTER FOUR: THE BORDER BATTLE CANNOT BE CEDED

1. Eusebio Elizondo, United States Conference of Catholic Bishops, Committee on Migration, letter to Jeh Johnson, March 26, 2014, http://www.washingtonpost.com/r/2010-2019/WashingtonPost/2014/03/31/Editorial-Opinion/Graphics/1717%20DHSenforce.pdf.

2. Pew Research Center, FactTank, "Catholics and Other Christians Support Immigration Reform, But Say Faith Plays a Small Role," by Michael Lipka, April 1, 2014, http://www.pewresearch.org/fact-tank/2014/04/01/catholics-other-christians-support-immigration-reform-but-say-faith-plays-small-role/, accessed April 19, 2015.

3. Plimoth Plantation, "Mayflower and the Mayflower Compact," http://www.plimoth.org/learn/just-kids/homework-help/mayflower-and-mayflower-compact, accessed April 19, 2015.

4. Ann Coulter, "For Death by ISIS You Have to Go Out, but Illegals Deliver!," WND, February 25, 2015, http://www.wnd.com/2015/02/for-death-by-isis-you-have-to-go-out-but-illegals-deliver/.

5. W. Gardner Selby, "Judicial Watch Says ISIS Operating a Camp in Mexico—Near El Paso," PolitiFact, April 17, 2015, http://www.politifact.com/texas/statements/2015/apr/17/judicial-watch/judicial-watch-says-isis-has-camp-mexico-and-near-/.

6. Jana Winter, "Feds Issue Terror Watch for the Texas/Mexico Border," Fox News, May 26, 2010, http://www.foxnews.com/us/2010/05/26/terror-alert-mexican-border/.

7. Thomas Jefferson, Notes of the State of Virginia, Query VIII, on the website of the Yale Law School's Avalon Project, accessed September 2, http://avalon.law.yale.edu/18th_century/jeffvir.asp.

8. Steven A. Camarota and Jessica Vaughan, "Immigration and Crime: Assessing a Conflicted Issue," Center for Immigration Studies, November 2009, http://cis.org/ImmigrantCrime.

9. Mark Hugo Lopez and Michael T. Light, "A Rising Share: Hispanics and Federal Crime," Pew Hispanic Center, February 18, 2009, http://www.pewhispanic.org/files/reports/104.pdf, p. i.

10. Ibid., p. ii.

11. Michael T. Light, Mark Hugo Lopez, and Gonzalez Barrera, "The Rise of Federal Immigration Crimes," Pew Research Center, Hispanic Trends, March 18, 2014, http://www.pewhispanic.org/2014/03/18/the-rise-of-federal-immigration-crimes/#fnref-20132-10.

12. Camarota and Vaughan, "Immigration and Crime."

13. Mitt Romney, at the 2007 GOP debate, St. Anselm College, June 3, 2007, quoted in "Mitt Romney on Immigration," OnTheIssues, http://mittromneycentral.com/on-the-issues/immigration/.

14. Jennifer Overend Prior, *Primary Source Fluency Activities: Early America* (Huntington Beach, CA: Shell Education, 2004), 132.

15. Cory Marshall, "FBI Investigating National Park assault near Wilcox," KGUN9-TV, August 29, 2013, http://www.jrn.com/kgun9/news/FBI-investigating-an-assault-on-a-60-year-old-woman-221633701.html.

16. Mark Potter, "Border Insecurity: Arizona Ranchers Frustrated over Smugglers, Crime," NBC News, June 21, 2014, http://www.nbcnews.com/news/us-news/border-insecurity-arizona-ranchers-frustrated-over-smugglers-crime-n106711.

17. Derek Jordan, "Gaxiola Found Not Competent to Stand Trial," *Willcox Range News*, February 25, 2015, http://www.willcoxrangenews.com/news/article_b1987fda-bc6d-11e4-bf60-17d4410c981a.html.

18. Potter, "Border Insecurity."

19. Alexander Bolton, "Reid: Southern border is secure," *The Hill*, July 15, 2014, http://thehill.com/homenews/senate/212328-reid-southern-border-is-secure.

20. Andrew Johnson, "Harry Reid: $1.7 Million Sale of My Home Will Create 60 Jobs!" *The Corner* (blog), June 9, 2014, http://www.nationalreview.com/corner/379884/harry-reid-17-million-sale-my-home-will-create-60-jobs-andrew-johnson.

21. Fox Nation, "Exclusive: Kate Steinle's Parents Reflect on Her Legacy and Final Moments," July 14, 2015, http://nation.foxnews.com/2015/07/13/exclusive-kate-steinles-parents-reflect-her-legacy-and-final-moments.

22. Cornell Barnard, "Man Accused in San Francisco Pier 14 Shooting Admits to Crime," ABC7News, July 5, 2015, http://abc7news.com/news/exclusive-pier-14-shooting-suspect-admits-to-crime/830325.

23. Chuck Ross, "Francisco Sanchez, Kate Steinle's Killer, Used 30 Aliases over the Course of a 25-Year Life of Crime," *Daily Caller*, July 8, 2015, http://dailycaller. com/2015/07/08/francisco-sanchez-kate-steinles-killer-used-30-aliases-over-the-course-of-a-25-year-life-of-crime/.

24. Michelle Moons, "Murderer: I Chose SF Because It Was a Sanctuary City," *Breitbart*, July 6, 2015, http://www.breitbart.com/california/2015/07/06/murderer-says-he-chose-san-francisco-because-it-is-a-sanctuary-city/.

25. AWR Hawkins, "Nancy Pelosi: Sanctuary City Policies Are Not the Problem, Guns Are," *Breitbart*, July 23, 2015, http://www.breitbart.com/california/2015/07/23/ nancy-pelosi-sanctuary-city-policies-are-not-the-problem-guns-are.

26. Alan Gomez, "'Sanctuary Cities' Not Changing Policies After San Francisco Shooting," *USA Today*, July 11, 2015, http://www.usatoday.com/story/news/nation/2015/07/11/sanctuary-cities-not-changing-san-francisco-shooting/29979357/.

27. Ashley Herzog, "Illegal Immigrant Held Woman as Sex Slave for 18 Months," *Right Wing News*, May 19, 2014, http://rightwingnews.com/uncategorized/illegal-immigrant-held-woman-as-sex-slave-for-18-months/.

28. Jim Hoft, "Illegal Immigrant Oscar Ayala-Arizmendi Imprisons Woman in Chains," *The Gateway Pundit* (blog), May 17, 2014, http://www.thegatewaypundit. com/2014/05/illegal-immigrant-imprisons-woman-in-chains-repeatedly-beats-rapes-her-for-18-months-video/.

29. Herzog, "Illegal Immigrant Held Woman as Sex Slave for 18 Months."

30. King Staff, "Investigators: Edmonds rape suspect deported nine times," KING 5, May 27, 2010, http://www.king5.com/story/local/2015/03/12/12867316/.

31. Ibid.

32. Bridget Clerkin, "Immigrant found guilty in cold case sexual assault of Princeton woman," nj.com, May 9, 2014, http://www.nj.com/mercer/index.ssf/2014/05/immigrant_found_guilty_in_cold_case_sexual_assault_of_princeton_woman.html.

33. The White House, Office of the Press Secretary, "Remarks by the President in Address to the Nation on Immigration," November 20, 2014, https://www.whitehouse.gov/ the-press-office/2014/11/20/remarks-president-address-nation-immigration.

34. Amanda Sakuma, "House passes clean bill to fund Department of Homeland Security," MSNBC, March 3, 2015, http://www.msnbc.com/msnbc/boehner-call-vote-clean-dhs-funding-bill.

35. Department of Homeland Security, "Deferred Action for Childhood Arrivals," http:// www.dhs.gov/deferred-action-childhood-arrivals, accessed March 14, 2015.

36. Immigration Policy Center, "A Guide to the Immigration Accountability Executive Action," http://www.immigrationpolicy.org/special-reports/guide-immigration-accountability-executive-action#deferredaction, accessed March 1, 2015.

37. Silvio Canto Jr., "Did President Obama's Rhetoric Create This Mess on the Border?" *American Thinker*, June 11, 2014, http://www.americanthinker.com/blog/2014/06/did_president_obamas_rhetoric_create_this_mess_on_the_border.html.

38. Miguel Otarola, "300 more immigrant children shipped to Arizona," Republic, June 8, 2014, http://www.azcentral.com/story/news/arizona/2014/06/06/arizona-illegal-immigrant-children-brewer/10113105/.

39. Kellen Howard, "Feds flying illegal immigrant minors to Alaska, Hawaii; 30K transported across U.S.," *Washington Times*, August 2, 2014, http://www.washingtontimes.com/news/2014/aug/2/feds-flying-illegal-immigrant-minors-hawaii-alaska/.

40. Brandon Darby, "Thousands of Illegal Immigrants Bused Across U.S. into Cities," *Breitbart*, June 30, 2014, http://www.breitbart.com/texas/2014/06/30/thousands-of-illegal-immigrants-bused-across-us/.

41. Fox News, "Protests turn back buses carrying illegal immigrant children," July 2, 2014, http://www.foxnews.com/us/2014/07/02/protests-force-buses-carrying-illegal-immigrant-children-to-be-rerouted/.

42. Brian Hayes, "Obama Dumping of Illegal Alien Children in Focus as Mystery Virus Spreads Rapidly Across 10 States," Top Right News, September 9, 2014, http://toprightnews.com/?p=5726.

43. Michael Martinez and John Newsome, "Respiratory Virus Suspected in Midwest Children's Hospitalizations," CNN, September 6, 2014, http://www.cnn.com/2014/09/06/health/respiratory-virus-midwest/.

44. Phil Gingrey, letter to Thomas R. Frieden, July 7, 2014, posted on the website of Judicial Watch, http://www.judicialwatch.org/wp-content/uploads/2014/07/Gingrey-Letter-to-CDC-on-Public-Health-Crisis.pdf.

45. FoxNews.com, "Pelosi calls surge of illegal immigrant children an 'opportunity,'" June 29, 2014, Fox News, http://www.foxnews.com/politics/2014/06/29/pelosi-calls-surge-illegal-immigrant-children-opportunity/.

46. Jeannie DeAngelis, "Nancy Pelosi's 'Baby Jesus' Argument," *American Thinker*, July 23, 2014, http://www.americanthinker.com/blog/2014/07/nancy_pelosis_baby_jesus_argument.html.

47. U.S. Immigration and Customs Enforcement, "Updated Facts on ICE's 287(g) Program," http://www.ice.gov/factsheets/287g-reform, accessed April 20, 2015.

48. FoxNews.com, "Businesses to receive incentive for hiring illegal immigrants, report says," Fox News, November 27, 2014, http://www.foxnews.com/politics/2014/11/27/businesses-to-receive-incentive-to-hire-illegal-immigrants-report-says/.

49. Lauren Carroll, "Does Obamacare Give Businesses a $3,000 Incentive to Hire Illegal Immigrants?" PolitiFact.com, December 2, 2014, http://www.politifact.com/truth-o-meter/article/2014/dec/02/does-obamacare-give-businesses-incentive-hire-ille/.

50. Tony Lee, "Chamber of Commerce: We've Never Supported Amnesty," Breitbart, July 17, 2014, http://www.breitbart.com/big-government/2014/07/17/chamber-of-commerce-we-ve-never-supported-amnesty/.

51. Dan Merica and Kevin Bohn, "Chamber to 'pull out all the stops' to pass immigration reform in 2014," Political Ticker (blog), January 8, 2014, http://politicalticker.blogs.cnn.com/2014/01/08/chamber-to-pull-out-all-the-stops-to-pass-immigration-reform-in-2014/.

52. Franklin Graham, Twitter @Franklin_Graham, April 20, 2015, https://twitter.com/Franklin_Graham/status/590235266423590912.

CHAPTER FIVE: DEBT IS A DEVICE OF THE DEVIL

1. "If We had been True to the Constitution," National Center for Constitutional Studies website, accessed September 2, 2015, http://www.nccs.net/2008-11-if-we-had-been-true-to-the-constitution.php.

2. Bloomberg, "How Roosevelt Secretly Ended the God Standard," Bloomberg View, March 21, 2013, http://www.bloomberg.com/news/articles/2013-03-21/how-franklin-roosevelt-secretly-ended-the-gold-standard.

3. Foundation for Economic Education, "Money: The Great Gold Robbery," http://fee.org/freeman/detail/money-the-great-gold-robbery, accessed March 16, 2015. No longer accessible.

4. Franklin D. Roosevelt, Executive Order 6102: Forbidding the Hording of [sic] Gold Coin, Gold Bullion and Gold Certificates, April 4, 1933, http://www.uhuh.com/laws/donncoll/eo/1933/EO6102.TXT.

5. History.com, "This Day in History, June 5, 1933: FDR Takes United States off Gold Standard," http://www.history.com/this-day-in-history/fdr-takes-united-states-off-gold-standard, accessed March 16, 2015.

6. W. Cleon Skousen, "The History of American Money," CMI Gold & Silver, http://www.cmi-gold-silver.com/history-american-money/, accessed March 16. 2015.

7. J. D. Alt, "The Strange Reality of Fiat Money," New Economic Perspectives, posted January 2, 2013, http://neweconomicperspectives.org/2013/01/the-strange-reality-of-fiat-money.html.

8. Lewis E. Lehrman, "The Nixon Shock Heard 'Round the World," Wall Street Journal, August 15, 2011, http://www.wsj.com/articles/SB10001424053111904007304576494073418802358.

9. Sandra Kollen Chizoni, "Nixon Ends Convertibility of US Dollars to Gold and Announces Wage/Price Controls," Federal Reserve History, http://www.federalreservehistory.org/Events/DetailView/33, accessed March 16, 2015.

10. Lehrman, "The Nixon Shock Heard 'Round the World."

11. Ron Paul, "Honest Money," RonPaul.com, http://www.ronpaul.com/fiat-money-inflation-federal-reserve-2/, accessed March 16, 2015.

12. Simon Johnson, "Ron Paul and the Banks," *Economix* (blog), January 5, 2012, http://economix.blogs.nytimes.com/2012/01/05/ron-paul-and-the-banks/?_r=0.

13. Martin Shubik, The Theory of Money and Financial Institutions, vol. 1 (n.p.: Massachusetts Institute of Technology, 1999), 60.

14. Wolters Kluwer, "Federal Tax Law Keeps Piling Up," CCH, http://www.cch.com/taxlawpileup.pdf, accessed March 19, 2015.

15. Sean Kennedy and Alexandra Booze, 2014 Congressional Pig Book Summary (Washington, DC: Citizens Against Government Waste, 2014), 2, http://cagw.org/sites/default/files/pdf/Pig%20Book%2014.pdf.

16. USADebtClock.com, accessed October 15, 2015 http://usadebtclock.com/.

17. Mike Patton, "Who Owns the Most US Debt?" *Forbes*, October 28, 2014, http://www.forbes.com/sites/mikepatton/2014/10/28/who-owns-the-most-u-s-debt/.

18. US Government Accountability Office, "Improper Payments: Government-Wide Estimates and Use of Death Data to Help Prevent Payments to Deceased Individuals," GAO-15-82T, March 16, 2015, http://www.gao.gov/products/GAO-15-482T.

19. Patton, "Who Owns the Most US Debt?"

20. James Dorn, "The Debt Threat: A Risk to US-China Relations?" *Brown Journal of World Affairs* 14, no. 2 (Spring/Summer 2008): 153, http://object.cato.org/sites/cato.org/files/articles/dorn_bjwa_142.pdf.

21. J. D. Foster, "The Many Real Dangers of Soaring National Debt," Heritage Foundation, June 18, 2013, http://www.heritage.org/research/reports/2013/06/the-many-real-dangers-of-soaring-national-debt.

22. D. Andrew Austin and Mindy Levit, "The Debt Limit: History and Recent Increases," Congressional Research Service, October 28, 2014, p. 4, http://www.senate.gov/CRSReports/crs-publish.cfm?pid=%270E%2C*P\%3F%3D%23%20%20%20%0A.

23. Ibid, summary page.

24. Paul Kengor, "Congress Makes History: This is a Big Deal . . . Congress Has Cut Spending Two Consecutive Years," *Human Events*, November 3, 2014, http://humanevents.com/2014/11/03/congress-makes-history-this-is-a-big-deal-congress-has-cut-spending-two-consecutive-years/.

25. R. A., "The Economist Explains: What is Quantitative Easing?" *Economist*, March 9, 2015, http://www.economist.com/blogs/economist-explains/2015/03/economist-explains-5.

26. Ibid.

27. King World News, "Paul Craig Roberts Stunning 2015 Predictions—at Any Time the West Can Collapse," December 19, 2014, http://kingworldnews.com/paul-craig-roberts-stunning-2015-predictions-time-west-can-collapse/. See also the website of Paul Craig Roberts, http://www.paulcraigroberts.org/2015/03/17/economy-recovered-way/, accessed September 3, 2015.

CHAPTER SIX: BE BOLD: WE ARE BOSSES OF PRESIDENTS, POLITICIANS AND POLICE

1. US Census Bureau, "Federal Government Civilian Employment and Payroll Data," American Fact Finder, March 2013, http://factfinder.census.gov/faces/tableservices/jsf/pages/productview.xhtml?src=bkmk.

2. Carma Hogue, "Government Organization Summary Report: 2012," US Census Bureau, September 26, 2013, http://www2.census.gov/govs/cog/g12_org.pdf.

3. US Census Bureau, "State Government Employment and Payroll Data: March 2013," American Fact Finder, March 2013, http://factfinder.census.gov/faces/tableservices/jsf/pages/productview.xhtml?src=bkmk, accessed March 25, 2015.

4. US Census Bureau, "Local Government Employment and Payroll Data: March 2013," American Fact Finder, March 2013, at http://www.census.gov/govs/apes/.

5. Robert Jesse Willhide, "Annual Survey of Public Employment & Payroll Summary Report: 2013," US Census Bureau, December 19, 2014, http://www2.census.gov/govs/apes/2013_summary_report.pdf, p. 3.

6. Ibid.

7. Ibid.

8. Taxpayer Advocate Service, MSP #2, "IRS BUDGET: The IRS Desperately Needs More Funding to Serve Taxpayers and Increase Voluntary Compliance," IRS.gov, accessed March 28, 2015, http://www.taxpayeradvocate.irs.gov/userfiles/file/2013FullReport/IRS-BUDGET-The-IRS-Desperately-Needs-More-Funding-to-Serve-Taxpayers-and-Increase-Voluntary-Compliance.pdf.

9. The Fred W. Smith National Library for the Study of George Washington at Mount Vernon, George Washington's Mount Vernon, "Spurious Quotations," http://www.mountvernon.org/research-collections/digital-encyclopedia/article/spurious-quotations/, accessed March 28, 2015.

10. Legistorm, "About Member of Congress Salaries," http://www.legistorm.com/member_of_congress_salaries.html, accessed March 28, 2015.

11. Robert Longley, "Presidential Pay and Compensation," About News, http://usgovinfo. about.com/od/thepresidentandcabinet/a/presidentialpay.htm, accessed March 28, 2015.

12. Todd Campbell, "How Does Your Income Stack Up Against the Average American's?" *The Motley Fool*, January 18, 2015, http://www.fool.com/investing/general/2015/01/18/how-does-your-income-stack-up-against-the-average.aspx.

13. Longley, "Presidential Pay and Compensation."

14. National Institute on Retirement Security, "Who Killed the Private Sector DB Plan?" http://www.nirsonline.org/index.php?option=com_content&task=view&id=607&Itemid=49, accessed March 28, 2015.

15. Lou Carlozo, "Pensions Are Taking the Long, Lonely Road to Retirement," *U.S. News and World Report*, July 20, 2015, http://money.usnews.com/money/personal-finance/mutual-funds/articles/2015/07/20/pensions-are-taking-the-long-lonely-road-to-retirement.

16 Katelin P. Isaacs, Retirement Benefits for Members of Congress (Congressional Research Service, June 31, 2015), Summary Section, http://www.senate.gov/CRSReports/crs-publish.cfm?pid=%270E%2C*PLC8%22%40%20%20%0A.

17. Rob Hotakainen, "A $130,500 pension? Some in Congress say no, but most cash in," McClatchy DC, November 25, 2014, http://www.mcclatchydc.com/2014/11/25/248084/a-130500-pension-some-in-congress.html.

18. Annie Mach and Ada Cornell, "Health Benefits for Members of Congress and Certain Congressional Staff," Congressional Research Service, February 8, 2014, https://fas.org/sgp/crs/misc/R43194.pdf, pp. 7–8.

19. Bridget Bowman, "Malpractice Suit Raises Questions About Congress' Doctor," *Roll Call*, June 2, 2015, http://blogs.rollcall.com/hill-blotter/malpractice-suit-raises-questions-about-congress-doctor/.

20. Mach and Cornell, "Health Benefits for Members of Congress and Certain Congressional Staff," 8.

21. Corbin Hiar, "Congressional Perks: Lawmakers' Most Surprising Benefits," Center for Public Integrity, November 23, 2011, http://www.publicintegrity.org/2011/11/23/7495/congressional-perks-lawmakers-most-surprising-benefits.

22. Arlette Saenz and Erin Dooley, "Here's How Much Less Congress Works Than You Do," ABC News, August 4, 2014, http://abcnews.go.com/Politics/heres-congress-works/story?id=24810354.

23. Joshua Green, "The Pampered World of Congressional Air Travel," *Bloomberg*, April 30, 2013, http://www.bloomberg.com/bw/articles/2013-04-30/the-pampered-world-of-congressional-air-travel.

24. Sean Williams, "10 Perks Congress Has That You Don't," *The Motley Fool*, October 20, 2013, http://www.fool.com/investing/general/2013/10/20/10-perks-congress-has-that-you-dont.aspx.

25. Ibid.

26. US Securities and Exchange Commission, "2013 Insider Trading Policy," Section II, "Penalties; Sanctions," http://www.sec.gov/Archives/edgar/data/25743/000138713113000737/ex14_02.htm, accessed March 29, 2015.

27. Steven Dennis and Jay Hunter, "Wealth of Congress Jumps $150 Million," *Roll Call*, October 22, 2014, http://blogs.rollcall.com/hill-blotter/wealth-of-congress-jumps-150-million-50-richest/.

28. Russ Choma, "One Member of Congress = 18 American Households: Lawmakers' Personal Finances far From Average," Center for Responsive Politics, January 12, 2015, http://www.opensecrets.org/news/2015/01/one-member-of-congress-18-american-households-lawmakers-personal-finances-far-from-average/.

29. "Andrew Jackson: Farewell Address, March 4, 1837, on the website of the Miller Center at the University of Virginia, http://millercenter.org/president/speeches/speech-3644.

CHAPTER 7: DUST OFF THE CONSTITUTION

1. Todd Starnes, "School's Nation of Islam Handout Paints Founding Fathers as Racists," Fox News, October 27, 2014, http://www.foxnews.com/opinion/2014/10/27/school-nation-islam-handout-paints-founding-fathers-as-racists.

2. Olivia Caridi, "Mother, superintendent respond to school's Nation of Islam handout," WCYB.com, October 29, 2014, http://www.wcyb.com/news/mother-superintendent-respond-to-schools-nation-of-islam-handout/29416188; Gina Cassini, "America's Elementary School Kids Taught That America's Founding Fathers Were Racist," *Top Right News*, January 31, 2015, http://toprightnews.com/elementary-school-kids-taught-founding-fathers-were-racists/.

3. Mike Opelka, "Was the Boston Tea Party Terrorism? Texas Schools Are Teaching Just That (and More)," *TheBlaze*, November 20, 2012, http://www.theblaze.com/stories/2012/11/20/was-the-boston-tea-party-terrorism-texas-schools-are-teaching-just-that-and-more/.

4. CSCOPE, World History/Social Studies, Unit 12, "Terrorism," Instructional Procedures, p. 2, http://api.ning.com/files/jG4ce1PlU97SzLPU*fOW3-jYoYtgbSraedaRO-sGgrmhQBBH9SG1LhEXNSk7f2Ts4NZKWPwfUeexiXCWpI*NFwVw5RS82MED5/Terrorism.pdf, accessed April 27, 2015.

5. Opelka, "Was the Boston Tea Party Terrorism?"

6. Danette Clark, "Pearson Common Core Expert: 'Was George Washington Any Different from Palestinian Terrorists?'" EAGNews.org, July 7, 2014, http://eagnews.org/pearson-common-core-expert-was-george-washington-any-different-from-palestinian-terrorists/.

7. Media Trackers, "Wisconsin Teachers' Guide Compares Ferguson Riots to the Boston Tea Party," EAGNews.org, December 3, 2014, http://eagnews.org/wisconsin-teachers-guide-compares-ferguson-riots-to-the-boston-tea-party/.

8. Mike Kaechele, "Ferguson vs. Boston," on Mike Kaechele's blog, August 18, 2014, http://www.michaelkaechele.com/ferguson-vs-boston/.

9. Ibid.

10. David Carter et al., "Understanding Law Enforcement Intelligence Processes," Report to the Office of University Programs, Science and Technology Directorate, US Department of Homeland Security (College Park, MD: National Consortium for the Study of Terrorism and Responses to Terrorism, July 2014), 7–8, https://www.start.umd.edu/pubs/START_UnderstandingLawEnforcementIntelligenceProcesses_July2014.pdf.

11. Homeland Security, Office of Intelligence and Analysis, "Intelligence Assessment: Sovereign Citizen Extremist Ideology Will Drive Violence at Home, During Travel, and at Government Facilities," IA-0105-15, February 15, 2015, http://cloudfront-assets.reason.com/media/pdf/Sovereign_Citizen_Extremist_Ideology_2-5-15.pdf, p. 1.

12. David Carter et al., "Understanding Law Enforcement Intelligence Processes," (July 2014), 7.

13. Judicial Watch, "Defense Department Teaching Documents Suggest Mainstream Conservative Views 'Extremist,'" August 22, 2013, http://www.judicialwatch.org/press-room/press-releases/judicial-watch-defense-department-teaching-documents-suggest-mainstream-conservative-views-extremist/.

14. Ibid.

15. Defense Equal Opportunity Management Institute, "About DEOMI," https://www.deomi.org/AboutDEOMI/AboutDEOMIIndex.cfm, accessed April 30, 2015.

16. DEOMI, EOAC Student Guide: Extremism (January 2013), introduction, obtained by Judicial Watch, http://www.judicialwatch.org/wp-content/uploads/2013/08/2161-docs.pdf, p. 35.

17. Ibid., 45.

18. Ibid., 43, emphasis added.

19. Michael German (ACLU national security policy counsel) and Ann Brick (ACLU staff attorney), letter on "DOD's Level I Antiterrorism Awareness Training," June 10, 2009, https://www.aclu.org/sites/default/files/images/general/asset_upload_file89_39820.pdf, 1–2.

20. CNN, "Bush signs landmark Medicare bill into law," CNN.com, Politics, December 8, 2003, http://www.cnn.com/2003/ALLPOLITICS/12/08/elec04.medicare/.

21. Sheryl Gay Stolberg and Robert Pear, "Obama Signs Health Care Overhaul Bill, with a Flourish," New York Times, March 23, 2010, http://www.nytimes.com/2010/03/24/health/policy/24health.html.

22. "From Thomas Jefferson to Edward Carrington, 16 January 1787," Founders Online, National Archives, http://founders.archives.gov/documents/Jefferson/01-11-02-0047, upd. June 29, 2015.

23. Glenn Kessler, "How many pages of regulations for Obamacare?" Washington Post, May 15, 2013, http://www.washingtonpost.com/blogs/fact-checker/post/how-many-pages-of-regulations-for-obamacare/2013/05/14/61eec914-bcf9-11e2-9b09-1638ac-c3942e_blog.html.

24. See http://constitutioncenter.org/constitution-day, accessed May 2, 2015.

25. National Archives, The Center for Legislative Archives, "Lesson Plans: Teaching Six Big Ideas in the Constitution," http://www.archives.gov/legislative/resources/education/constitution/, accessed May 2, 2015.

26. PBS, "Constitution USA with Peter Sagal," About Constitution USA, http://www.pbs.org/tpt/constitution-usa-peter-sagal/about/#.VUT8p5OAS1k, accessed May 2, 2015.

27. Architect of the Capitol, "Quotations" (a list of some of the quotations and inscriptions found in the buildings on Capitol Hill), http://www.aoc.gov/facts/quotations, accessed May 2, 2015.

28. Holly Burrito's Bucket/Americas Foundation, "The Ten Commandments in the floor of the National Archives," PhotoBucket, accessed May 2, 2015, http://s869.photobucket.com/user/HolyBurrito/media/Americas%20Foundation/DECALOG_IN_FLR_OF_NATL_ARCHIVES.jpg.html.

29. John J. Miller "The Horns of Moses," Hey Miller: The Official Website of John J. Miller, January 29, 2010, http://www.heymiller.com/2010/01/the-horns-of-moses/.

30. Carl Limbacher and NewsMax.com Staff, "U.S. Supreme Court Has Its Own Ten Commandments," NewsMax.com, August 21, 2003, posted by "kattracks" on the Free Republic website, at http://www.freerepublic.com/focus/f-news/967880/posts.

31. "In the year of our Lord" from which we get our abbreviation AD, comes from the Latin phrase anno Domini, rendered more fully anno Domini nostri Iesu Christi, "in the year of Our Lord Jesus Christ."

32. Monticello.org, "Quotations on the Jefferson Memorial," http://www.monticello.org/site/jefferson/quotations-jefferson-memorial, accessed May 2, 2015.

33. John Jay, letter to John Murray, October 12, 1816, in *John Jay: The Correspondence and Public Papers of John Jay*, vol. 4 (1794–1826), ed. Henry P. Johnston (New York: G. P. Putnam's Sons, 1890–93), http://oll.libertyfund.org/titles/jay-the-correspondence-and-public-papers-of-john-jay-vol-4-1794-1826.

CHAPTER 8: EXECUTIVE ORDERS OUGHT TO BE OUTLAWED

1. National Archives, Constitution of the United States, Article 2, Sections 2–3, http://www.archives.gov/exhibits/charters/constitution_transcript.html, accessed May 5, 2015.
2. Cornell University Law School, Legal Information Institute, "Executive Power: An Overview," https://www.law.cornell.edu/wex/executive_power, accessed May 5, 2015.
3. Mike Emanuel, "'I've Got a Pen': Obama Raises Hackles With Executive Actions," Fox News, January 20, 2014, http://www.foxnews.com/politics/2014/01/20/ive-got-pen-obama-raises-hackles-with-executive-action-push/.
4. The following table is taken from Gerhard Peters and John T. Woolley, "Executive Orders," The American Presidency Project, Ed. John T. Woolley and Gerhard Peters, Santa Barbara, CA, 1999-2015. Available from the World Wide Web: http://www.presidency.ucsb.edu/data./orders.php. (website no longer accessible in its chart form).
5. Jeremy Diamond, "Second Round for Arizona Sheriff's Case Against Obama Immigration Orders," CNN, May 4, 2015, http://www.cnn.com/2015/05/04/politics/joe-arpaio-obama-immigration-executive-action-lawsuit/.
6. The White House, Office of the Press Secretary, "FACT SHEET: Reducing Greenhouse Gas Emissions in the Federal Government and Across the Supply Chain," March 19, 2015, https://www.whitehouse.gov/the-press-office/2015/03/19/fact-sheet-reducing-greenhouse-gas-emissions-federal-government-and-acro.
7. Ibid.
8. The White House, "FACT SHEET: Reducing Greenhouse Gas Emissions in the Federal Government."
9. Bill Clinton, Statement on Kosovo, March 24, 1999, Miller Center, http://millercenter.org/president/speeches/speech-3932.
10. William J. Clinton, Executive Order 13119 of April 13, 1999: "Designation of Federal Republic of Yugoslavia (Serbia–Montenegro), Albania, the Airspace Above and Adjacent Waters a Combat Zone," Federal Register 64, no. 73 (April 16, 1999), http://www.gpo.gov/fdsys/pkg/FR-1999-04-16/pdf/99-9738.pdf.
11. Geoffrey S. Corn, "Clinton, Kosovo and the Final Destruction of the War Powers Resolution," William & Mary Law Review 42, no. 4 (2001): 1176–83, http://scholarship.law.wm.edu/cgi/viewcontent.cgi?article=1474&context=wmlr.

12. Ibid.

13. James Phillips and James H. Anderson, "Lessons from the War in Kosovo," Heritage Foundation, July 22, 1999, http://www.heritage.org/research/reports/1999/07/lessons-from-the-war-in-kosovo.

14. Corn, "Clinton, Kosovo and the Final Destruction of the War Powers Resolution," 1178–79.

15. Phillips and Anderson, "Lessons from the War in Kosovo."

16. Erik C. Rusnak, "The Straw That Broke the Camel's Back? Grand Staircase-Escalante National Monument Antiquates the Antiquities Act," Ohio State Law Journal 64, no. 669 (2003): 669–70, http://isites.harvard.edu/fs/docs/icb.topic983317.files/Readings%20November%209/Rusnak.pdf.

17. "Joint Release: Hatch and Lee Sponsor Grand Staircase-Escalante National Monument Grazing Protection Act," Senate website for Orrin Hatch, February 4, 2015, http://www.hatch.senate.gov/public/index.cfm/2015/2/joint-release-hatch-and-lee-sponsor-grand-staircase-escalante-national-monument-grazing-protection-act.

18. D.F. Oliveria, "Clinton Land Grab Concerns Us All: Pure Arrogance: Public Lands Too Important for One Man to Decide," Spokesman-Review, November 8, 1996, http://www.spokesman.com/stories/1996/nov/08/clinton-land-grab-concerns-us-all-pure-arrogance/.

19. Thomas Jefferson, in "Quotes from the Founding Fathers," Renew America, March 13, 2009, http://www.renewamerica.com/article/090313.

20. Richard Salsman, "When It Comes to Abuse of Presidential Power, Obama Is a Mere Piker," Forbes, January 28, 2013, http://www.forbes.com/sites/richardsalsman/2013/01/28/when-it-comes-to-abuse-of-presidential-power-obama-is-a-mere-piker/.

21. Abraham Lincoln, Executive Order: Authorizing General Winfield Scott to Suspend the Writ of Habeus Corpus, American Presidency Project, July 2, 1861, http://www.presidency.ucsb.edu/ws/index.php?pid=69791.

22. History, "This Day in History, May 6, 1933: FDR Creates the WPA," http://www.history.com/this-day-in-history/fdr-creates-the-wpa, accessed May 9, 2015.

23. George W. Bush, Executive Order Establishing Office of Homeland Security, White House website, October 8, 2001, http://georgewbush-whitehouse.archives.gov/news/releases/2001/10/20011008-2.html.

24. See Abraham Lincoln "The Emancipation Proclamation," January 1, 1863, on the website of the National Archives & Records Administration, http://www.archives.gov/exhibits/featured_documents/emancipation_proclamation/.

25. T. J. Halstead, "Executive Orders: Issuance and Revocation," March 19, 2001, archive.is, http://archive.is/FCDeR.

26. Ibid.
27. Ibid.

CHAPTER 9: CHRISTIANITY DOESN'T MEAN DEFENSELESSNESS:
THE SECOND AMENDMENT SAVES

1. Molly Reilly, "Obama Addresses Gun Control Following Aurora Shooting," Huffington Post, July 25, 2012, http://www.huffingtonpost.com/2012/07/25/obama-gun-control_n_1704246.html.
2. The White House, Office of the Press Secretary, "Remarks by the President at Sandy Hook Interfaith Prayer Vigil," December 16, 2012, https://www.whitehouse.gov/the-press-office/2012/12/16/remarks-president-sandy-hook-interfaith-prayer-vigil.
3. Ibid.
4. The White House, "Now Is the Time: The President's plan to protect our children and our communities by reducing gun violence," January 16, 2013, https://www.whitehouse.gov/sites/default/files/docs/wh_now_is_the_time_full.pdf.
5. National Conference of State Legislatures, "Summary: President Obama's Gun-Control Proposals," http://www.ncsl.org/research/civil-and-criminal-justice/summary-president-obama-gun-proposals.aspx, accessed May 12, 2015.
6. Michael D. Shear, "President Obama Honors Navy Yard Victims," *New York Times*, September 22, 2013, http://www.nytimes.com/2013/09/23/us/obama-to-attend-memorial-service-for-victims-of-navy-yard-shooting.html.
7. Gosia Wozniaka, "Troutdale Shooting: A 15-year-old with Guns in a Guitar Case," Christian Science Monitor, June 11, 2014, http://www.csmonitor.com/USA/Latest-News-Wires/2014/0611/Troutdale-shooting-A-15-year-old-with-guns-in-a-guitar-case-video.
8. Mark Landler and Lee Van Der Voo, "Oregon Shooting Draws Obama's Outrage on Gun Laws," New York Times, June 10, 2014, http://www.nytimes.com/2014/06/11/us/troutdale-oregon-reynolds-high-school-shooting.html.
9. Associated Press, "President Obama Expresses Frustration After OR School Shooting," Fox 12 Oregon, June 10, 2014, http://www.kptv.com/story/25745176/president-obama-expresses-frustration-after-school-shooting.
10. Linda Bloom and Kathy L. Gilbert, "Faith Leaders Join Call to End Gun Violence," the United Methodist Church, December 21, 2012, http://www.umc.org/news-and-media/faith-leaders-join-call-to-end-gun-violence.
11. Ibid.
12. Faiths United to Prevent Gun Violence, "Supporters," http://faithsagainstgunviolence.org/about/supporters/, accessed May 14, 2015.

13. Faiths United to Prevent Gun Violence, http://faithsagainstgunviolence.org/, accessed May 14, 2015.

14. Snopes, Dalai Lama, statement made in May 2001, as reported by the *Seattle Times*, in answer to a question from a student about how to react to a potential school shooter, http://www.snopes.com/politics/guns/dalailama.asp, accessed May 16, 2015.

15. Thomas Jefferson, letter to William Smith, November 13, 1787, Library of Congress, http://www.loc.gov/exhibits/jefferson/105.html.

16. Stephen P. Halbrook, "How the Nazis Used Gun Control," National Review, December 2, 2013, http://www.nationalreview.com/article/365103/how-nazis-used-gun-control-stephen-p-halbrook.

17. Bernard E. Harcourt, Chicago Public Law and Legal Theory Working Paper No. 67: On Gun Registration, the NRA, Adolf Hitler and Nazi Gun Laws: Exploding the Gun Culture Wars (University of Chicago, 2004), 2–4, http://www.law.uchicago.edu/files/files/67-harcourt.pdf.

18. Jews for the Preservation of Firearms Ownership, "The Genocide Chart," copyright JPFO.org 2002, http://jpfo.org/filegen-a-m/deathgc.htm, accessed October 17, 2017.

19. WSB-TV 2 Atlanta, "Police: Woman Shot Intruder 9 Times in Self-Defense," May 11, 2011, http://www.wsbtv.com/news/news/police-woman-shot-intruder-9-times-in-self-defense/nFB7g/.

20. Richard Nance, "14-Year-Old Boy Shoots Armed Intruder in Home," *Guns&Ammo*, July 2, 2012, http://www.gunsandammo.com/blogs/defend-thyself/14-year-old-boy-shoots-armed-intruder-i-home/.

21. WGCL-TV Atlanta, "Homeowner Shoots Intruder in Walton County," CBS46.com, upd. February 1, 2013, http://www.cbs46.com/story/20506821/homeowner-shoots-intruder-in.

22. Valerie Schremp Hahn, "Husband and Wife Shoot at Gunmen Who Try to Enter Their St. Louis Home, Killing 1, Police Say," St. Louis Post-Dispatch, June 11, 2014, http://www.stltoday.com/news/local/crime-and-courts/husband-and-wife-open-fire-on-gunmen-who-try-to/article_29109617-bc56-534f-82e6-d36ccba40c38.html.

23. Dustin Wilson, "Authorities: Homeowner Shoots, Kills Intruder in Catawba County," WCNC, February 23, 2015, http://www.wcnc.com/story/news/crime/2015/02/23/authorities-homeowner-shoot-intruder-in-catawba-county/23879563/.

24. The Heritage Foundation, "Solutions 2014: Protecting Second Amendment Rights," *Talking Points*, http://solutions.heritage.org/guns/, accessed May 15, 2015.

CHAPTER 10: TAKE ON THE LOCAL FIRST, THEN THE FEDERAL

1. James Madison or Alexander Hamilton, Federalist No. 51: "The Structure of the Government Must Furnish the Proper Checks and Balances Between the Different Departments," from the New York Packet, February 8, 1788, Library of Congress, http://thomas.loc.gov/home/histdox/fed_51.html.

2. The Constitution Society, "The Federalist No. 51," http://www.constitution.org/fed/federa51.htm, accessed May 23, 2015.

3. Madison or Hamilton, Federalist No. 51, emphasis added.

4. The Library of Congress, "The Federalist Papers," http://thomas.loc.gov/home/histdox/fedpapers.html, accessed May 23, 2015.

5. Madison or Hamilton, Federalist No. 51.

6. James Madison Federalist No. 46: "The Influence of the State and Federal Governments Compared," from the New York Packet, January 29, 1788, Library of Congress, http://thomas.loc.gov/home/histdox/fed_46.html.

7. Ibid.

8. Virginia Institute for Public Policy, http://www.virginiainstitute.org/, accessed May 28, 2015.

9. John Taylor, interview with author, May 22, 2015.

10. See Tertium Quids' website at http://www.tertiumquids.org/, accessed May 28, 2015.

11. Tertium Quids, "Freedom & Prosperity Agenda: A Citizens' Agenda for Better State Government," http://www.tertiumquids.org/agenda.html, accessed May 28, 2015.

12. Taylor, interview with author.

13. Ibid.

14. Ibid.

15. Ibid.

16. Ibid.

17. Ibid.

18. Ibid.

19. Emily Brown, "Timeline: Michael Brown Shooting in Ferguson, Missouri," USA Today, December 2, 2014, http://www.usatoday.com/story/news/nation/2014/08/14/michael-brown-ferguson-missouri-timeline/14051827/.

20. Michelle Ye Hee Lee, "'Hands Up, Don't Shoot' Did Not Happen in Ferguson," Fact Checker (blog), March 19, 2015, http://www.washingtonpost.com/blogs/fact-checker/wp/2015/03/19/hands-up-dont-shoot-did-not-happen-in-ferguson/.

21. Matt Apuzzo, "After Ferguson Unrest, Senate Reviews Use of Military-Style Gear by Police," New York Times, September 9, 2014, http://www.nytimes.com/2014/09/10/us/ferguson-unrest-senate-police-weapons-hearing.html?_r=2.

22. Steve Watson, "Rand Paul Plans Bill to End Police Militarization," Infowars.com, December 23, 2014, http://www.infowars.com/rand-paul-plans-bill-to-end-police-militarization/; "Reps. Johnson, Labrador Introduce Bill to De-Militarize Police," Rep. Hank Johnson's congressional website, September 16, 2014, http://hankjohnson. house.gov/press-release/reps-johnson-labrador-introduce-bill-de-militarize-police.

23. Mike Lillis, "Obama Orders Review of Police Militarization," *The Hill*, January 16, 2015, http://thehill.com/homenews/administration/229816-obama-orders-review-of-police-militarization; Devlin Barrett, "Attorney General Eric Holder Urges Broad Review of Police Tactics," *Wall Street Journal*, October 8, 2014, http://www.wsj.com/articles/attorney-general-eric-holder-urges-broad-review-of-police-tactics-1412769602.

24. David Weigel, "How Police Unions Stopped Congress from 'Militarized' Reform," Bloomberg, November 25, 2014, http://www.bloomberg.com/politics/articles/2014-11-25/how-police-unions-stopped-congress-from-militarization-reform; Julia Edwards, "Obama Sets New Limits on Police Use of Military Equipment," Reuters, May 18, 2015, http://www.reuters.com/article/2015/05/18/us-usa-race-obama-idUSKBN0O30UQ20150518.

25. Ted Sherman, "Christie Orders New Oversight of Surplus Military Gear by Police," NJ.com, March 17, 2015, http://www.nj.com/news/index.ssf/2015/03/christie_orders_new_oversight_of_police_military_g.html.

26. Tenth Amendment Center, "First in the Country: New Jersey Law a First Step to Stop Federal Militarization of Local Police," March 18, 2015, http://blog.tenthamendmentcenter.com/2015/03/first-in-the-country-new-jersey-law-a-first-step-to-stop-federal-militarization-of-local-police/.

27. David Morton, "Bill Would Ban Police Using Military Gear in Tennessee," Nooga.com, January 20, 2015, http://nooga.com/168884/bill-would-ban-police-using-military-gear-in-tennessee/.

28. IWB, "New Hampshire Bill Proposes Ban on Cops Receiving Military-Grade Weapons," *InvestmentWatch*, January 29, 2015, http://investmentwatchblog.com/police-state-new-hampshire-bill-proposes-ban-on-cops-receiving-military-grade-weapons/.

29. Alex Dobuzinskis, "Two California Cities Are Giving Up the Mine-Resistant Vehicles Their Police Departments Acquired," *Business Insider*, August 29, 2014, http://www.businessinsider.com/california-cities-mraps-2014-8.

30. Brian Wright, "Supervisor Requests Audit of PCSO Military Equipment," CopaMonitor.com, August 26, 2014, http://www.copamonitor.com/news/around_pinal/article_9d29e812-2d58-11e4-aeb6-0019bb2963f4.html.

31. Taylor, interview with author.

CHAPTER 11: THE PRESS IS SECULAR—BE YOUR OWN WATCHDOG

1. Richard L. Strauss, "Be Honest—The Story of Ananias and Sapphira," Bible.org, https://bible.org/seriespage/12-be-honest-story-ananias-and-sapphira, accessed May 31, 2015.

2. John Daniel Davidson, "Three Lies About Obamacare Jonathan Gruber Accidentally Revealed," Federalist, November 24, 2014, http://thefederalist.com/2014/11/24/three-lies-about-obamacare-jonathan-gruber-accidentally-revealed/.

3. Cokie Roberts, on *This Week*, December 20, 2009, quoted on the Empowered Citizens News Network website, http://www.ecnn.com/chump-change/once-morons-understand-obamacare-theyll-love-it/.

4. "Dezinformatsia," Patriot Post Wednesday Chronicle, January 27, 2010, http://patriotpost.us/digests/4824.

5. "MSNBC's Ed Schultz Erupts: Republicans Want to See You Dead!" YouTube video, 0:33, uploaded September 25, 2009, by "DronetekPolitics," https://www.youtube.com/watch?v=zRFMuvXG52g.

6. John Fund, "Passing Lane," Wall Street Journal, July 9, 2001, http://www.wsj.com/articles/SB994653540253364880.

7. Lars Willnat and David H. Weaver, The American Journalist in the Digital Age: Key Findings, (Bloomington, IN: School of Journalism, Indiana University, 2014), 13, http://news.indiana.edu/releases/iu/2014/05/2013-american-journalist-key-findings.pdf.

8. John Perazzo, "In the Tank: A Statistical Analysis of Media Bias," FrontPageMag.com, October 31, 2008, http://archive.frontpagemag.com/readArticle.aspx?ARTID=32928.

9. Ibid.

10. Tim Groseclose and Jeffrey Milyo, "A Measure of Media Bias," *Quarterly Journal of Economics* 120, no. 4 (November 2005): 1204–6, http://www.sscnet.ucla.edu/polisci/faculty/groseclose/pdfs/MediaBias.pdf.

11. Perazzo, "In the Tank."

12. Gallup, "Religion," http://www.gallup.com/poll/1690/religion.aspx, accessed June 1, 2015.

13. Ibid.

14. Pew Research Center, "Values and the Press," May 23, 2004, http://www.people-press.org/2004/05/23/iv-values-and-the-press/.

15. Ibid.

16. Ibid.

17. Pew Research Center Global Attitudes survey, "Global Views on Morality," 2013, http://www.pewglobal.org/2014/04/15/global-morality/, accessed June 1, 2015.

18. Pew Research Center Global Attitudes Survey, "Global Views on Morality: United States," 2013, http://www.pewglobal.org/2014/04/15/global-morality/country/united-states/, accessed June 1, 2015.

19. Warner Todd Huston, "The Top 50 Liberal Media Bias Examples," Western Journalism, December 10, 2011, http://www.westernjournalism.com/top-50-examples-liberal-media-bias/.

20. Warner Todd Huston, "Obama's Propagandistic Iconography: the Making of a Messiah," Publius Forum, June 22, 2008, http://www.publiusforum.com/2008/06/22/obamas-propagandistic-iconography-the-making-of-a-messiah/.

21. Roger Aronoff, "George Stephanopoulos: Objective Journalist, Wednesday's Example of Media Bias," *Student News Daily*, May 20, 2015, http://www.studentnewsdaily.com/example-of-media-bias/george-stephanopoulos-objective-journalist/.

22. Ibid.

23. See George Stephanopoulos, All Too Human: A Political Education (n.p.: Thorndike Press, 1999), https://books.google.com/books/about/All_Too_Human.html?id=YsHmpqx0Qb0C.

24. Jim Rutenberg, "From Spin Doctor to Reporter to Anchor," *Business Day*, June 10, 2002, http://www.nytimes.com/2002/06/10/business/from-spin-doctor-to-reporter-to-anchor.html?pagewanted=1.

CHAPTER 12: STAND FAST IN THE FACE OF THE PROGRESSIVE, ATHEIST ONSLAUGHT

1. Huffington Post, author page on Jeff Schweitzer, http://www.huffingtonpost.com/jeff-schweitzer/, accessed June 6, 2015.

2. Jeff Schweitzer, "Founding Fathers: We Are Not a Christian Nation," *The Blog*, February 26, 2015, http://www.huffingtonpost.com/jeff-schweitzer/founding-fathers-we-are-n_b_6761840.html.

3. "The Barbary Treaties, 1786–1816: Treaty of Peace and Friendship, Signed at Tripoli November 4, 1796," the Avalon Project, Yale Law School, http://avalon.law.yale.edu/18th_century/bar1796t.asp#art11, Article 11, accessed June 6, 2015.

4. Alex Holt, "Countdown Host Says Founding Father Reached Out to Muslims," PolitiFact.com, May 11, 2010, http://www.politifact.com/truth-o-meter/statements/2010/may/11/keith-olbermann/countdown-host-says-founding-father-reached-out-mu/.

5. John Adams, letter to Thomas Jefferson, June 28, 1813, in Dave Miller, "The Treaty of Tripoli and America's Founders," Apologetics Press, http://www.apologeticspress.org/APContent.aspx?category=7&article=4520, accessed June 6, 2015.

6. John Adams, "Proclamation: Recommending a National Day of Humiliation, Fasting and Prayer," March 6, 1799, American Presidency Project, http://www.presidency. ucsb.edu/ws/?pid=65675.

7. Schweitzer, "Founding Fathers."

8. Mark David Hall, "Did America Have a Christian Founding?" (lecture), Heritage Foundation, June 7, 2011, http://www.heritage.org/research/lecture/2011/06/did-america-have-a-christian-founding.

9. Ibid.

10. Frank Zindler, "Ethics Without Gods," American Atheists, http://atheists.org/activism/resources/ethics, accessed September 17, 2015.

11. Roger Wolsey, "16 Ways Progressive Christians Interpret the Bible," *The Holy Kiss* (blog), January 21, 2014, http://www.patheos.com/blogs/rogerwolsey/2014/01/16-ways-progressive-christians-interpret-the-bible/.

12. Ibid

13. Todd Starnes, "School District Says Feds Forced Policy That Allows Transgender Kids to Use Bathrooms of Their Choice," Fox News, May 7, 2015, http://www.foxnews. com/opinion/2015/05/07/parents-pastors-try-to-block-school-s-transgender-policy. html.

14. Hailey Branson-Potts, "Gender-Neutral Single-Stall Restrooms Now Required in West Hollywood," *Los Angeles Times*, January 13, 2015, http://www.latimes.com/ local/lanow/la-me-ln-weho-gender-neutral-restroom-20150113-story.html.

15. David Muscato, "Today I'm Saying Goodbye to My Old Self," Patheos, November 17, 2014, http://www.patheos.com/blogs/friendlyatheist/2014/11/17/today-im-saying-goodbye-to-my-old-self/.

16. Chris Stedman, "Why Atheists Should Care About Transgender Issues: A Conversation with Kayley Whalen," Religion News Service, May 10, 2014, http://chrissted-man.religionnews.com/2014/05/10/why-atheists-should-care-about-transgender-issues-a-conversation-with-kayley-whalen/.

17. Gary Gates, "How Many People Are Lesbian, Gay, Bisexual and Transgender?" the Williams Institute, April 2011, http://williamsinstitute.law.ucla.edu/wp-content/uploads/Gates-How-Many-People-LGBT-Apr-2011.pdf, p. 2.

18. Michael Lipka, "Millennials Increasingly Are Driving Growth of 'Nones,'" Pew Research Center Facttank, May 12, 2015, http://www.pewresearch.org/fact-tank/2015/05/12/millennials-increasingly-are-driving-growth-of-nones/.

19. Ibid.

20. Ibid.

21. John Jessup, "'I Would Go to Jail over Jesus' Name,' says Public Official," Charisma News, July 8, 2014, http://www.charismanews.com/us/44596-i-would-go-to-jail-over-jesus-name-says-public-official.

22. Ibid.

23. Reuters, "In 'Brazen Defiance' of Court, Maryland Official Opens Meeting with a Prayer That References Jesus," March 27, 2014, http://www.huffingtonpost.com/2014/03/27/maryland-local-official-d_n_5045122.html.

CHAPTER 13: GET IN THE BATTLE OF PRINCIPALITIES

1. Phil Cooke, "2015 National Day of Prayer Themed, 'Lord, Hear Our Cry,'" Charisma News, April 3, 2015, http://www.charismanews.com/us/49031-2015-national-day-of-prayer-themed-lord-hear-our-cry.

2. Ibid.

3. See Jack Graham, "About Prestonwood Baptist Church," http://www.jackgraham.org/about/our-church, accessed June 16, 2015.

4. Eric Owens, "Sad, Lonely Atheists Gather for Weeklong Benediction of Nothingness, Fundraising," Daily Caller, May 6, 2015, http://dailycaller.com/2015/05/06/atheists-gather-for-weeklong-benediction-of-nothingness-fundraising/.

5. US House of Representatives, Office of the Chaplain, "First Prayer of the Continental Congress, 1774," http://chaplain.house.gov/archive/continental.html, accessed June 17, 2015.

6. "Proposed Seal for the United States," Religion and the Founding of the American Public, the website of the Library of Congress, http://www.loc.gov/exhibits/religion/rel04.html, accessed June 18, 2015.

7. BibleScripture.net, "1776 National Day of Humiliation, Fasting and Prayer," http://biblescripture.net/Day.html, accessed June 18, 2015.

8. "Congressional Thanksgiving Day Proclamation," Religion and the Founding of the American Public, Library of Congress

9. Military Religious Freedom Foundation, "Michael L. 'Mikey' Weinstein, Esq. – MRFF Founder & President," http://www.militaryreligiousfreedom.org/about/michael-l-mikey-weinstein/, accessed June 18, 2015.

10. "Settling the West" and "Northwest Ordinance," Religion and the Founding of the American Public, Library of Congress.

11. The Franklin quotes that follow are taken from David Barton, "Founding Fathers on Prayer," WallBuilders, May 1, 2013, http://www.wallbuilders.com/libissuesarticles.asp?id=144096.

12. Jim Allison, "The Franklin Prayer Myth," The Constitutional Principle: Separation of Church and State, http://candst.tripod.com/franklin.htm, accessed July 29, 2015.

13. Barton "Founding Fathers on Prayer."

14. Allison "The Franklin Prayer Myth."

15. James Madison, Federalist No. 37, "Concerning the Difficulties of the Convention in Devising a Proper Form of Government," January 11, 1788, Constitution Society, http://www.constitution.org/fed/federa37.htm, accessed June 18, 2015.

16. Alexander Hamilton, Statement after the Constitutional Convention, 1787, posted by Steve Straub, "Alexander Hamilton: The Constitution Could Not Have Been Written Without the Finger of God," The Federalist Papers Project, http://www.thefederalistpapers.org/founders/hamilton/alexander-hamilton-statement-after-the-constitutional-convention-1787, accessed June 18, 2015.

17. Congressional Prayer Caucus Foundation, 219 Prayer, CPCF, http://cpcfoundation.com/pray-for-america/, accessed September 23, 2015.

18. Congressional Prayer Caucus Foundation, "Pray USA Initiative Exploding," CPCF blog, June 3, 2015, http://cpcfoundation.com/prayusa-initiative-exploding/.

19. Congressional Prayer Caucus Foundation, Initiatives, http://cpcfoundation.com/initiatives/, accessed June 19, 2015.

CHAPTER 14: LOOKING FOR A FEW GOOD JONAHS

1. Gilbert Keith Chesterton, What I Saw in America, repr. (BiblioBazaar, 2009), 7.

2. "Ambassador Ken Blackwell: 'Shining a Bright Light on Obama's Atrocities,'" YouTube video, from a speech by Ambassador Ken Blackwell, a fellow at the Family Research Council, 22:44, posted by "JoeMillerUS," June 22, 2015, https://www.youtube.com/watch?v=plV7ezLCTbs.

3. Ibid.

4. Obergefell et al v. Hodges, 576 U.S. _____ (6th Cir. 2015), http://www.supremecourt.gov/opinions/14pdf/14-556_3204.pdf.

5. JoeMillerUS, "Ambassador Ken Blackwell: 'Shining a Bright Light on Obama's Atrocities.'"

6. Leo Hohmann, "Is There Still Hope for America?" WND, June 26, 2015, http://www.wnd.com/2015/06/is-there-still-hope-for-america/.

7. Ibid.

8. News Room, "Court Contradicts Constitution," American Pastors Network, June 26, 2015, http://www.americanpastorsnetwork.net/2015/06/26/court-contradicts-constitution/.

9. Carl Gallups, e-mail to author, June 26, 2015.

10. Awake America, "Who We Are: Dr. Chuck Harding," http://awakeamericaonline.org/who-we-are.html, accessed June 24, 2015.

11. Chuck Harding, telephone interview with author and email to author.

12. Ibid.

13. Public Religion Research Institute, "Survey: Most Americans Believe Protests Make the Country Better; Support Decreases Dramatically Among Whites If Protesters Are Identified as Black," June 23, 2015, http://publicreligion.org/research/2015/06/survey-americans-believe-protests-make-country-better-support-decreases-dramatically-protesters-identified-black/#.VY3ZW0aAS1l

14. Ibid.

15. Ibid.

16. Carl Gallups, interview with author and email to author, June 2015.

17. The Guttmacher Institute, "Fact Sheet: Induced Abortion in the United States," July 2014, http://www.guttmacher.org/pubs/fb_induced_abortion.html.

18. Ibid.

19. Ibid.

20. Gallups, interview with author and email to author.

21. Tim Ryan, "In Context: What Obama Said about 'Fundamentally Transforming' the Nation," PolitiFact.com, February 6, 2014, http://www.politifact.com/truth-o-meter/article/2014/feb/06/what-barack-obama-has-said-about-fundamentally-tra/.

22. Walter Brandimarte and Daniel Bases, "United States Loses Prized AAA Credit Rating from S&P," Reuters, August 7, 2011, http://www.reuters.com/article/2011/08/07/us-usa-debt-downgrade-idUSTRE7746VF20110807.

23. Tara Fowler, "Did Middle School Students Receive Fifty Shades of Grey–Themed Word Search Puzzles?" People, February 12, 2015, http://www.people.com/article/middle-school-fifty-shades-word-search.

24. Gallups, interview with author and e-mail to author.

25. Harding, telephone interview and e-mail to author.

26. The story and comments that follow are from Steve Yount, "T. D. Jakes: 'We Cannot Remain Silent on This Issue,'" Charisma News, January 16, 2015, http://www.charismanews.com/us/47925-t-d-jakes-we-cannot-remain-silent-on-this-issue.

27. Ronnie Floyd, "My Plea," on the National Day of Prayer website, June 2, 2015, http://nationaldayofprayer.org/my-plea/.

28. Bethany Blankley, "From the Pulpit to the Polls: Political Pastors Return to America's Roots," Western Journalism, January 27, 2015, http://www.westernjournalism.com/pulpit-polls-political-pastors-return-americas-roots/.

29. T. Jefferson, "Glenn Interviews Jerry Falwell Jr.," Glenn Beck, June 25, 2010, http://www.glennbeck.com/content/articles/article/198/42325/.

30. "Ambassador Ken Blackwell: 'Shining a Bright Light on Obama's Atrocities.'"

31. Author telephone/email interview with Dr. Chuck Harding, June 2015, notes maintained at author's residence.

32. Author telephone/email interview with Dr. Chuck Harding, June 2015, notes maintained at author's residence.

CHAPTER 15: CHRISTIANS, WAKE UP! THE CULTURE WAR IS RAGING

1. Hunter Walker, "Ted Cruz Says 'Lawless' Supreme Court Rulings Have Led to 'Some of the Darkest 24 Hours in Our Nation's History," *Business Insider*, June 26, 2015, http://www.businessinsider.com/cruz-supreme-court-rulings-mean-the-darkest-24-hours-in-history-2015-6.

2. Sherif Gergis, "After Obergefell: The Effects on Law, Culture and Religion," *Catholic World Report*, June 29, 2015, http://www.catholicworldreport.com/Item/3991/after_iobergefelli_the_effects_on_law_culture_and_religion.aspx.

3. Bureau of Labor and Industries, "Before the Commissioner of the Bureau of Labor and Industries of the State of Oregon: In the Matter of Melissa Elaine Klein, dba, Sweet Cakes by Melissa, and Aaron Wayne Klein, dba, Sweet Cakes by Melissa," http://www.oregon.gov/boli/SiteAssets/pages/press/Sweet%20Cakes%20FO.pdf, 42, 71, accessed July 5, 2015.

4. Todd Starnes, "Christian Bakers Fined $135,000 For Refusing to Make Wedding Cake for Lesbians," Fox News, July 3, 2015, http://www.foxnews.com/opinion/2015/07/03/christian-bakers-fined-135000-for-refusing-to-make-wedding-cake-for-lesbians.html.

5. Ibid.

6. Miranda Blue, "Herb Titus: Christians Must Defy Gay Marriage Ruling or Abandon Government to Heathens and Satan," *Right Wing Watch*, July 7, 2015, http://www.rightwingwatch.org/content/herb-titus-christians-must-defy-gay-marriage-ruling-or-abandon-government-heathens-satan.

7. Franklin Graham, Facebook post, June 5, 2015, post, https://www.facebook.com/FranklinGraham?ref=br_rs. This posting has since been removed, but it can be viewed in Joe Borlik, "Franklin Graham slams Wells Fargo for featuring same-sex couple in ad; urges boycott," Fox 8, June 6, 2015, http://myfox8.com/2015/06/06/franklin-graham-slams-wells-fargo-for-featuring-same-sex-couple-in-ad-urges-boycott/.

8. The Shepherd's Guide, "Your Christian Connection," http://www.shepherdsguide.com/, accessed July 5, 2015.

9. *Christian Business Marketplace*, Frequently Asked Questions, http://www.christianbusinessmarketplace.com/cbm-faqs/, accessed October 16, 2015.

10. Todd Starnes, "Oregon Puts Gag Order on Persecuted Christian Bakers," American Dispatch, July 6, 2015, http://www.charismanews.com/opinion/american-dispatch/50401-oregon-puts-gag-order-on-persecuted-christian-bakers.

11. Kelsey Harkness, "State Silences Bakers Who Refused to Make Cake for Lesbian Couple, Fines Them $135K," Daily Signal, July 2, 2015, http://dailysignal.com/2015/07/02/state-silences-bakers-who-refused-to-make-cake-for-lesbian-couple-fines-them-135k/.

12. Kim LaCapria, "Bitter Baker Battle," Snopes.com, July 3, 2015, http://m.snopes.com/2015/07/03/sweet-cakes-melissa-damages/.

13. Rand Paul, "Rand Paul: Government Should Get Out of the Marriage Business Altogether," Time, June 28, 2015, http://time.com/3939374/rand-paul-gay-marriage-supreme-court/.

14. Gordon L. Anderson, "Why Christians Should Oppose a Government Definition of Marriage," blog.ganderson.us, May 16, 2011, http://blog.ganderson.us/2011/05/why-christians-should-oppose-a-government-definition-of-marriage/.

15. Ibid.

16. Ashby Jones, "Why Do We Need the State's Permission to Get Married Anyway?" Wall Street Journal Law Blog, January 14, 2010, http://blogs.wsj.com/law/2010/01/14/why-do-we-need-to-ask-the-state-for-permission-to-get-married-anyway/.

17. Ibid.

18. Ibid.

19. Blue, "Herb Titus."

20. See Emord & Associates, P.C., Jonathan W. Emord, Esq., http://www.emord.com/Jonathan-Emord.html, accessed July 7, 2015.

21. Robert Scott Bell, "FDA Dragon Slayer Jonathan Emord, Presidential Politics, Ron Paul's Compassionate Use H.R. 6342, Rosie O'Donnell's Heart Attack, FDA Team Visits Grandma's 'Drug' Soap, Endometriosis Cures, Chelation Therapy, Obese Antibiotics, Selenium, Silica and More on The Robert Scott Bell Show," The Robert Scott Bell Show blog, August 22, 2012, http://www.robertscottbell.com/blog/fda-dragon-slayer-jonathan-emord-presidential-politics-ron-pauls-compassionate-use-h-r-6342-rosie-o-donnels-heart-attack-fda-team-visits-grandmas-drug-soap-endometrio-sis-cures-chela/.

22. Jonathan Emord, e-mail interview with author, July 2015.

23. David Harsanyi, "Time for a Divorce," Townhall.com, August 6, 2010, http://townhall.com/columnists/davidharsanyi/2010/08/06/time_for_a_divorce/page/full.

24. The following story and quotes are from Robert Scott Bell, telephone interview with author, July 2015.

25. Boundaries For Effective Ministry, "Marriage Without License Prevents 'Strange Gods' from Controlling Families," http://www.boundaries-for-effective-ministry.org/ marriage-without-license.html, accessed July 8, 2015.

26. Bell, telephone interview with author.

27. Charlie Butts, "Fine, Gag Order Not Deterring Christian Bakers," *OneNewsNow*, July 7, 2015, http://www.onenewsnow.com/culture/2015/07/07/fine-gag-order-not-deterring-christian-bakers.

CHAPTER 16: CHURCHES TO THE RESCUE—HOPEFULLY

1. Efrem Graham, "Luis Palau Festival Draws 60,000 to Central Park," CBN News, July 11, 2015, http://www.cbn.com/cbnnews/us/2015/July/Luis-Palau-Festival-Draws-60000-to-Central-Park/.

2. Adelle M. Banks, "Q & A: Evangelist Luis Palau, 80, Gears Up for NYC 'CityFest,'" Religion News Service, July 8, 2015, http://www.religionnews.com/2015/07/08/qa-evangelist-luis-palau-80-gears-nyc-cityfest/.

3. Ibid.

4. Graham, "Luis Palau Festival Draws 60,000 to Central Park."

5. Franklin Graham, "Franklin Graham: 'This Is a Defining Moment for Our Nation,'" Billy Graham Evangelistic Association, July 7, 2015, http://billygraham.org/story/ franklin-graham-this-is-a-defining-moment-for-our-nation/.

6. Ibid.

7. Talk Radio Network, *The Sam Sorbo Show*, http://www.trncorporate.com/host/ the_sam_sorbo_show.

8. From my recollection of our discussion on *The Sam Sorbo Show* in mid-2014.

9. Hallowell, "Hollywood Actor."

10. David Treybig, "Seven Churches of Revelation," Life, Hope & Truth, http://lifehope-andtruth.com/prophecy/revelation/seven-churches-of-revelation/, accessed July 13, 2015.

11. Chelsen Vicari, "How the Liberal, Progressive Infestation of the Church Threatens America's Future," TPNN, August 29, 2015, http://www.tpnn.com/2014/08/29/ how-the-liberal-progressive-infestation-of-the-church-threatens-americas-future/.

12. Hallowell, "Hollywood Actor."

13. The Church Law Group, "Is the Johnson Amendment on Its Way Out?" http:// churchlawgroup.com/resources/blog/is-the-johnson-amendment-on-its-way-out/, accessed July 15, 2015.

14. Alliance Defending Freedom, "IRS Remains Mum on Pulpit Freedom Sunday," April 19, 2012, http://www.adflegal.org/detailspages/commentary-details/irs-remains-mum-on-pulpit-freedom-sunday#Sunday+in+2008+to+challenge+the+constitutionality+of+the+Johnson+Amendment.++We+believe+that+it+is+unconstitutional+for+the+government+to+attempt+in+any+way+to+censor+a+pastor%E2%80%99s+sermon., accessed July 15, 2015.

15. Erick W. Stanley, "Pulpit Freedom Sunday 2011—A Success by All Accounts," Alliance Defending Freedom, November 1, 2011, http://www.adflegal.org/detailspages/blog-details/allianceedge/2011/11/01/pulpit-freedom-sunday-2011---a-success-by-all-accounts.

16. Alliance Defending Freedom, "Pulpit Freedom Sunday 2013: Speaking Truth to the Culture," July 9, 2013, http://www.adflegal.org/detailspages/blog-details/allianceedge/2013/07/09/pulpit-freedom-sunday-2013-speaking-truth-to-the-culture-1.

17. See United States District Court, Western District of Wisconsin, *Freedom from Religion Foundation Inc. and Triangle FFRF v. Steven Miller*, acting commissioner for the Internal Revenue Service, Case 12-CV-946, Complaint, http://ffrf.org/images/uploads/legal/990lawsuit.PDF, accessed July 18, 2015.

18. Mark A. Kellner, "IRS Agrees to Investigate Churches That Preach Politics After Settling With Atheist Lobbying Group," *Deseret National News*, July 31, 2014, http://national.deseretnews.com/article/2016/irs-agrees-to-investigate-churches-that-preach-politics-after-settling-with-atheist-lobbying-group.html.

19. Alliance Defending Freedom, "ADF Joins Panel Discussion on Vague Tax Laws Muzzling Nonprofits, Churches," January 28, 2015, http://www.adfmedia.org/News/PRDetail/4360.

20. Alice Speri, "Atheists and Religious Conservatives Battle over the Right to Preach Politics in Church," Vice News, August 6, 2014, https://news.vice.com/article/atheists-and-religious-conservatives-battle-over-the-right-to-preach-politics-in-church.

21. Rebecca Markert (staff attorney, FFRF), letter to Nanette Downing (Internal Revenue Service), November 6, 2012, http://ffrf.org/uploads/legal/madison_letter.pdf, p. 1.

22. Ibid., 2.

23. Mission America, "Pulpit Freedom Proposed," Research and Trends column, Evangelism Connection, September 2013, http://community.elevatorup.com/missionamerica/assets/2013_09evangelism-connection.htm.

24. Commission on Accountability and Policy for Religious Organizations, "Commission Recommendation—Government Regulation of Political Speech—Proposed Solutions," point 5, Examples: A, http://religiouspolicycommission.org/Content/Proposed-Solutions, accessed July 18, 2015.

25. Zachary A. Goldfarb and Karen Tumulty, "IRS Admits Targeting Conservatives for Tax Scrutiny in 2012 Election," *Washington Post*, May 10, 2013, http://www.washingtonpost.com/business/economy/irs-admits-targeting-conservatives-for-tax-scrutiny-in-2012-election/2013/05/10/3b6a0ada-b987-11e2-92f3-f291801936b8_story.html.

26. Susan Crabtree, "Obama to Jon Stewart: IRS Never Targeted Conservatives," *Washington Examiner*, July 21, 2015, http://www.washingtonexaminer.com/obama-to-jon-stewart-irs-never-targeted-conservatives/article/2568699.

27. Ibid.

28. Jazz Shaw, "Judge Orders IRS to Release List of Targeted Conservative Nonprofit Groups," *Hot Air*, April 4, 2015, http://hotair.com/archives/2015/04/04/judge-orders-irs-to-release-list-of-targeted-conservative-nonprofit-groups/.

29. Quin Hillyer, "The IRS's God Complex," National Review, August 4, 2014, http://www.nationalreview.com/article/384454/irss-god-complex-quin-hillyer.

30. Catherine Millard, "Preachers and Pulpits of the American Revolution," ChristianHeritageMins.org, http://www.christianheritagemins.org/articles/Preachers%20and%20Pulpits%20of%20the%20American%20Revolution.pdf, accessed July 18, 2015.

31. The Episcopal Church, "Muhlenberg, John Peter Gabriel," http://www.episcopalchurch.org/library/glossary/muhlenberg-john-peter-gabriel, accessed July 18, 2015.

32. The Library of Congress, "Religion and the Founding of the American Republic: Revolution Justified by God," http://www.loc.gov/exhibits/religion/rel03.html, accessed July 18, 2015.

33. Jonathan Mayhew, "A Discourse Concerning Unlimited Submission and Non-Resistance to the Higher Powers" (1750), LawAndLiberty.org, http://lawandliberty.org/mayhew.htm, accessed July 18, 2015.

CHAPTER 17: A CRASH COURSE IN LETTING GOD LEAD

1. Ronald Reagan, "The Shining City upon a Hill—Reagan," OriginsofNations.org, January 5, 1974, http://www.originofnations.org/books,%20papers/quotes%20etc/Reagan_The%20Shining%20City%20Upon%20A%20Hill%20speech.htm.

2. Luke 18:8 KJV.

INDEX

Pew Research Center, 60, 179, 197
Philadelphia, PA, 14–15, 16
Pierce, Franklin, number of executive orders issued by president, 128
Pledge of Allegiance, 48
Police State USA (Chumley), xiii, 258
political activism, 168, 282
political parties, 6, 11, 21, 280, 281. *See in general chap. 1, "Partisan Politics Won't Win the Nation"* (4–22)
PolitiFact, 74, 188
Polk, James K., number of executive orders issued by president, 128
pork-barrel spending, 83
Potter's House, 228, 230
prayer, 143, 167, 176, 189, 199, 202, 203–4, 205, 206, 209–13, 229, 232, 254, 256, 257, 278, 280, 283
    in public schools, percent in the news profession who condemn, 176
Pray USA, 213
Presbyterian Church USA, 145
presidents, number of executive orders issued by our (table), 128–29
press, the. *See in general chap. 11, "The Press Is Secular"* (169–85)
principalities, xiv, 203, 209, 210, 215, 254, 283
progressives, 186, 190, 192–93, 194, 196–97, 198, 200, 276, 282
Property and Environment Research Center, 19
Public Law 89-10, 39
Public Religion Research Institute (PRRI), 221
public schools. *See* schools
Pulpit Free Sunday, 263, 264

Q

quantitative easing (QE), 87–88, 281
Quarterly Journal of Economics, 175
Qu'ran, 49

R

racist skinheads, 113, 114
Rasmussen Reports, 5–6, 7
Reagan, Ronald, 20, 90, 129, 139, 175, 248, 276
"Reconciled Church" (summit), 227–28
Reid, Harry, 63
Reid, Landra, 63
Religion News Service, 195, 255
Religious Freedom Restoration Act, xii
repentance, 203, 206, 209, 213, 232, 233, 257, 261, 278, 280
Republican Party (*also* GOP), 9, 11, 12–13, 16, 225, 280
Republicans, 9, 11, 13, 68, 145, 173, 174, 175, 187, 221, 262
Reuters, 181–82
Revelation, book of, 260
right to bear arms, 141. See *Second Amendment*
RINOs (Republicans in Name Only), 12
Roberts, Cokie, 172
Roberts, Paul Craig, 90–91
Robison, James, 227
Rodriguez, Samuel, 228
Rogers, William, 211–12
Rohrer, Sam, 219
Roll Call, 105
Rolling Stone, 181–82
Romney, Mitt, 61
Roosevelt, Franklin, 78–79, 129, 137

WND Books

PRESENTS

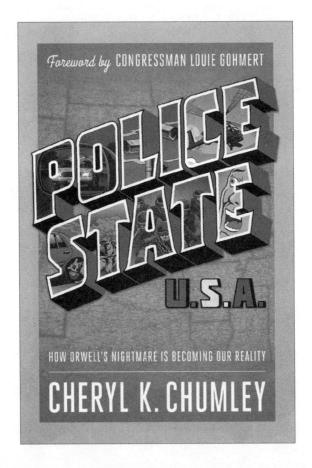

Foreword by CONGRESSMAN LOUIE GOHMERT

POLICE STATE U.S.A.

HOW ORWELL'S NIGHTMARE IS BECOMING OUR REALITY

CHERYL K. CHUMLEY

Police State USA explains how America is standing on the cusp of a police state, what led to this state—including environmental and corporate influences, as well as media spin and lies—and how we might overcome and recapture our freedoms, as envisioned by the Founding Fathers. But it's not too late to reverse the police state.

WND Books   •   A **WND** COMPANY   •   WASHINGTON DC   •   WNDBOOKS.COM

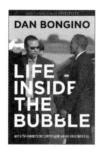
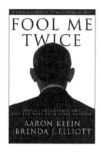

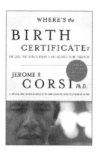

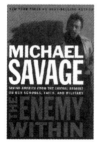
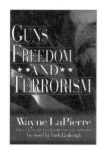
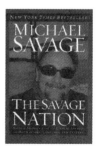